The Dark and Light Gods

The Dark and Light Gods:

Essays on the Self in Modern Literature*

by

Donald Gutierrez

*"... gods, strange gods, come forth from the forest into the clearing of my known self, and then go back."
—D. H. Lawrence,
Studies in Classic American Literature

The Whitston Publishing Company
Troy, New York
1987

To My Wife's Family—

Hans and Norma Zander
and
Gary and Margie Greene

ACKNOWLEDGEMENTS

I wish to thank the following book publishers, journals, and reviews for granting me permission to quote from the books, journals, and reviews listed below:

Beacon Press, for permission to quote from Viktor E. Frankl, *Man's Search for Meaning: An Introduction to Logotherapy* (1959).

Johns Hopkins University Press, for permission to reprint my article "Incarceration and Torture: The Self in Extremity," in *Human Rights Quarterly*, August 1984. This essay has been enlarged for the book.

Human Rights Quarterly, for permission to reprint my article "Incarceration and Torture: The Self in Extremity."

Alfred A. Knopf, Inc., for permission to quote from Diane Johnson, *The Shadow Knows* (1974) and Jacobo Timerman, *Prisoner Without a Name. Cell Without a Number* (1974).

Nassau Review, Nassau Community College, SUNY, Garden City, New York, for permission to reprint my article "Henry James' *The Beast in the Jungle:* The Ego as Self-Devourer," v. 5, no. 2, 1986.

New American Library, for permission to quote from Thomas Hardy, *Tess of the Durbervilles* (1964).

New Directions Publishing Corporation, for permission to quote from Louis-Ferdinand Céline's *Journey to the End of the Night* (Copyright 1952 by Louis Ferdinand Céline, translated by Ralph Mannheim.

Laurence Pollinger Limited and the Frieda Lawrence Ravagli Estate, for permission to quote from D. H. Lawrence, *Sex, Literature, and Censorship*, edited by Harry T. Moore (1959).

Hodder & Stoughton Limited, for permission to quote from Viktor E. Frankl's *Man's Search for Meaning: An Introduction to Logotherapy* (1959).

Viking Penguin, Inc., for permission to quote from Saul Bellow, *Mosby's Memoirs and Other Stories* (1959).

I wish in addition to thank Kingsley Widmer for his good advice on parts of the manuscript, and my school Western New Mexico University which awarded me a one-year Sabbatical during which some of this book was written. I am indebted as well to the WNMU Faculty Research Committee for summer grant support on the D. H. Lawrence chapter. I am also indebted to Professor Howard Lambert, a former WNMU colleague, for his generous support, and to Jean Goode, President of Whitston Publishing Company, for her ongoing support of my work.

Other Books
by Donald Gutierrez

Lapsing Out: Embodiments of Death and Rebirth in the Last Writings of D. H. Lawrence, (1980)

The Maze in the Mind and the World: Labyrinths in Modern Literature, The Whitston Publishing Company (1985)

Subject-Object Relations in Wordsworth and Lawrence (1986)

Contents

Preface

This study attempts to examine the character of the self in selected works of modern prose. More precisely, it is concerned with examining the existence or reality of the self through a scrutiny of late 19th and 20th century works of fiction and prose non-fiction that embody and test the self.

Such an enterprise is likely to be "self"-fulfilling or tendentious. It would show its hand at every juncture, from the authors and works chosen to the interpretations and conclusions elicited from them. Most literary studies of this nature are unavoidably committed to a particular perspective or attitude on the topic, for the self is, of all topics, one of the hardest to write about dispassionately or objectively. Most people, if they even think about the self, are likely to assume and accept its existence. The self seems too integral to our deepest sense of our own being to warrant questioning; it is or seems as much a part of our existence, even of the same repository of existence, as our breathing. It is rooted in old traditions in Western culture that relate it to the very pith of our physicality, mentality, and emotional substance and experience, and through Plato and Christianity has been regarded as being concentrated more finely and even ultimately in the soul, our best and most ideal or most spiritual self.

Yet there are also traditions in Western thought that deny the existence of the self. They can be isolated or are implied in writers like Pascal, La Rochefoucauld, and Hume, and find their counterpart in certain areas of 20th century art and thought. The idea that the self does not exist, or no longer exists, or that the character of the age is destroying it, is implied in some of the radical scepticism and nihilism of Modernist literature, beginning with Dostoyevsky's Underground Man in *Notes from Underground*, and continuing in the socially fractured self of Kafka's hunted and questing protagonists, of Beckett's disembodied voices and minds, of William Burroughs' drugged zombies.

Yet these and other profoundly pessimistic and even nihilistic writers, by the very substance and force of their case for the disintegration of the self, also imply that it once existed or even still exists, if only marginally. Their work ultimately makes no sense unless we recognize the assumption in the Modernist writers that only a self can disintegrate, only a being once consistent, coherent, and unified, or generally thought to be so, can lose these attributes.

I begin the main section on fiction with Fyodor Dostoyevsky's *Notes from Underground* because it has become the definitive exposure in Modernist fiction of the confessional, perverse private sensibility. At an early stage of a tradition of fiction focussing on the self and its permutations, this work has gone far in probing a crucial dimension of the self—the self in the psychological extremity of deeply masochistic self-revelation. Dostoyevsky's Underground Man represents the first full-scale dramatization in Western literature of self- and social alienation. What in part makes *Notes* complex is that we cannot believe everything the Underground Man says. Yet we can, or should, I will argue, accept a lot of it. Further, and disturbingly, some of the self-revelation reflects on the reader as well; the Underground Man is a mirror, if a distorted one, of dark areas in our own constellation of selves, which in part might account in reading Dostoyevsky's novella for a peculiar painfulness that goes beyond esthetic identification or repulsion.

Notes reveals a self in all the horror of progressing towards—and virtually recording its progression towards—its own damnation; as such, it obliquely reflects its heritage in a religious sensibility the very disappearance of which has made the culture of the self such a bristling problem and intense concern for modern people.

Despite its deeply buried religious roots, *Notes* possesses a sharp Modernist edge that contrasts vividly with the second chosen fiction. Thomas Hardy's *Tess of the Durbervilles* is, by comparison, conventional in narrative technique. Yet in its conception and presentation of an alienated hero (or heroine), it is, rustic guise notwithstanding, strikingly modern. Bereft, alone, innocent, Tess (a "Pure Woman") bears a burden of anguish and guilt almost "modern" in a harshness and injustice verging on nihilism. Tess may have her "place" (although that too is crucially ambiguous socially, because of her status as both plebian and patrician), but in her "self-actualizing" individuality, she possesses a tragic dignity and integrity. As such, she (or *Tess*) deserves to be part of a fictional panoply of modern varieties of the self.

In *The Beast in the Jungle*, Henry James depicts the partly
farcical, partly tragic, spectacle of the self as extraordinary egotist.
One danger of the self is excessive concern with the core of self-
consciousness, the ego. In *Beast*, this psycho-philosophical orientation takes the "romantic" form of the (deluded) sense of a great
purpose or destiny for an individual. In the blindly selfish pursuit of this goal, everything is sacrificed—love, career, the Other,
ultimately, the self of the egotistic quester. In view of the 20th
century fascination with self-realization (a master theme in D. H.
Lawrence's work, for example), *Beast* represents a stunning
cautionary tale for the time.

Another paradigm of the modern self is strikingly and
complexly exhibited in another early Modernist classic, Joseph
Conrad's *Lord Jim*. This novel, which focusses almost cruelly
on the metaphysics of cowardice and illusion in a young ship's
officer, conveys its endless epistemological permutations of self
and Other through the use of one of the most striking narrative
techniques in modern literature, a point-of-view structure that,
dividing the protagonist into subject and object, narrator and
narrated, provides extraordinary psychological and philosophical
involutions of the divided self. *Lord Jim* is indeed so subtle in
its epistemological character that it oscillates between narrative
subject and object focus. Consequently, Jim, in some respects a
degraded object, also becomes, through narrator Marlow's ambivalent obsession and sympathy with Jim and his metaphysical
quest, an almost exalted subject. Like Dostoyevsky's protagonist,
Jim, or Marlow's "study" of him, also reflects on the reader.
Jim's Jump from the *Patna* also rebounds within the reader,
challenging his own deepest resources of courage and of liability
towards cowardice, self-delusion, and rationalization. And
Marlow's identification with Jim is at times so intense and so
intimate, that the changing gamut of Self and Other collapses or
coalesces into a unity of subject and "object," a kind of tacit
community of selves. It is a "community" of noble aspiration
and self-degraded consciousness, which, in its endless ambivalence and ambiguity, seems part of the very essence of the
modern multivalence of definitions of the self.

The next work chosen, Ferdinand-Louis Céline's *Journey
to the End of the Night*, again presents a Dostoyevskian anti-
hero, but now in a far greater expansion of relation to society. If
Dostoyevsky's Underground Man viciously and insightfully inti-

mates that 19th century conceptions of the perfect or ideal society, and thus of the perfect human being, are unattainable, at least along rationalist lines, *Journey* embodies in part an updated version of *Notes*, by depicting modern society in a condition of advanced corruption. Céline's protagonist, one of the more salient anti-heroes in Modernist literature, is relevant to a study of the self in fiction because he shows the rottenness and brutality at the heart of modern society in the very process of exposing his own "sod" of a self. However, part of my thesis about Bardamu is that, as anti-heroes go, he is not so bad; he even possesses a significant residual integrity that reflects very negatively on early 20th century society.

The post World-War-One *Journey* and the post World-War-Two novel, *Invisible Man*, by Ralph Ellison, exhibit an affinity in desperation in Céline's pre-Existentialist savage world of barely controlled hysteria and Ellison's nightmare of racist and exploitative hallucination. Ellison's *Invisible Man* is attractive for a study of the self, first, for its subtle, reflexive use of the symbolism of black and white. Part of the artistry of Ellison's novel is that the racial, psychological, and philosophical significances are interrelated. If, let us say, a White man responds negatively or "blackly" to a Black, is it his own darkness or "blackness" propelling him? If so, how far does his projection of himself on the Black not only miss the Black, but contribute to creating a new or evil person mainly existent in his own mind and thus in himself? The relevance for a study of self in *Invisible Man* is that racism is a tragic farce of false identifications. Thus, rather than identifying the essence of the racial self, racism confounds the self in ignorantly or maliciously projecting a synthetic image that causes and results in hatred, fear, and a pursuit of the self into extremity. Like most of the fictions chosen for this study, Ellison's narrator engages in both an outward quest of self-definition, and an inward searching and progression. The nameless protagonist of *Invisible Man* moves from South to North, from Southern innocent to Northern, Big-city sophisticate, ending up, like some other Modernist heroes and anti-heroes, as another Underground Man. Unlike the ambiguous protagonists of Dostoyevsky, Céline, and James, however, Ellison's self-searcher, activating the mystical sentiment from T. S. Eliot's *Four Quartets*, will not only find his end in his beginning, but his beginning in his end as well. Out of his new acceptance of his own racial darkness promises to come a new person, neither "nigger" or manipulated social radical—someone, some self, tough, seasoned, and beyond classification, perhaps a basic result of genuine self-hood.

Giving attention to Saul Bellows's novella "Leaving the Yellow House" allows one to focus on elderly women. Not an easy period of life for a writer to deal with, old age is held by Carl Jung to be the time of the maturation of self, the delicious ripening period of individuation. That, instead, old age can be a worsening nightmare is a reality not readily faced. Bellow's novella is arresting because it shows an elderly woman forced on her self after all the props she depends on as part of a number of insufficient or artificial selves are removed from her by a combination of circumstances and the thrust of her life's selves. Like the Yeats persona in his late verse, she descends into the desolation of reality. Yet she also ascends into a new, mystic self. Hardly one of Bellow's hyper-glamorized female characters, Hattie is a remarkable creation of character and new spiritual being in a desert of place and being.

For a contemporary woman's representation of self in a recent novel, I have chosen Diane Johnson's 1976 novel *The Shadow Knows*. A satiric Gothic of contemporary domestic and racial tensions, fear, and violence, *Shadow* is remarkable for the way the fears, guilt, and suspicions of the age reverberate through its specific material. As much as any fiction chosen for this study, *Shadow* exhibits the enormous vulnerability and durability of self (or of selves) under the stress of fear and violence and of an increasingly menacing society. With the exception of elderly people and children, women, and especially small women, are very sensitive to certain orders of danger. As Johnson says in an interview, women, particularly women alienated from husbands or from mentally unbalanced people, experience whole dimensions of apprehension, anxiety, and terror that the average man seldom conceives of. In this sense, as in others, *Shadow* explores female sensibility with authority, yet creates a governing sensibility in the prime character that men too can identify with. In so doing, it valuably exhibits self through the protagonist of Johnson's novel being intelligent and sensitive enough to be aware of the evil within herself. Thus, the sense of an evil, menacing external Other is deepened by a corresponding sense of inner devils. This combination makes *Shadow* a rewarding fiction of opposing selves in a tension of peril and significant growth.

All of the preceding works are fiction. To provide a different perspective of the self to this study, I have chosen two subjects in non-fiction prose that amplify the possibilities of a scrutiny of the self. One is sex, the other is incarceration and torture. Despite the fame and high availability of D. H. Lawrence's late Nineteen-Twenties essay, "Pornography and Obscenity," the piece has received very little analysis or criticism. Yet there is much in the essay that could profit from analysis, comparison, and elaboration, particularly when related to the idea of self. Lawrence, seldom one to take sex at its face value, defines in this essay what he dramatizes in his fiction: that sex is rooted in our soul or deepest self, and thus is a manifestation of what we most deeply are. This definition becomes terrifying if related, as I attempt to do, to our contemporary erotic culture, where assumptions and permissibilities about sexual relations, experience, and sex commercialization either make the author of *Lady Chatterley's Lover* seem like a Puritan, or suggest that areas of our society today are dangerously corrupt and threaten to destroy our intrinsic being. In this landmark essay, as in his other work, Lawrence indicates an identity of self and sex that is both frightening and liberating in our age of *Playboy*, *Hustler Magazine*, and video-cassette pornography stars, and intimates too a libertarian dimension in himself seldom credited.

If sex is the arrow of the self in an extremity of privacy, incarceration and torture project the self in the public sphere, albeit a rather special public sphere—the underworld of prisons, slave-work and concentration camps, sports arenas and public buildings turned by tyrannic regimes into sequestered and hidden detention zones of torture. The self under the electrodes and the sadistic knife, the self facing itself and its tormentors in weeks, months, and years of sordid and isolated incarceration, the self trying to accept the ghastly present of physical and mental agony, cruelty, and imprisoned time as eternity because it knows that to lapse into the "normal" and thus paradisical past is a perilous temptation—these considerations comprise the self in a kind of extremity of misery and terror all too typical of the 20th century, from the early political prisoners under Czarist Russia to the contemporary prisoners of conscience that abound in many nations.

What is left of the self under the exactions of deliberate or sustained torment? What about the self is revealed, and what subtracted, by torture and confinement? To probe these questions, I have focussed mainly on two fascinatingly contrastive books, Viktor E. Frankl's *The Search for Meaning: From the Concentration Camp to Logotherapy*, and Jacobo Timerman's *Prisoner Without a Name, Cell Without a Number*, the first work about life in the German concentration camps, the other about imprisonment and torture in Argentina during the 1970s. Also included by way of testing these two works in their conceptions of endurance (and being tested by them in turn) is an exposition of part III of George Orwell's *1984*. In addition, I have made allusions, sometimes extensive, to such key authorities on the subject as Bruno Bettelheim, Jean-Paul Sartre, Aleksandr Solzhenitsyn, Terrence Des Pres, and Oriani Fallaci in an attempt to round out the topic with other witnesses and meditators. Frankl and Timerman provide two contrastive styles of survival in institutional extremity; both say something acute about the self in extremity, at its very core: the decision to be or remain human, or to disintegrate. In ending the book with an examination of psychic extremity under coercive social conditions, I attempt thereby to bring the study by intimation back to the "torturous" self-explorations of Dostoyevsky's anti-self character. The implied circularity—from the condition of torture victims back to that of an ontologically desperate and self-tortured Underground man—form a modern gamut of the self in extremity, between which all the other selves from literature in this book take their own distinctive place. It is my hope that a sufficient variety of analyzed selves are exhibited to comprise an adequate statement on the modern self.

The self, both an intriguing idea because of its ostensible inscrutability, and a concept of being we generally take for granted, is very much with us today, partly because, on the one hand, modern humanity knows that it is threatened as never before, while on the other hand feeling that self-realization for more than a few people is, poignantly, almost within reach. Our late 20th century sense of the self is so keen, so probed, so palpable that it seems to supplant the virtually modern loss of the concept of soul. This study tries to dramatize, then, part of our modern culture of the self through a close scrutiny of a representative number of works of literary art. The selves literary artists create may or may not be the last word on the subject, but we ignore their characters at more peril than might be generally realized.

I.

SELVES IN MODERN FICTION

Dostoyevsky's *Notes From Underground*:
Self-Degradation As Revelation Of Self

I

In a passage from Section VI of *A Treatise of Human Nature* entitled "Of Personal Identity," Hume begins his famous attack on the conception of the self: "If any impression give rise to the idea of self, that impression must continue invariably the same thro' the whole course of our lives; since self is suppos'd to exist after that manner. But there is no impression constant and invariable. Pain and pleasure, grief and joy, passions and sensations succeed each other, and never all exist at the same time. It cannot, therefore, be from any of these impressions, or from any other, that the idea of self is derived; and consequently there is no such idea."[1] Hume, as I understand him, is saying that there is no such idea as the self because there is no element ("impression") that is sufficiently permanent to allow one to orient his being upon it, and thus stabilize his sense of self. Dostoyevsky's famous-infamous character, the Underground Man, in the Modernist classic *Notes From Underground*, comes impressively close for such a scoundrel to refuting this area of Humean scepticism. Indeed, Dostoyevsky's anti-hero in a complex way challenges Hume's implicit nihilism by—iron-ically—the very force of his own nihilistic being. Joseph Frank in a splendid essay on *Notes* has written about the moral implications of the Underground Man's character: "Far from wishing to portray the underground man as the embodiment of *evil*, the whole of *Notes* is quite the opposite. Only in a world where human choice can make a difference, only where there is no absolute determinism, is any morality possible at all; and Dostoyevsky adroitly defends the Underground Man's 'capri-ciousness' as the necessary precondition for any morality whatsoever."[2] Quoting from *Notes*, Frank buttresses this key point a little later in his essay in stating that man, to assure himself of freedom and moral autonomy, will "deliberately and consciously desire something that is injurious, stupid, . . . just because he wants to have the right to desire for himself even what is very stupid and not be bound by an obligation to desire only what is very sensible," for this right "preserves what is most precious and most important to us, namely, our personality and our individuality" (Frank, p.14).

These insights seem significantly true. Frank's essay is also valuable for its rich sense of the literary and ideological culture nurturing (if by the spark of antithesis) Dostoyevsky's extraordinary novella. Yet, even Frank and other commentators strike me as failing to take a close look at the real horror of this story. This is understandable, for *Notes*, in its unrelenting depiction of a degraded human being analyzing and dramatizing his own degradation, is not pleasant to behold. Yet it should be beheld, because whether or not the Underground Man is our double, he is too close to us to ignore with impunity—or with a clear conscience.

Frank claims that the Underground Man is continually jousting with the basic values of a Utopian novel published in 1863 named *What Is To Be Done?* by the Utopist radical Nicolai C. Chernyshevsky. Chernyshevsky appears to embody some of the ideals of the European Enlightenment in his belief in the innate virtue and reasonableness of humanity. Though Dostoyevsky and his main character are not one and the same, Dostoyevsky too is hostile to these beliefs. Although, furthermore, the basis of his resistance is ultimately religious, Christian, his artistry in *Notes* resides in his capacity to create and motivate a virtually semi-diabolic character who both in his thinking, and, later (in the second section), in his actions towards people, embodies "precepts" and practices that are despicable and that refute ready acceptance of innate human nobility. This in fact is one of the "discussions" going on in the story.

Another discussion is comprised of the narrator with himself in the sense that the narrator is irrevocably self-divided, and acutely aware of his division; he is continually doing things that he does and does not want to do. Indeed, anyone so deeply motivated as he is by spite and perversity (key words in the story), and who has his intelligence, is bound to possess a strong sense of his own dividedness. And if the Underground Man (or, more accurately, *The Man Who Lives in a Mousehole*, as Andrew A. MacAndrew translates the title) is also literary and intellectual, he comes disturbingly close to being like many bookish people. I suggest then that *Notes* is a deeply disturbing work because it graphs with close, if sometimes feverish, attentiveness the dissolution of a soul, the symbolic killing of a self, which in important respects is not so different from "ourselves." And If I find Frank's points about the narrator's moral significance inadequate, it is not because they are untrue but because his commentary and most commentaries on this still shocking work do not give us a sufficiently concrete sense of the horror of degradation and disintegration of being that Dostoyevsky somewhat sadistically exhibits for us. If I attempt to look into this dark pit at some length, it is not to extend Dostoyevsky's sadism. Rather, I wish to examine and assess the character of the degradation of *Notes* as an example of the extraordinary resiliency of the self, and to witness how far a self can go in its willed decomposition and still retain an identity.

II

Part of what makes this disagreable fiction curiously readable and even appealing is its comic aspect as well as the distance it projects between author and narrator. The work has been called comic and tragic,[3] and in fact those two designations fairly accurately describe the two main sections and the modal progression of the work. At the start of Section One there is a disclaimer by "Dostoyevsky" of any biographical connection with the narrator in his statement that the work is fictitious, though "people like the author of these notes may, and indeed must, exist in our society. . . . "[4] The idea that the author of the "Notes" and Dostoyevsky are one and the same is essentially a naive tribute to Dostoyevsky's skill with confession as a fictional sub-genre (whatever private springs of frustration and rage *Notes* might have welled from).[5] The whole trajectory of the work by its very nature would exclude "Dostoyevsky" as its author and victim, for that would be rather like Iago writing *Othello*.

Some of the complexity of *Notes* resides in its change of modes from comic to tragic, though the latter is implicit from the beginning, and is qualified by the irony of the Underground Man's self-deception and the profound sordidness of his existence.[6] Further, the comic dimension in Section One (which includes such attributes as farce, ridicule, and irony) helps to "objectify" the work distancing Dostoyevsky from its particularly dangerous authorial self-incriminativeness (a problem I will examine later in this study when dealing with Ferdinand-Louis Céline). And the comedy helps to make the "tragic" impact greater by preceding it, which disorients our expectations.

One of the first actions in the story of our "mouse-man" concerns the officer in a tavern whose way he gets into as the latter is playing billiards. Being moved by the officer as if he were an object constitutes one of our anti-hero's first-mentioned degradations, which he examines, probes, tastes and re-tastes with a masochistic assiduity and torment typical of a strain in literature from the Romantics on to the present. His complaint that he had ' "been treated as one treats a fly," '(p. 30), embodies a descriptive motif of the narrator recurring throughout the story. The Officer (Man of Action) is large and burly, and our narrator (the Intellectual, the Man of Thought) is "small and thin," but he still thinks he could make trouble. Duelling is out because the officer looks like a man who could break our protagonist in two with one hand. This gives occasion for the narrator's proclivity to paradox and self-delusion, which in this instance is that though he acts like a coward "when the chips are down", (p. 130) he is not a coward at heart. Besides exemplifying the sub-genre of the degradational confession, this revelation is true in the highly qualified sense that although our narrator would never confront the Officer, he nevertheless exhibits a certain audacious candor in the extreme soul-stripping revealed by his notes.

But our anti-hero does confront the Officer, if in his own ridiculously comic way. First, he responds to the first insult in a literary mode, by caricature in a short story, then in a "beautiful" letter to the Officer that he never mails. Considering that the letter is written two years after the event in the tavern, the narrator is clearly obsessed with the incident, and with his psychological opposite. But he finally has his satisfaction. He discovers that the Officer often goes for a walk on Nevsky Avenue. Accentuating the motif of his degradation, the narrator admits that he " ' scurried along like a mouse in a most undignified way, skipping out of the path of important gentlemen, guards, officers, and ladies' " (p.132). He notices that the Officer always walks straight ahead, over or through anyone. His plan is to show his mettle—and make up for his past

humilation by the Officer—by bumping into him. He realizes
that he'll get the worst of the encounter, but at least he will not
have backed down. But he does back down, for, in his first
attempt he skips aside. The same night, however, he accidentally encounters the Officer again: " 'I closed my eyes and we
banged hard against each other, shoulder against shoulder. I
didn't yield an inch and walked past him as equal! He never
even turned around, *pretending* [italics added—D.G.] not to
have noticed a thing . . . Of course I got the worse of the
collision, for he was much heavier.' " (p.135).

But that such an event is a symbolic victory for our
narrator is a dramatic indication of how degraded he feels he is.
And though the event is comically ridiculous, the comedy also
serves, as observed earlier, to distance both Dostoyevsky and
reader from this dangerously insidious individual. The episode
also provides the first substantially dramatized accounts of the
depth of the narrator's sense of his own degradation. On the one
hand he aspires to be the equal of a military officer, an official
man of action, while, on the other hand, knowing, or feeling,
that all the respectable people on Nevsky Avenue regard him as
a "pestiferous fly." Thus the incident harbors a vertical gamut of
the narrator's vivid realization of his own capacity for
humiliation, and, as he contains (as we all do) a force in him
resenting and resisting his being degraded, one becomes aware
that this man could be dangerous not only to himself, but to
others. In line with this possibility, the narrative modes of the
first section (called "The Mousehole" or "The Underground"),
which are confessional, unpleasantly comic, theoretical, private
in character, will change in the second or "action section" of the
novella.

To get a graphic idea of how the narrator's profound
nastiness and introspection confirm an idea of self, it is well to
start near the beginning of the story so as to take a closer look at
the narrator's inner life and thought. Forty years old the
Underground Man presents a picture of himself as being
hopelessly useless:

> I couldn't manage to make myself nasty or, for that matter, friend-
> ly, crooked or honest, a hero or an insect. Now I'm living out life in
> a corner, trying to console myself with the stupid, useless excuse
> that an intelligent man cannot turn himself into anything, that
> only a fool can make anything he wants out of himself. It's true

that an intelligent man of the nineteenth century is bound to be a
spineless creature, while the man of character, the man of action,
is, in most cases, of limited intelligence. (p.92).

Although the Underground Man often retracts his claims
that he is telling the truth, the truth in this passage possesses
some validity and general significance, for it intimates a sense of
fatality and powerlessness often felt by the intellectual in
modern society—and possibly a resultant if seldom overt self-
contempt as well. Yet the essential point is less whether the
Underground Man is really as useless as he thinks than that he
feels he is useless. Indeed, as he says later, he has felt that way
much of his life, from awkward, lonely days as a student to an
alienated condition as an office worker during his twenties. Yet
he is also candid enough to admit his nastiness. The one
student friend he has for a while he tries to dominate ruthlessly,
and in his office phase as a young man his relations with other
people are basically hostile; though he looks down on them, he
also feels that they despise him, and thus lives amidst social
conditions scarcely conducive to a stable or comforting sense of
self.

The narrator's candor in fact goes so far as to reveal what
has become a conventional theme of Modernist literature, that
consciousness (he calls it "lucidity") is a disease. His consciousness is "diseased" partly because he is a man violently at
odds with himself. The Underground Man indeed is, unless one
counts Diderot's Rameau's Nephew, the archetypal alienated
man in modern Western literature. His confessions are not
cathartic; they don't make him feel or be any better. If anything,
they make him worse. His self-conflict is too crudely put as Ego
versus Id. For one reason, the Id in this fiction would have too
much rationalistic and rationalizing intelligence on its side, or
the ego too much idinal savagery and violence. In the *Ego and
the Id*, Freud himself states that "The ego is not sharply
separated from the Id; its lower portion merges into it."[7] The
Underground Man's willingness to admit what a scum he is
cannot be understood in terms of a mechanistic conception of
the conflicts of Ego and Id in the Freudian schema. This could be
an important point, if true, because it suggests how harrowingly
penetrative and therapeutically irreducible Dostoyevsky's acrid
vision of the lost soul really is. In fact, one of the quiet yet basic
implications of *Notes* is the existence not only of the self but of

the "soul" as well in view of how degraded, how damned, this man really is. But the evidence of damnation does not emerge climactically until late in the story.

Nevertheless, we are prepared for it early in *Notes*, and time after time: " 'The more conscious I was of 'the good and the beautiful,' the deeper I sank into the mud [excrement], and the more likely I was to remain mired in it' " (p.94), a condition, he goes on to say, that he comes to feel is not accidental, but constitutes his "normal state," for, as he says in frightening words, " ' . . . finally I lost all desire to fight my depravity' " (p.94). This disintegration of his essential being is described in a famous passage shortly afterwards:

> I reached a point where I felt a secret, unhealthy, base little plea-
> sure in creeping back into my hole after some disgusting night in
> Petersburg and forcing myself to think that I had again done some-
> thing filthy, that what was done couldn't be undone. And I inward-
> ly gnawed at myself for it, tore at myself and ate myself away, un-
> til the bitterness turned into some shameful, accursed sweetishness
> and, finally into a great, unquestionable pleasure. Yes, yes, defin-
> itely a pleasure! I mean it! And that's why I started out on this
> subject: I want to find out whether others experience this sort of
> pleasure too . . . I derived pleasure precisely from the blinding reali-
> zation of my degradation; because I felt I was already up against
> the wall; that it was horrible but couldn't be otherwise; that there
> was no way out and was no longer possible to make myself into a dif-
> ferent person; that even if there were still enough time and faith
> left to become different, I wouldn't want to change myself; and
> that, even if I wanted to, I still wouldn't have done anything about
> it because, actually, there wasn't anything to change into. (p.94).

Frank offers an insight into this key passage worth considering: "The ambiguous 'delight' of the Underground Man
arises from the moral-emotive response of his *human nature* to
the blank nullity of the *laws of nature*. It signifies his refusal to
abdicate his conscience and submit silently to determinism,
even though his reason assures him that there is nothing he can
really do to change for the better. The 'masochism' of the
Underground Man thus has a *reverse* significance from that
usually attributed to it. Instead of being a sign of pathological ab-
normality, it is in reality an indication of the Underground
Man's paradoxical spiritual health—his preservation of his
moral sense.' "[8]

This is a powerful insight into *Notes*, but Frank fails to

confront the literal reality of the text sufficiently. Deriving pleasure from the "blinding realization" of one's degradation in a gesture opposed to determinism may really be a sign of spiritual health or of a preserved moral sense. Moreover, it may indeed be more than a clinically-disposed-of case of masochism. But *Notes* is first and "blindingly" a realization of degradation so intense, so acrid, that the reader is meant to taste it, to feel it in his bones.

Being degraded is a common experience (if more common to some than to others), and can be experienced without the *via negativa* of Frank's exaltation of the exit. The Underground Man is cunning enough to know that he is not untypical, but his claiming more normality than he should is really typical of his proclivity to rationalize, as is his claim that he could not change, assuming he wanted to, because there is nothing to change into, no other kind of person to be. But the real reason he doesn't change is because he doesn't want to change. The Underground Man *wills* himself into a corner, denies and destroys any capacity for change or growth by a perverse "act" of will. His action is a willed non-action, a kind of moral sloth that any sentient person is bound to have experienced. So, though his masochism does harbor, as Frank says, a kind of moral energy, it is qualified by a deadly level of acedia in his nature. At the end of the episode with the prostitute Liza, the Underground Man asserts that " 'all I did was carry to the limit what you haven't dared to push even half way—taking your cowardice for reasonableness, thus making yourselves feel better.' " (p.203). This, again, is an ugly, self-serving rationalization—but it is sufficiently true to give us pause, and to suggest that the Underground Man is not merely, as Sacvan Bercovitch claims, the victim of Dostoyevsky's irony. For, if he were, he would not be the compelling, fascinating (if obnoxious) figure that he is. Conscience does make cowards of us all, said another self-divided individual, and to be called coward by as loathsome a person as the Undergroundling, if not a pungent insult, is certainly an involvement of the reader in the narrative that (as I shall consider later) bears significance. Dostoyevsky's basic if oblique point may be that the realization through "conscience" (which includes consciousness, and even Lawrentian "unconsciousness") about our "cowardice" and deep self-delusion may help us to struggle toward some measure of worth or integrity, but it would be very hard.

The narrator shortly after the "secret . . . pleasure" passage admits that there are moments when he " 'liked to have his face slapped' " (p.95). Though he claims that this pleasure would be the "pleasure and despair" (p.95), though, further, it could be said that this last qualification represents the moral motif that Frank observes, one has also to face the full force here of both "pleasure" and of "despair." What our Underground Man is implying is that the humiliation of a face-slapping would give him *sexual* satisfaction; he might experience an ejaculation, perhaps even an orgasm, at this physical humiliation (and there is a real sense in which the whole narrative is one long sado-masochistic ejaculation).

The other term in this oxymoronic combination, despair, lends the needed ontological depth to this symbolic sexual degradation. Indeed, this is the term of potential salvation, despite the status of despair as a cardinal sin in Catholicism. For it would be worse if degradation were not responded to in *any* way, with no affect at all. This *would* be damnation, and though it is a state found in 20th century literature (as in William Burroughs' *Naked Lunch*), affectless despair represents nihilism, and is perhaps further than Dostoyevsky, with his religious affiliation, wanted to go. Indeed, the moral sense glittering dimly at the bottom of this abyss of confession is, as Frank points out, what gives *Notes* part of its considerable if oblique moral energy. Yet whatever moral character this novella harbors must also absorb the moral extremity embodied in the real possibility that our anti-hero is a sex-soiled soul; his despair itself could mean damnation.

Dostoyevsky's sense of degradation is more than excoriating; it is deeply piercing, penetrating all our egoistic defenses, threatening to blight our very core of being. In the quotation following, we continue to hear about the Underground Man's sense of resentment of the tavern Officer, but it is presented in broad enough terms to qualify strongly as one of the most overwhelming passages of metaphysical degradation in literature:

> In addition to being disgraced in the first place, the poor mouse manages to mire itself in more mud as a result of its questions and doubts. And each question brings us so many more unanswered questions that a fatal pool of sticky muck is formed, consisting of the mouse's doubts and torments as well as of the gobs of spit aimed at it by the practical men of action, who stand around like judges and dictators and laugh lustily at it till their throats are sore. Of course, the only thing left for it to do is to shrug its puny shoulders,

and, affecting a scornful smile, scurry off ignominiously to its mouse-hole. And there, in its repulsive, evilsmelling nest, the downtrodden, ridiculed mouse plunges immediately into a cold, poisonous, and—most important—never-ending hatred. For forty years, it will remember the humiliation in all its ignominious details, each time adding some new point, more abject still, endlessly taunting and tormenting itself. Although ashamed of its own thoughts, the mouse will remember everything, go over it again, and again, then think up possible additional humiliations. (p.97).

III

I am suggesting that the core of the narrator's degradation is sexual, literally, a claim I will elaborate later in the chapter. But it is also necessary to suggest in this last torturous confession, that something resides within or beneath the sexual element here, and that it is central to the meaning of the story itself. " 'Desire,' " says our man " ' . . . is the manifestation of life itself—of all life—and encompasses everything from reason down to scratching oneself' "(p.112). When he goes on to assert that " 'I . . . instinctively want to live, to exercise all the aspects of life in me and not only reason . . .,' " (p.112), we also realize that a major thematic tension girding the work is that of objectivity versus subjectivity. Implied more specifically above as reason versus desire, this tension amounts within the elusive contexts of *Notes* to an opposition between ideology and *libido*, basic life energy.

Students of Dostoyevsky have observed that he is making an attack in *Notes* on reason because 19th century ideologists like Chernyshevsky, influenced by 18th century European optimistic rationalism, asserted that rationality will solve or resolve all human problems, the consummation of which is imagized in the glittering metaphor of the Crystal Palace. An ideal of realized objectivism, this gaudy architectural symbol of the 19th century European ideologue represents a world free of whim, impulse, perversity, will, desire. But Dostoyevsky implies throughout *Notes* that these elements are not only essential to human experience, significance, and value; human life lacks ultimate moral possibility without them. In this light, Dostoyevsky, through his "untermënsch," is not a social

reactionary resisting 19th century Western radical rationalism;
he is also, and significantly, an early Modernist artist claiming
like Thomas Hardy in "In Tenebris, II," that "If way there be to a
better, it demand a full look at the worst." This credal battle-cry,
so familiar to us now through the heritage of Modernist and
vanguard writers and artists, makes an early and disguised
appearance in the narrator of *Notes*, who more than once is
described, if in self-deprecatory terms, as being a literary intellectual.   Ultimately, of course, it is his literary "father,"
Dostoyevsky himself, who is the Modernist Ur-father here, but
the role is shared with his unheroic "son," and there is a subtle
sense in which one can regard the Underground Man as both a
"poét maudit" and a travesty of one.

Through this travesty Dostoyevsky conveys a number of
Modernist attitudes and values now taken for granted as part of
our modern art culture. That that "culture" should appear in
such despicable and bristling form lends force to Kingsley
Widmer's reminder in the title of his monograph on literary
modernism, *Edges of Extremity*, that modernism as a cultural
heritage remains explosive and subversive if properly understood. For all the iconoclastic posturings and symbolic preten-
tiousness of Hermann Hesse and Harry Haller in *Steppenwolf*,
Dostoyevsky's mouse-man is, except in one significant respect
that I will broach later, a far more impressive literary realization
of primal rebellion than Hesse's romanticized rebel-intellectual.
Dostoyevsky and his narrator not only want to throw rocks at
the crystal palace; they really want to strip all of us naked, and
exhibit ourselves in the "glass" of satire. Thus Dostoyevsky's
partial defense of libido, instinct, and caprice, even in their most
revulsive embodiments, becomes the most radical gesture
conceivable, and antedates Freud's idea of a biological
libertarianism that resists cultural or societal control. This
instinctual subjectivism goes beyond political revolution to
render a basically ontological gesture of liberation through self-
liberation. Before we build the Good Society, *Notes* graphically
implies, we must first recognize and confront the totality of
human nature. Dostoyevsky is suggesting that we will never
have a good society, let alone a "Crystal Palace," until we have
confronted the Underground Man in ourselves.

But how bad, how perverse, is the Underground Man? To
find out, to see how much suffering he can masochistically
absorb and sadistically impose, we must look into the climactic

episodes of this novella, the Zverkov dinner-party and the subsequent episode involving the young prostitute Liza.

IV

A basic condition of alienation is loneliness. Solitary, the Underground Man yearns for human contact. Yet his human contacts invariably result in disastrous personal experiences that re-enforce his misanthropy and his self-loathing. Thus, the narrator is trapped in a vicious circle. One day, feeling desperately lonely, he is driven to visit a former school acquaintance named Simonov who with two other school acquaintances of the narrator is planning a going-away party for an army officer named Zverkov, a friend of theirs. This Zverkov is elegant, handsome, debonair, and, by his own estimation, a woman's man. He is also a large man (although almost everyone in this novella is bigger, apparently, than the narrator, a factor partly defining his plight). Thus, Zverkov harbors a doubles relationship (in the narrator's mind) with the Officer who had treated him like an object in the tavern. Zverkov is again the Man of Action, further glamorized by the adulation of Simonov and the other former school mates, and by his own boasting about amorous conquests. He is, in other words, the complete opposite of our anti-hero, the type the latter most loathes and feels threatened by. This temperamental and physical contrast is important, because it helps organize the novella in several ways. First, it not only focuses on the Man of Exploits: it also suggests in a fundamental way the real resolution of the narrator's on-going conflict with the Nevsky-Prospect Officer and the type he represents. We recall that the narrator, in an understandable self-delusion, had felt that he had taken the last round by having the impulsive audacity to bump into the Officer on the Prospect. The outcome of his engagement with the Man of Action in the form of Officer Zverkov is not only that he loses the next round—he loses a great deal more.

When the Underground Man arrives at Simonov's place, Simonov and his cronies, who represent "society" for the rest of the narrative, are surprised and displeased to see him: " 'Apparently I was something like a housefly in their eyes . . . I had not expected that much contempt' "(p.140). He hears (or overhears) the plans for the party for Zverkov.   The narrator impulsively decides to invite himself to the party, partly out of spite to himself and to the others (who had hated him in school).   The sensible, self-respecting thing to have done under the circumstances would have been to withdraw, but it is necessary with the Underground Man to keep the "principle" of perversity in mind continually.   He invites himself to the dinner party precisely because it is made clear by the others that he is not wanted: " ' . . . you never got along with Zverkov,' " he is pointedly informed (p.143).

Indeed, he shouldn't invite himself, he shouldn't go, for he will get involved in a train of disastrous events.   Yet by not being sensible or "rational" here he will certainly undergo suffering, the one state, he and Dostoyevsky think, that the Crystal Palace will banish.   But even more deeply, there is perhaps something psychologically healthy beneath this perversity.   The narrator invites himself to a social event whose planners frankly don't want him to attend.   In inviting himself he is giving himself the opportunity or chance to be *accepted*, to have social judgement reversed.   He wants in a way to be accepted. Acceptance is hardly what happens, yet to an extent it is a wholesome social impulse, and part of the same urge that drives him out of his lonely dwelling to have refreshening contact with other human beings.   Alongside the narrator's perversity, spite, and sado-masochism is a desire for the inspiriting life of a social concourse and social approval.

After leaving Simonov's, he asks himself why he forced himself into the party, and realizes it is "spite":   " 'I'd go just to spite them, and the more wrong, the more tactless it was for me to go, the more certainly I'd go' "(p.145).   Another reason for going, perhaps partly rationalization, is given a little later: " 'Had I not gone, I'd have taunted myself for the rest of my life: "so you didn't have the guts to face *reality*, eh?" ' "(p.148).   When the narrator says right after this that " 'I wanted to show the lot of them that I wasn't the coward I myself thought I was,' " we realize how profoundly divided he is between his inner and social being, and what a hopeless task he is undertaking. Though he is respected neither by others nor by himself, the fact remains that some spark of survival as self-respect persists in him.   It is that spark, as well as the consequences of his perversity, that turns *Notes* from confessional comedy and satire into a sordid ontological tragedy transcending its polemical role in the context of 19th century Russian and European cultural politics.

Matters get off to a bad start by the narrator not being informed that the dinner-party time has been changed to an hour later. Thus he is the first to arrive, and must endure the peculiar ignominy of the guest who arrives too early for an event because he is not considered important enough to be informed of a time change. The rest of the party finally arrives, and after some superficial and patronizing sociability towards the narrator from Zverkov, the latent animosities re-emerge, which result in the narrator being ignored and thus savagely isolated. He thinks of leaving but doesn't. He also *doesn't* enjoy the pain this whole incident is giving him, and instead of being masochistic (or only masochistic), he becomes aggressive and hostile, even attacking Zverkov himself, the life and light of the party.

His attacking Zverkov while the latter is in the middle of relating an amorous conquest is significant. Our anti-hero, whose courage here derives from a rage of frustration and humiliation, even refuses to toast the Hero Zverkov, to everyone's amazed disgust. He proposes his own toast in which he declares his hatred of " 'smut and those who talk smut. Especially the latter' "(p.155). Zverkov is deeply offended, and the others rain insults on the narrator, who responds with a challenge of a duel that is laughed down. The others move from the table to a sofa, leaving the narrator alone and totally ignoring him, as he sits drenched in vindictiveness, self-pity, and simulated scorn.

Again he feels he should leave, but remains, out of "spite." He is suffering badly, and the suffering continues for three hours, as he paces back and forth by the table, pretending to ignore the carousing Zverkov party nearby:

> 'Now and then, with a stabbing, sickening pain, it occured to me that ten, twenty, perhaps forty years might pass and I'd still remember these, the most ridiculous and painful minutes of my life, with horror and disgust. One could not have gone further out of one's way than I had to inflict upon myself the cruelest of humiliations.'(p.157).

Finally breaking down, the Underground Man asks for forgiveness, but is scorned by the whole dinner group, including Zverkov (who says " '*You* couldn't offend *me* under any circum-

stances!' ") (p.157). Finding out that the group is on its way to a
brothel, the narrator allows this last degradation to lead to a
worse one by asking Simonov to lend him money so that he too
can join the gang. Simonov first turns him down brutally, then
after our narrator pleads with him (" 'I clutched at his coat. It
was a nightmare' ") (p.158), almost throws the money at the
narrator. Left alone, in a state of "horrible anguish," the narrator
decides to go to the same brothel, where he thinks he will make
atonement to his self-debasement by demanding forgiveness
from Zverkov, or slapping his face.

V

Fortunately yet unfortunately, the Underground Man gets
to the brothel too late to make contact with the Zverkov group.
At desperately loose ends with himself, and in a very nasty
mood, he selects a young woman named Liza to go to bed with.
After intercourse, still feeling degraded and vicious, he launches
a formidably insidious attack on the young prostitute. He
describes her bleak future as a prostitute, and contrasts it with
various images of happy family life with a sadistic, malignant
imaginativeness that is "literary" in its cogency and articu-
lateness, if pathological in motivation. First, he stresses her
enslaved condition in the brothel: " 'You'll never buy yourself
out. It's as though you'd sold your soul to the devil' "(p.189).
When at one point in his discourse Liza says that the narrator
sounds like a book, he takes this remark in the worst sense, and
thus begins to describe her condition with a penetrative
viciousness:

> 'I tell you, when I came to just now and found myself here with you,
> I felt sick. As a matter of fact, people only come here when they're
> drunk. But if I'd met you somewhere else, and you'd led a decent
> life, I'd have trailed after you and probably fallen in love with
> you too . . . now I know that all I have to do is whistle and, whether
> you want to or not, you have to come with me . . . Just ask yourself
> what you're . . . selling into bondage. It's your soul you're selling,
> your soul, over which you have no power. You're selling it along
> with your body. You offer your love to the first drunkard who comes
> along, to tramp upon'(p.175).

The narrator continues pouring it on, virtually anni-
hilating any fantasies Liza may have woven to protect herself
from her sordid present life. He says that her "house lover"
doesn't, couldn't, really love her, that if she asked him to marry
her, he'd probably beat her, that she will age quickly and before
long the brothel-owner will make her feel very unwanted,
insulting her as she sinks lower and lower (" 'You'll lose
everything; everything will go without return—youth, hopes,
looks—and at 22 you'll look 35.' ") He also mentions possible
diseases she well could catch. Like another prostitute who ends
up beaten and bleeding, weeping in front of a particularly brutal
whorehouse called the Haymarket (as women do, claims the
narrator, who have finally reached the bottom), Liza is shown
the most harrowing degradation as her sure future in the mirror
of the narrator's diabolical art. Moreover, as this woman, Liza's
projected double, sits weeping and bleeding and swearing,
"'drunken soldiers and cabbies gathered around her and taunted
her'"(p.177); this nightmare would be Liza's fate as well.

Nor does the Underground Man stop here. He describes
Liza in the future, aging and despised, told openly by the brothel-
keeper that she should die, and that " 'they'll stow you
somewhere in the dirtiest corner of the basement. And as you
lie dying in the dank darkness, what will you think about in
your loneliness?' " (p.178). As if this were not enough, he
describes what people will feel towards her after she is dead: "'no
one will come to your grave, there'll not be a tear, not a sigh, not
a prayer over you . . . it'll be as if you'd never even existed'"
(p.179).

There is art in this interminable exercise of psychological
skin-stripping, as well as enormous spite, the venom stored up
until the whole personality of the narrator resembles a tautened
scorpion's tail. If he wants to break Liza's heart, turn her inside
out, he has succeeded, but he has gone too far, and no longer
enjoys this slow, thorough destruction of another human being
(" 'the fact is, I'd never, never witnessed such despair' ") (p.179).
Yet somehow, as the narrator tries to leave, Liza, undergoing an
extraordinary rebirth of spirit, all but embraces him. He in turn
unwisely gives her his address, thus setting the scene for the
final and worst degradation of the entire narrative.

The experience with Liza bothers him far more than the
Zverkov-party events preceding it. He doesn't seem to know
why this is so, though he is worried that she will come to his

mousehole and see him in all his squalor. But it is possible that the deeper reason for his disturbance and worry about Liza is that he realizes he has aroused a soul in her. This he cannot stand, because he cannot summon the soul-lifting "sincerity" he was taken by Liza as having the night before in the brothel when he actually was trying to destroy her.

One problem about Liza appearing at the narrator's dwelling is the exposure of his bizarrely masochistic relationship with his servant Apollon. Their relationship exhibits the social and psychological irony of a servant who is master of his master. Apollon, who lisps, and is haughty and imperturbable, is dependent on the narrator only for his wages, and it is money alone that provides the latter with any power over the impudently imperious servant. Otherwise, Apollon embodies another dimension of humiliation of the narrator, intensified by the atmosphere of oblique homosexuality in this domestic situation, the cold tension and slightly nightmarish invasion of territorial space and proprieties of two men living together in hostile emotional intimacy. The relationship is basically frustrating to the Underground Man because, except for Liza, Apollon is the one person he is in a social position to dominate or even crush. Unfortunately for the narrator and Liza, Apollon is indomitable.

Thus what sets up the climactic scene of the narrator's damnation is Liza's entering his place at the very moment he is bashing himself hysterically on the rock of Apollon's imperturbability. She accidentally and blamelessly sees her hero disgracing himself with his own servant. Profoundly humiliated, the narrator is determined to make Liza " 'pay dearly for *everything*' "(p.192). "Everything" is italicized in the text to give it weight, and it should have weight, for in effect Liza is sacrificed for the narrator's lifetime of degradation. She indeed is to pay for *everything*, though this penalty harbors the deeper horror and disgrace for the narrator that she is innocent, and one of life's victims. Sold, as she informs the narrator, by her parents (p.171), she is now subjected to the worst viciousness conceivable by the Underground Man.

Not realizing what the narrator really feels, Liza admits that she wants to leave the brothel for good. But the narrator who is in an agony (or ecstasy) of hypersensitivity and resentment, takes offense at her mild resentment at his five-minute lapses of angry, selfish silence. His vindictive fury pours over her like lava:

'Why did you come? Answer me!' I shouted in a rage. 'All right, my girl, I'll tell you why: you came because of all the 'touching' things I said the other night. But, for your information, I was laughing at you then, just as I'm laughing at you now. Why are you trembling? Yes, I say I was laughing. I had been insulted at a dinner party just before I came by the fellows who preceded me. I came to your place to take a punch at one of them, the officer, but I was too late. I had to vent my spite on someone else, and you happened to be around, so I poured my resentment out on you and had a good laugh. I'd been insulted, so I wanted to insult back'(p.195).

The narrator is kicking someone who is down, in this case, a woman. Although he claims that " 'My cynicism had crushed her,' " she will rebound even from this fiendish cruelty. The narrator, if nothing else, is honest with her about why he hates her. He also says, " 'I can only play with words or dream inside my head; in real life, all I want is for you to vanish into the ground!' "(p.196). And in an ecstasy of self-abasement, the narrator exposes himself totally:

. . . you alone are responsible for everything because you happened to be at hand, because I'm a louse, because I'm the most disgusting, most laughable, pettiest, most stupid, and most envious of all the worms of the earth—which are in no way better than me, but which, hell knows why, never feel embarrassed. But me—all my life I've let all sorts of scum push me around—that's just like me! And do you think I care if you don't understand all this? What concern of mine are you? What concern is it of mine whether or not you rot in that house? Don't you realize that when I've finished telling you all this, I'll hate you just because you were here and listened to me? Why, a man only bares his soul like this once in a lifetime . . . (pp.196-97)

Liza's response to all of this "existential" venom and masochistic exhibitionism is saintly, if disastrous for her; she embraces him in the one great and only act of self-sacrificing empathy in the entire work. At this point, the narrator feels that a role-reversal from the previous night has taken place: " ' . . . she now had the heroic role, and I was the beaten-down, crushed creature she had been . . . ' "(p.189). His abjectness at this moment stimulates (the word is carefully chosen) the narrator to " 'dominate and possess. Passion burned in my eyes as I fiercely clasped her hands. Ah, how I hated her, and how furiously I was drawn to her at the moment . . . she threw herself at me in rapture' " (p. 198).

Aside from Liza's dreadful misinterpretation of the narrator's cast of mind here, his ambivalence, which he will convey towards Liza a minute later as lust and vindictive degrading hatred, damns him. This ambivalence is the effect of all his pent-up misery and social despicableness, and he gets rid of it in the worst way he can—by literally pouring it, transformed into irrational hate, into another, vulnerable, innocent human being who, further, is deluded about the true nature of his passion until it is too late: " 'A quarter of an hour later . . . she knew everything, for I had subjected her to the ultimate insult, but . . . no need to go into detail. She had guessed that my outburst of passion had actually been an act of revenge, a new effort to humiliate her, and that now, to my almost impersonal hatred, there was added a *personal* hatred for her' "(p.199).

Now he personally hates Liza because he has been vindictive towards her, making him feel guilt that he converts self-protectively into hatred of the prostitute. What is the "ultimate insult" to Liza that our narrator doesn't want to go into? To convey vindictive or spiteful anger, the occasionally savage Mellors in D. H. Lawrence's *Lady Chatterley's Lover* sodomizes his beloved Connie on one dark "night of sensual passion." Lawrence further complicates and obscures this scene by implying doctrinal, heuristic values in Mellor's act. The analogous scene in *Notes* is briefer, and without having to spell things out (he couldn't have, anyway, given the literary censorship of the time), Dostoyevsky, I think, is suggesting that the narrator sodomizes Liza in a way that makes his true attitude towards her quite clear.

In thus demeaning the girl, the narrator also demeans himself. At least, he must think he does, for what follows indicates some guilty self-examination and semi-justification. He says that for him, love is only "bullying and dominating" (p.199); love is a struggle " 'starting with hatred and ending in the subjection of the loved object . . . ' "(p.199). Thus the Underground Man in effect justifies the maltreatment he has received from those stronger or more successful than himself by his willingness to behave or feel even more vindictiveness towards those weaker than or defenseless towards him.

Although the narrator is frequently described by critics and scholars as the ultimate sensibility in early modern alienation, the forerunner of the despised or dispossessed characters of Beckett, Céline, Henry Miller, B. Traven, it can also be said that by virtue of the narrator's sado-masochistic character structure and conduct, he affirms the repressive social and power structure of his day and society by acting like a person (low) in the pecking order. He thus loses the final, residual, desperate integrity that might have been sustained in surmounting a brutal social order by refusing to trample on or mistreat the one vulnerable human being lower on the pole than himself. In this extreme, intentional degrading of Liza, he condemns himself socially by justifying the very power and social hierarchy that makes him feel not only like a mouse, but like a worm.

But buggery, if it occurs, is not the last viciousness imposed by the narrator upon the young prostitute. A worse and final one remains, though it proceeds from the former, as the former proceeds from the narrator's humiliation by the Officer in the tavern. As Liza starts to leave, the narrator rushes after her, and puts some money in her hand. Yet he has an immediate revulsion to his brutal gesture: " 'The cruelty was so contrived and such *bad literature* that I couldn't bear it myself and leaped away to a far corner of the room; after that, full of shame and despair, I rushed after Liza" (p.200). He can't find her, and, on returning to the room, finds the money he gave her on the table. Although the narrator has devastated the young prostitute, she maintains her integrity in a final, decisive gesture that makes his deliberate viciousness towards her impotent. Not unlike Hardy's Tess D'Urberville, Liza rises to the occasion, and whatever degradation or deprivation she is likely to encounter in a future probably made darker by the Underground Man's complex sadism, she can remember her dignified rejection of the narrator's "whore-money" with just pride.

On finding the money, the narrator runs out again looking for Liza. He realizes, though, that even if he found her, it would only lead to the compulsive cycle of repentance followed (the next day) by hatred " 'because I kissed her feet today. . . . As though I hadn't found out today for the *hundredth time* [italics added] what I'm really worth? As though I could prevent myself from torturing her!' " (p.201). This passage is followed by the hideous self-deception that his grave insult to Liza would actually do her good, even redeem and "purify" her, through hatred or even forgiveness. This is certainly, as Frank has observed,[9] a gross rationalization, and is part of the narrator's continuing self-debasement. But the preceding passage, indicating the Underground Man's habitual oscillation between penitence and viciousness, constitutes a broad way of describing his alternate masochism and sadism, an activity which also functions as part of the internal organization of *Notes*. Kissing her feet one day, verbally tearing her apart the next, the Underground Man occupies a circle of compulsively, irrevocably vicious and self-degrading impulses from which he will never escape. Such, again, is his damnation.

That his damnation is significantly sexual in character is important. The sexual motif, though not omnipresent in *Notes*, serves both as one of its major elements, and as its primary "plot" determinant. It is not accidental that the narrator's attack on Zverkov is made as the latter is making sexual boasts. This attack in turn leads to his drastic rupture with the Zverkov party, resulting in his three hours of deeply rankling isolation that finally degrades him into offering rejected apologies. All these dovetailed rejections and humiliations, interwoven by their relation to sexual topics and values, so dehumanize the narrator and desensitize his self-respect and even his sense of self, that he finally abases himself definitively by asking money of a man who has just scorned him—in order to have sex at a brothel, as part of a party of men who have treated him with the utmost contempt. In this psychological context, sex becomes a means through which the humiliation becomes ontological, a shaft driven through the narrator's selfhood. So transfixed, the narrator's still musters a little *"libido"*—he wants to insult Zverkov, provoke a duel, and save or at least partially redeem his honor (although as he has no honor, this is not easily accomplished). But as he well knows, this revenge of honor is an absurd fantasy, born of reading too much Russian romantic literature (Lermontov, Saltikov-Schredin, Pushkin). The ironic contrast effected here by Dostoyevsky with the heroes of the 19th century romance fictions, while satirizing that tradition, also makes Dostoyevsky's anti-hero look all the worse. Even had the Zverkov party still been at the brothel when the narrator arrived, he would either have lacked the courage to attack Zverkov physically, or if he had challenged him in any way, would have again been mocked, or perhaps, in one of his typical and extreme emotional reversals, have found himself kissing Zverkov's boots. And, in any event, what kind of a threat is a mouse or a fly to anyone?

Nevertheless, a literary or intellectual fly with a dangerous flair for words and a deep need to vindicate his soiled soul at *someone's* expense, *is* dangerous to anyone vulnerable to him. Liza thus becomes his victim, and it is through sex that the narrator virtually attempts to destroy her. Ironically, he first inadvertently gives her a kind of spiritual rebirth in the brothel. At his lodging the next day, he demolishes Liza's resurrectionary mood again, out of vindictive spite, though he is not able to destroy her selfhood. But he does devastate her, and does so by sexual and verbal means. Whatever the nature of his second (and last) sexual encounter with Liza, sodomy or otherwise, it embodies an attitude that would shove her towards the Haymarket.

VI

The damnation of the Underground Man is his entrapment by a habitual orientation towards hatred and self-hatred born of his incapacity to meet life and society in self-respecting terms. This evaluation of course means taking Dostoyevsky's protagonist literally. Yet a literal interpretation does not detract from the numerous symbolic readings of Dostoyevsky's Underground Man. Some of these interpretations are both impressive and true. Dostoyevsky's underling *is* the unreconstructed individualist, the man or person that no ameliorative, let alone utopian, society can tolerate or assimilate, because his very existence undermines its rationale for or claims to excellence. He exemplifies human nature inaccessible to rational social planning. He will always suffer or cause suffering, irregardless of any societal or theoretical assumption that suffering and perversity can be legislated out of existence. His very spitefulness is, ultimately, part of the essence of his (and our) humanity, if humanity is regarded as what is left in the viscera of rebellious subjectivity against any totalitarian polity of repressive control. And, as Dostoyevsky's creature satirizing the rationalist ideologues of the 19th century (Owen, Fourier, Chernyshevsky, Marx), the Underground Man reverberates with further significance. He is the anti-Romanticist retort to swashbuckling heroism and to Organizational Man; he is as well the prototype of the protagonist as fascinating scum or bum prominent in Modernist literature. Unheroic, anti-humane, he is the Residual Man of the modern era.

But the Underground Man is first and basically his literal self, without which all the formidable symbolic meanings would not exist. He is first and foremost, and for whatever reason, an intelligent human being of disturbingly fascinating nastiness. He has his primary significance on that level, in that sphere. And it is on that level of literalness that his selfhood is most vividly projected and shown in the process of damning itself. The narrator's damnation of self is part of the literal reality of the story, and derives from this position more of its considerable force than critics have allowed. It does so because people don't like looking steadily into a cesspool, yet it is only by so doing that one can fully realize the nature or cause of the power of this characterization.

But if *Notes* is a story of damnation, partly registered through sex, if it is as well an extremely reflexive confessional, it goes well beyond being an isolated instance readily dismissed as being pathologically unique. Indeed, in an electrifying tactic effective in its being placed at the end of the narrative, Dostoyevsky has the Underground Man indicate (to cite a key passage again) that he holds a higher opinion of himself than of the reader: " '. . . All I did was carry to the limit what you haven't dared to push even halfway—taking your cowardice for reasonableness, thus making yourself feel better. So I may still turn out to be more *alive* than you in the end' "(p.203). This passage is preceded by an overt attack on literature that romanticizes reality, for, and it is a central, pre-Eliotic attitude in *Notes*, human beings don't want to face reality—" 'we're all cripples to some degree' " (p.202). Although Bercovitch has argued convincingly that we cannot take the Underground Man at his own word because he is at times deeply self-deluded, it reduces the depth and thrust of the story *not* to take the narrator seriously here. He may be self-deluded, like many people; yet, again, like other deeply-divided protagonists of Modern literature, he reveals alarming perceptivity into human nature in the very act of discrediting himself.

Without transforming the narrator into a T.S. Eliot, one can still claim that Dostoyevsky's partial affirmation of him, without substantially enhancing the narrator's status, is made at the reader's expense. The narrator may be a swine, but at least he knows and accepts that he is, wallowing in the mire of his own degradation. He actually exhibits a kind of perverse metaphysical courage (though he also displays masochism, extreme compulsiveness, and self-deception) in his obsession to examine and reveal the abysses of his own being. Most of the rest of us would *not* do this—out of "reasonableness." The Underground Man calls our bluff; we lack his confessional gutsiness and pleasure in self-exposure, his fortitude and masochism in confronting extremely upsetting "material" in our experience, and *thus* we are less alive than he. To make matters even softer for ourselves, we (some of us) embrace a literary vision of life—"romanticism"—that lies about reality. Indeed, the narrator accuses us of being generally confused and disoriented: " 'Left alone without literature, we immediately become entangled and lost—we don't know what to join, what to keep up with; what to love, what to hate; what to respect, what to despise! We even find it painful to be men. . . . We're stillborn. . . .' " (p.203).

"Stillborn"—again the accusation of the reader being dead, or unrealized, because he is unchallenged, disoriented, indecisive. The Underground Man is, among other things, a travesty of Hamlet. He is a man who can never satisfactorily resolve "the whips and scorns of time," and who will let almost anyone tweak him by the nose, because of his radical self- and social-alienation. This little man, this agony of convoluted self, disturbs us both because he is in his very self a mockery of the likelihood of a Good Society, and because he is the Shadow or idinal side to our "real me," threatening too in the acuity and frenzied vitality of his intelligence. He also is perturbing because he reaches out of the text and holds us responsible for our worst self or selves. Rather than being merely a disintegrated self, the Underground Man is a person feverishly alive at his core of nihilistic individuality. By existing so intensely at this terrible center of negatively bared being, he suggests that some substance of self is at the bottom of human nature, and leaves little room for the reader to decide how deeply his self-scrutiny sounds our being as well. One of the most devastating accounts in fiction of self-damnation, *Notes* harbors the profound obverse implication that if there is a self to damn, there is also a self to cherish.

Notes

[1]David Hume, *A Treatise of Human Nature* (Oxford, England: Clarendon Press, 1967) 251-252.

[2]Joseph Frank, "Nihilism and *Notes from Underground,*" *Sewanee Review*, v.30, 1961, 12.

[3]Frank, Ibid, (pp.26,27). George Steiner relates the tragic character of *Notes* to the *narrator's* inadequate manhood: "The tragedy of the Underground Man is, literally, his retreat from manhood. This retreat is made explicit through the cruel impotence of his assault on Liza" (*Tolstoy or Dostoyevsky: An Essay in the Old Criticism.* (New York: Knopf, 1959), 225.

[4]Fyodor Dostoyevsky, *Notes from Underground* . . . (New York: NAL, 1961), 90. All further references to this text in this chapter are to this edition.

[5]Some Dostoyevsky scholars feel that there are areas of similarity between Dostoyevsky and his protagonist in *Notes.* Avraham Yarmolinsky claims that " . . . Dostoyevsky makes him [the Underground Man], to some extent, his own spokesman. Indeed, the wretch took more from his creator than his ideas—he embodied a potentiality of the author's nature." (*Dostoyevsky: a Life*) (New York: Harcourt, Brace, 1934), 192. According to Boyce Gibson, "Dostoyevsky certainly does not identify with his anti-hero . . . [yet] something of the Underground enters into the world view of Dostoyevsky himself. His anti-rationalism, his antipathy to scientific paradigms, his sense of freedom as unlimited opportunity for good and for evil . . . —all this is pure Dostoyevsky." (*The Religion of Dostoyevsky* (London: SCM Press Ltd., 1973), 82-83. Walter Kaufman goes to the extreme of regarding Dostoyevsky and his narrator as virtually having as much in common as the author and protagonist in the autobiographical works of Augustine, Pascal, and Rousseau. (*Existentialism from Dostoyevsky to Sartre* (New York: Meridian, 1956), 12-13.

[6]For a treatment of irony in *Notes* see Sacvan Bercovitch, "Dramatic Irony in *Notes from Underground,*" *Slavic and East European Journal*, v.VIII, no.3 (1964).

[7]Sigmund Freud, *The Ego and the Id* (London: Hogarth Press, 1959), 28.

[8]Frank, Op. cit., 9-10.

[9]Frank, Op. cit., 31.

Hardy's *Tess of the Durbervilles*:
The Self in Tragic Love

I

In one of the big narrative shocks halfway through Thomas Hardy's *Tess of the Durbervilles*, the heroine of this novel says to her newly-wed husband Angel Clare (who has just confessed to an earlier weekend fling with a strange woman):

> 'Forgive me as you are forgiven. I *forgive* Angel.'
>
> 'You—yes, you do.'
>
> 'But you do not forgive me?'
>
> 'Oh, Tess, forgiveness does not apply to the case! You were one person; now you are another.'[1]

Shortly afterwards, Tess defends herself further, only to find her sense of self—and her *self*—flatly rejected by her present husband and former lover:

> 'I thought, Angel, that you loved me—me, my very self! If it is I you do love, oh how can it be that you look and speak so? It frightens me! Having begun to love you, I love you forever—in all changes, in all disgraces, because you are yourself. I ask no more. Then how can you, O my husband, stop loving me?'
>
> 'I repeat, the woman I have been loving is not you.'
>
> 'But who?'
>
> 'Another woman in your shape.' (p.246)

Angel soon tells Tess that he forgives her, but "forgiveness is not all." (p.249). Angel Clare's wife soon finds out what remains for her in the way of suffering, including virtual abandonment by her husband for a long time.

This scene is not only one of the most heartbreaking in a novel filled with grief and misery (especially for Tess); it is also a crisis in the work that tests the determinism that Hardy's plots are often accused of. One facet of the passage, tragic in nature, is that an individual cannot escape the past, that past and present (and future) form an inexorable chain of cause and effect, action and consequence.

Tess is regarded by her husband—and by Victorian society—as if she had committed the cardinal sin. Yet Tess was seduced, perhaps even partly forced, and by a "cousin." Further, she is only sixteen years old at the time of the incident, and sizably resists her seducer and all the circumstances (which include her parents and their poverty) forcing her into his company.

What could be regarded as highly, even excessively, deterministic in the novel is that the die is already cast for Tess by her seduction-rape by Alec. Indeed, that event triggers the action for the entire novel. But whether it determines or even pre-determines the effects should be questioned. Had Angel Clare been a different kind of man, Tess's past might not have made any real difference. The fact, furthermore, that she confesses her sexual past is a tribute to her integrity. It can be argued that Hardy's choice of a Clare—a conventional prude in his working moral values if not in his "advanced" thinking— - registers Hardy's forcing hand. Yet does it? Is it so unlikely for a young woman to encounter an Alec and then a Clare, basic male types? The encounters could have been reversed, and the story would have been another, quite different, one. But the likelihood of the Alec, then Angel, sequence is hardly rigged. If it is certainly Tess's bad fortune, the sequence is also part of life's patterns of chance (though the narrative is also given authority by the economic desperation that would make the Durbeyfields alert to improving their economic lot—or that of Tess).

More irony is embedded in the central, confessional scene. Before Tess makes her confession, Angel makes his: "He then told her of that time in his life to which allusion had been made when, tossed about by doubts and difficulties in London, like a cork in the waves, he plunged into eight-and-forty hours' dissipation with a stranger. 'Happily I awoke almost immediately to a sense of my folly,' he continued, 'I would have no more to say to her, and I came home.' "(p. 243). Several revealing truths emerge here that suggest that Angel is mis-

named.   One is that he voluntarily enters a two-day, two-night
bout of fornication.   Indeed, he "plunged" into it, which suggests
an orgy.   No one seduced, let alone raped Angel.   Also, rather
smugly, he forgives himself and accentuates his being the *same*
self after the plunge that he was before by stating that he
"awoke" to a sense of his error—" 'almost immediately' ",
though "8-and-40 hours" might strike one as a rather slow
immediateness.   Further, to accentuate his moral smugness,
Angel appears to drop the woman abruptly (" 'I would have no
more to say to her,' "), and can return quietly and unscathed to
his middle-class life and status.   Asked if he is forgiven, his lover
Tess "pressed his hand tightly for an answer' "(p.243).

A reader in the 1980's has to exert his moral and historical
imagination to see how a society could have blamed Tess more
than Angel.   Surely she is the victim, and Angel's experience is
much harder to condone.   Yet even in our era Angel's conduct
would be excused as a "young man sowing his wild oats"; Tess,
on the other hand, some would regard as suspect for letting
herself be led into a wood in the first place, but how much
worldly wisdom are we to expect from a 16-year-old rural girl?

Indeed, Tess tells her mother that she should have been
warned about such things.   The fact remains that Angel
experiences his fornication voluntarily, and leaves it when he
wishes to.   Tess is, after a *week* of trying physical and emotional
events, almost forced into hers, and, rather than being forgiven
by either society or her husband, is condemned.   To make matters worse, Angel, the free-thinking son of a parson, takes on
society's attitude towards promiscuous women—he becomes the
superego in the work, despite, perhaps in part because of, his
own more serious sexual derelection.   Further, Tess partly
absorbs Angel's moral severity, and judges herself by *his* harsh
standards.   Only late in the narrative does she relent on herself,
and fling some just recriminations back at Angel: " 'Oh why
have you treated me so monstrously, Angel! I do not deserve it.
. . . I can never, never forgive you. . . . It is all injustice I have
received at your hands!' "(p.377).   Too little too late, and she
ultimately accepts him, when he returns from Brazil "worn and
unhandsome as he had become" from an illness picked up in his
place of self-imposed exile.

This attention to the key confession scene is intended to
dramatize the central idea of this chapter—that *Tess* is remarkable for its "portrait" in early modern literature of a tragic her-

oine whose essential being is indeed the sameness or integrity of her self, despite its undergoing a series of shocks, violence, and social and family pressures that would disfigure or even destroy a lesser person. *Tess* is imposingly and memorably a novel about self, about a great female self. This self is tragic,[2] not so much in the traditional classic sense of a great figure who through a major flaw experiences ruin and, finally, realization or illumination. Rather, Tess's tragic substance consists of a great capacity for experiencing large adversity and suffering yet sustaining an identity that in her case constitutes a nobility of self.

Something of the tragic "stature" essential to classical tragedy is suggested through the ambiguity surrounding Tess's double name of Durbeyfield and Durberville. Hardy achieves many significant effects with this ambiguity. One of them is the lower-class, peasant Durbeyfield side from her mother (from whom, however, she also, we are told, acquires her beauty). The Durberville line on her father's side not only has found its lowest point in her boozing, irresponsible father, but there is the implication—obliquely diminishing the determinism with which Hardy plots are so often indicted—that the "Durbervilles" of the world brought about the condition of the Durbeyfields. Thus, near the end of the novel, when Tess's family is dispossessed of its lease upon the death of the family line and must wander from town to town like tramps, barely surviving, we see how a symbolic history of class spoliation can be located—even in one family:

> Thus the Durbeyfields, once d'Urbervilles, saw descending upon them the destiny which, no doubt, when they were among the Olympians of the county, they had caused to descend many a time, and severely enough, upon the heads of such landless ones as they themselves were now. So do flux and reflux—the rhythm of change—alternate and persist in everything under the sky. (p.371)

One encounters allusions throughout *Tess* to the Durberfield-peasant and Durberville-aristocrat strain, and witnesses how these discrete selves are—often falsely—identified and projected by other key characters. But the real Tess, the tragic figure, is another Tess, so complex a mixture of "Durbeyfield"-"Durberville" as to suggest that the essential Tess is *above* class. Part of this tragic and more genuine selfhood transcends class through Tess's continual identifications with nature.[3]

In the Talbothays section, as Tess and Angel are being drawn to each other, both their existence and attraction are repeatedly presented through nature. One night Tess hears Angel playing a stringed instrument. The setting is more than setting:

> It was a typical summer evening in June, the atmosphere being in such delicate equilibrium and so transmissive that inanimate objects seemed endowed with two or three senses, if not five. There was no distinction between the near and the far, and an auditor felt close to everything within the horizon. The soundlessness impressed her as a positive entity rather than as the mere negation of sound. It was broken by the strumming of strings. (p.138)

The endowment of "inanimate" objects with senses (two, three, even five, suggesting a human status), the obliteration of distance ("the near and the far"), the soundlessness, all add to a "sense" of human mergence with the now animated "objects". In addition, there is Hardy's description of an "uncultivated" garden full of "rank grass, which sent up mists of pollen at a touch," and with "tall, blooming weeds emitting offensive odors," a "profusion of growth" by which Tess gathers "cuckoo-spittle on her skirt, cracking snails that were underfoot, staining her hands with thistle—milks and slugslime . . . "—not exactly Romantic imagery of blooming love (p.139). It suggests the danger, the risk, of "natural" involvement, of the release and pursuit of the passions. Yet it is part of Tess's gift for nature and of her rich creative imagination to regard the pollen as Angel's "notes made visible, and the dampness of the garden the weeping of the garden's sensibility" (p.139).

Tess in effect seems to merge with nature, to be at one with it. Soon Angel becomes aware of her presence, and becomes aware also of her heightened sensitivity to nature, which forms part of his growing realization that she is not an average dairy maid. This motif of Tess's union with nature blends with another important element, Tess's sense, never sufficient to quell her deep feeling of moral responsibility for her life, that the present and the past are dissociated. Society *and* her conscience in effect inform her that experience is a moral continuity, that what one did—or, in her case, what happened to one—in the past rules the present. The result, as she accurately states it late in the novel, is "Once victim, always victim" (p.351). Yet at times, and this is part of the essential rhythm of hope and despair in *Tess*, the past does seem surmountable:

> After wearing and wasting her palpitating heart with every engine of regret that lonely inexperience could devise, common sense had illumined her. She felt that she would do well to be useful again—to taste anew sweet independence at any price. The past was past; whatever it had been, it was no more at hand. Whatever its consequences, time would close over them; they would all in a few years be as if they had never been, and she herself grassed down and forgotten. Meanwhile the trees were just as green as before; the birds sang and the sun shone as clearly now as ever. The familiar surroundings had not darkened because of her grief. . . . (pp. 106-07)

Nature, despite human folly and evil and greed, goes on, and what is natural in Tess—and it is very deep—identifies with the natural living forces of life. Even "Hardy's" voice affirms the split between society and nature, and the important sense in which convention is not in accord with the singing birds and the shining sun: "Most of the misery had been generated by her conventional aspect, and not by her innate sensations"(p.107).

During the courtship of Tess and Angel, time and convention seem absent; the two lovers appear to occupy an Eden:

> Thus during this October month of wonderful afternoons, they roved along the meads by creeping paths which followed the brinks of trickling tributary brooks, hopping across by little wooden bridges to the other side and back again. They were never out of the sound of some purling weir, whose buzz accompanied their own murmuring, while the beams of the sun, almost as horizontal as the mead itself, formed a pollen of radiance over the landscape. They saw tiny blue fogs in the shadows of trees and hedges, all the time that there was bright sunshine elsewhere. (pp.210-11)

Later, on her way to Flintcomb Ash, where Tess seeks work in order to survive after Angel has left, she spends a frightening night in some bushes full of wounded and dying pheasants shot by hunters. Not only does she identify with the suffering birds and "their silent enduring of a night of agony" (p.297), but even uses them as a measure of absolute suffering by which to accept "the relativity of sorrows and the tolerable nature of her own, if she could once rise high enough to despise opinion" (p.297). Indeed all the images of animal life hinted in the novel (including a ratting scene later in the work at Flintcomb Ash) suggest through imagistic association that Tess herself is a part of the nature being mercilessly hunted down by severe human conventions:

> The birds had been driven down into this corner the day before by
> some shooting-party; and while those that had dropped dead un-
> der the shot or had died before nightfall had been searched for and
> carried off, many badly wounded birds had escaped and hidden
> themselves away or risen among the thick boughs, where they had
> maintained their position till they grew weaker with loss of blood
> in the night-time, when they had fallen one by one as she had
> heard them.
> She had occasionally caught glimpses of these men in girlhood,
> looking over hedges or peering through bushes and pointing their
> guns, . . . a bloodthirsty light in their eyes. (p.296)

Again we have, if indirectly, Hardy's judgement of
humans viciously assaulting natural life, including people closer
to nature than they. Tess's basic agony, besides her sense of guilt
about her being sexually violated by Alec, is that she *cannot*
"despise opinion . . . so long as it was held by Clare" (p.297). And
as it is so held, she too, like the birds, is "writhing in agony"
(p.296).

Tess's real nobility then resides in her being, as D. H.
Lawrence described the heroes in Homer, a "natural aristocrat."
Angel at one point describes her as a creature of nature, and, his
patronizing aside, he is more accurate than he is aware. Tess
may be a creature of nature, yet the fact that she trudges from
town to town, home to distant work place, becomes an itinerant
rural laborer, is all a measure of her inner nobility, her pride of
being self-sufficient, free of Angel's perfunctory marital support,
and even supportive of her own parents.

Yet Tess is not fully or truly one with nature. Her very
sense of her own worth, her sense of her moral self, is precisely
what makes her superior to both the nature of lower and
vulnerable animal life, as well as to the "nature" of the two male
principals, Alec and Angel; it is also what provokes in Tess her
"agon": "Walking among the sleeping birds in the hedges,
watching the skipping rabbits on a moonlit warren, or standing
under a pheasant-laden bough, she looked upon herself as a
figure of Guilt intruding into the haunts of Innocence." (p.101).
"It was they," the narrator says of the social world, "that were out
of harmony with the actual world, not she" (p.101). Thus,
though Tess is a tragic victim of a division of self, her division results from being victimized by the narrow moral standards of
her society rather than from any condemnable flaw in herself. It

is part of Hardy's peculiar achievement in the characterization of Tess that her predicament and ruin, rather than seeming sentimental or forced, communicate much of the force of a tragic experience. It does so, again, because of the very fullness and richness of Tess's self, qualities of breadth and depth of character also highlighted by the contrastive inadequacy of Alec and Angel.

II

At this point I would like to turn to these two male leads, for it is primarily between the opposed poles they occupy that Tess's self is challenged, developed, and ennobled.   Alec Durberville (alias Stokes) is introduced in terms of the stock villain of melodrama: "He had an almost swarthy complexion, with full lips . . . above which was a well-groomed black moustache with curled points. . . . Despite the touches of barbarism in his contours, there was a singular force in the gentleman's face and in his bold rolling eye." (p.51). There is no question that Alec suffers as a characterization from his stereotyping as a Scoundrel or Villain. Still, Hardy manages to avoid two-dimensional shallowness in characterizing Alec by endowing him with some genuine concern for Tess—only, however, after he has seduced-ravished her, thus, becoming the chief determinative and destructive agent in her life.

On parting with Tess after she decides to leave Trantridge, the Durberville estate, following the rape, Alec says: " 'I suppose I am a bad fellow . . . I was born bad, and I have lived bad, and I shall die bad in all probability. But . . . I won't be bad towards you again, Tess. And if certain circumstances should arise—you understand—in which you are in the least need, the least difficulty, send me one line and you shall have by return whatever you require' "(p.43). These are not the sentiments of an unmitigated blackguard. Granted, Alec still has designs on Tess. He implies that if she were to be his mistress, she would escape working in the fields or the dairies. This offer, this temptation, is a constant throughout the novel. Tess could escape her miserable drudgery if she were to accept Alec. Her lower class status throughout most of the story is thus a sign of her integrity, a sign, however, not understood by many of the people in the novel.

Alec's designs, further, evidence his infatuation with her. Alec is a slave to female flesh, and to Tess's in particular. Her mere appearance after not seeing her for years is enough to transform him (if we are to believe Hardy) instantly from an evangelical preacher back into the Old Adam. Alec's annihilation of his new religious self is declared in lines that clearly indicate his sense of self-degradation: " 'You may well despise me now! I thought I worshipped on the mountains, but I find I still serve in the groves!' " (p.341).

Although Tess finally lives with Alec, the conditions on which he makes her finally accept him do him little credit. He continually haunts her during the Flintcomb Ash section when she is undergoing brutal, mechanizing work. It is too pointedly significant that Alec is present at a "ratting," in a symbolic juxtaposition to the dehumanizing threshing machine in which Tess has been harnassed to work at a diabolically mechanical pace:

> She knew that Alex [Alec] d'Uberville was still on the scene, observing her from some point or other, though she could not say where. There was an excuse for his remaining, for when the threshed rick drew her near its final sheaves, a little ratting was always done, and men unconnected with the threshing sometimes dropped in for that performance—sporting characters of all descriptions,.... (p.353).

Alec's re-emergence as a "sporting" character underlines his role as the seducer-villain. As Donald Hall puts it, ".... Alec on this day is equally importunate, inhuman, and insatiable" (p.423). Like the human hunters of the pheasants earlier, Alec is aligned with both the rat-hunters and with the insistent brutality of the "threshing" machine. Having de-converted himself (through Tess's re-appearance), he pursues her remorselessly, attacking every area of vulnerability in her situation and condition (including her economically endangered parent). And his criticism of Angel, though rousing Tess to anger, even violence, has its force and cogency: " '. . . I think I am nearer to you than he [Angel] is. I, at any rate, try to help you out of trouble, but he does not . . .' "(p.350). Alec shortly after refers to Angel as a mule that Tess should leave, for which she strikes him with a glove. Her anger might partly mean that she realizes there is truth to Alec's insidious insights, as well as suggesting that Alec might be a convenient (and partly suitable) scapegoat for her repressed anger towards Angel for abandoning her. Whether Alec is finally sacrificed for Angel is worth considering later.

Alec, at any rate, is a little more complex than a mere seducer. He might not be the ideal mate for Tess; his love might only be infatuation, a carnal self-subjection. But, in his own fashion, he remains constant to an aspect of her. That he has "ruined" her life he is not entirely responsible for; Angel Clare also shares some of the blame. Alec's fragmentariness of self is one with his inadequate development or realization as a character type. His insufficiency of character and characterization coerces an Angel Clare on the narrative.

What is the nature of Angel Clare? It is of course "angelic": " . . . he was, in truth, more spiritual than animal; he had himself well in hand, and was singularly free from grossness. Though not cold-natured, he was rather bright than hot—less Byronic than Shelleyan; could love desperately, but with a love more especially inclined to the imaginative and ethereal . . . " (p.210). "Ethereal" is the word for this lover, this man of "fastidious emotion which could jealously guard the loved one against his very self" (p.210). Clearly Angel is a contrast to Alec. They are, and are meant to be direct opposites, embodiments of a light-dark male typology. Their very opportunities provide one reason why Tess is so vulnerable to Angel, and, indeed, why she continues to look up to him during most of his absence. Angel is all that Alec is not—mind, morality, a dangerous loftiness, vocational devotion. If Alec is "of the earth", Angel is of the sky ("Shelleyan").

Yet his love harbors some serious qualifications which limit his integrity, his sameness of self. Before the revelations scene, we are informed that Angel "loved her [Tess] dearly, though perhaps rather ideally and fancifully than with the impassioned thoroughness of her feeling for him" (p.221). "Ideally" and "fancifully," Angel's words—they contrast sizably, tragically, with the phrase ("impassioned thoroughness") describing Tess's nature as a lover. "Ideally" and "fancifully" are not complimentary terms here. One of Angel's defects is a lack of some of Alec's "grossness.". Some capacity for sensuous attraction in Angel might have helped him to bridge the gap caused by his shock that Tess was not "pure" (despite the important fact that he was not pure, either). Lacking animal warmth, physical "appetite," he can be ruthless when his basic conventionalness is threatened.[4]   When Tess tells Angel she had told him before getting married that she was not respectable, and thus did not want to marry him, but that he had urged the marriage, then breaks down and weeps, Angel's response is revealing —he is unmoved by her sobs: "Within the remote depths of his constitution, so gentle and affectionate as he was in general, there lay hidden a hard, logical deposit, like a vein of metal in a soft loam, which turned the edge of everything that attempted to traverse it"(p.258).

This inner hardness, in itself potentially good, combined with Angel's tendency towards "radiance," rather than "fire," and with his need to believe (" 'It [her past] is not a question of respectability, but one of principle' "(p.258), becomes a central destructive force in their relationship.   Angel even regards Alec as Tess's natural husband in an unwitting play on the word "nature" that discredits both Alec and Angel, Alec for his seduction and sexual forcing of Tess, and Angel for the violent unnaturalness of his coldness and of his conception of Tess's matrimonial status.

Further, Angel is condescending towards Tess during the confession sequence: " 'Tess—you are too, too—childish—uninformed—crude, I suppose!' "(p.225).   Earlier in the sequence he calls her an "unapprehending peasant woman,"(p.249)., surely a peculiarly gratuitous insult for a young woman who has had little experience yet has the inner fineness to defend herself against this contempt when she says   " 'I am only a peasant by position, not by nature!' "(p.249).

Despite the misery he inflicts on Tess, Angel feels sorry for himself as he plans to leave England for Brazil.   Telling one of his dairymaid admirers, Izz Huett, that he "has been badly used enough to wish for relief," and that "you are not to trust me in morals now"(p.287), he asks the love-stricken girl if she wants to go with him to Brazil.   After Izz agrees, she tells Angel that no one ever loved him more than Tess.   This is such a boost to Clare's vanity that he drops the Brazilian invitation to Izz, pretending it was just "idle talk."   Once again Angel looks very bad, revealing a profound, if "human," instability and vanity, but also revealing a terrible heartlessness towards the enamoured Izz who after losing Angel "flung herself down on the bank in a fit of racking anguish . . . "(p.289).   Whatever Angel's social or cultural credentials, his sense of the self and of the other is precarious, fastidious, and inhuman.   Not intentionally or maliciously cruel, he creates as much suffering as if he were being deliberately cruel. Unlike Tess's love, that of Angel Clare, as the narrator tells us, " 'had been a love which alters when it alteration finds' "(p.390).

III

Yet Tess by and large remains loyal to this man. This urges one to ask why Tess would kill Alec out of devotion to Angel. How is her sense of herself elaborated or realized (if it is) by this act of consummational homicide? Tess's expressed sentiments to Angel when he finds her in an expensive resort house in seaside Sandbourne offer an approach to these questions: " 'He [Alec] is upstairs. I hate him now because he told me a lie—that you would not come again; and you *have* come! These clothes are what he's put upon me: I didn't care what he did wi' me! But—will you go away, Angel, please and never come anymore ?' "(p.400).

Angel's mere appearance is enough to make Tess hate Alec, but, understandably, not enough—yet—to make her want to leave Alec. Though she doesn't regard herself as "belonging" to Alec, some ethical sense impels her to feel that her obligation is to Alec. This obligation, though compelling, is as thin and superficial as is the extent of their bond: " 'These clothes are what he's put upon me . . . ' " she tells Angel. Alec has made Tess "hers" in outward form only; she is now Mrs. Alec Durberville; she wears clothes he has bought for her. But the real, the essentially consistent, Tess is dormant. Thus it is not surprising for her to say " 'I didn't care what he did wi' me!' " —even marry her, a kind of death for Tess. Yet beneath or within the social persona—"Mrs. Alec Durberville"—Tess resides still.

But the old Tess, that great energy of primitive loyalties and violence, soon emerges in a talk with Alec that the house-owner, Mrs. Brooks, overhears after Angel leaves, which leads to Tess's fatal stabbing of Alec. In this speech one feels overpoweringly both Tess's sense that she has again been betrayed by Alec, and that she has lost Angel again " 'forever—and he will . . . only hate me! . . . Oh yes, I have lost him now—again, because of —you!' "(p.402).

The concentrated fury of this sense of Alec's betrayal and of the second loss of Angel plus "more and sharper words from Alec" combine to generate Tess's attack. One might be struck by the peculiarity of Tess's continuing guilt about Angel which reaches a climax in the narrative shortly after when Tess, fleeing the murder of Alec with Angel, says " ' . . . only, Angel, will you forgive me my sin against you, now I have killed him?' "(p.406).

Angel is now disposed, emotionally, to do little else but forgive her. His forgiveness is in order because in a way he is partly responsible for the motivation in Tess to Kill Alec, first, by rejecting her, and by contributing very crucially to the deep sense of guilt and responsibility she has carried around for years about her blamefulness in being seduced by Alec. But what deserves particular attention is the character of the logic and morality Tess embodies in her killing Alec as a sacrifice to Angel. Clearly it is not a Christian gesture; it is not moral or ethical in most senses of these terms. But from the perspective of a primitive vindictiveness and expiation, it makes emotional sense as well as possessing narrative logic. Her killing Alec does clear the path for Clare, and the fact that it does so temporarily, that it is in the most basic sense far more grave ethically than her seduction by Alec, and that Angel *accepts* Tess's slaying of Alec, suggests a radical change in Angel (though not in Tess). This change is so extreme as to suggest a dislocation of character in Angel. Not only does he accept Tess's murder of Alec but in effect participates in her flight which results in a brief "honeymoon" for the two reunited lovers outside of time and society. Even after this idyll—which contents Tess, though (even because) she knows she is doomed—she tells Angel:" ' . . . now I shall not live for you to despise me!' "(p.417).

The only way one can understand this "unrealistic" idolization of Angel is by regarding Alec as the prime repository for all of Tess's violent feelings, including some she must repress towards Angel, and, more unconsciously, towards society, convention, and life itself. Though Alec (and Tess) are to blame for Tess's condition of guilt and opprobrium, Angel deserves condemnation too, as do Tess's parents and Angel's brothers, by their social snobbery towards the "dairymaid" or "peasant" Tess, towards, that is, the Durbeyfield side of the family. Although Tess's fidelity to the cold, withdrawing, censorious Angel is impressive as a sign of her consistency of self, it also suggests a kind of Manichean simplification of her male world into black (Alec) and white (Angel). Nevertheless, this schema, if belied by the material of the novel in ways I have tried to suggest, is "true" for Tess because it "works"—that is, her moral identification of the two male principals supply a kind of fundamental energy for and structuring of her being that both perpetuates yet finally—and unavoidably—dooms it.

There is, then, an important sense in the organization of *Tess* in which Alec "prepares" Tess for Angel. By Alec being so readily identified in her mind with oppressive, violent male sensibility and thus male evil, she is totally disarmed by Angel's somewhat feminine ethereality. The more Alec wants her physically, the more Tess recoils. On the other hand, the less Angel wants her (or the more he is revulsed or inhibited physically by her sexual "immorality"), the deeper her dedication, the more profound her steadfastness.

Thus, Tess is trapped between the "natures" of the two men, one "physical," the other "spiritual"—both inadequate or false in their selfhood. She can only break free of her captivity by an absolute act of violence against her primal entrapper. It frees her, but only temporarily. She goes to sleep on a Stonehenge slab knowing from Angel that they will not meet after death. The brevity of her time with him after Alec's death is impressed upon her. Yet, as she soon says as the police arrive in the morning to arrest her for murder, " 'This happiness could not have lasted' "(p.417).

Significantly, Tess's killing of Alec deprives Angel of Tess, as if on some deeper level, she linked the two men in blame for her fate, and thus punished them both. This is less to imply that Alec and Angel comprise one allegorical or whole male character, than that they symbolize a moral gamut of the oppressive patriarchy of the day.

As Tess is hanged, "Hardy" with heavy irony states that "Justice was done," followed by the famous line about the President of the Immortals ending his sadistic fun with Tess's life. Yet this is only one more sign of male violence towards Tess, starting with Alec's physical brutality, Angel's sanctimonious condemnation, Farmer Groby's social and economic vindictiveness, the resultant deracinating pressures on her fatherless family, all consummated in and symbolized by a societal male deity. What makes Tess tragic through all these things *done* to her is the quality of the self resisting her encirclement by either rapacious or inhuman male conventions.

In an important passage based on Angel's surprise that Tess could make a place like a dairy assume such importance for him, Hardy makes a significant generalization:

> Many besides Angel have learnt that the magnitude of lives is not as to their external displacements, but as to their subjective experiences. The impressionable peasant leads a larger, fuller, more dramatic life than the pachydermatous king. Looking at it thus, he found that life was to be seen of the same magnitude here as elsewhere (p.170).

" . . . the magnitude of lives is . . . as to their subjective experience." The "impressionable" peasant is potentially a subject capable of deeper nature than the "pachydermatous king." This pre-Lawrentian characterological esthetic is profoundly equalitarian. Perhaps Hardy fudges on it by suggesting the aristocratic Durberville name, but the stress of his subjective treatment of Tess indicates that her nobility and her humanity—both one—are innate; they are not anything she has inherited through ancient family tradition. Hardy does not plunge into Tess's unconscious or pre-conscious, but he does follow her experiences, thoughts, and feelings closely.[5] Indeed the point of view of the novel is a restricted third person centered in Tess. Where she is or goes usually constitutes the center of the narrative; what she feels or thinks is its primary concern. Thus it is clear why the book gives off an overwhelming sense of Tess; quantitatively, it presents a lot of her. We are continually in her company.

Tess's fullness and range of being are compelling because she occupies so much of the novel and does so with memorable and deeply moving humanity. Adding to this impressiveness of stature is Tess's relation to a facet of theodicy in the novel. Asked by Angel during her courtship whether she wants to learn anything, she indicates she wants to do the hardest kind of learning; " 'I shouldn't mind learning why—why the sun do shine on the just and on the unjust alike. . . . But that's what the books will not tell me' "(p.143). Of course *Tess*, the whole novel itself, asks this large question, and like most tragic works, answers it obliquely. Tess wishes more than once in the novel that she were dead. Again, that is a response, perhaps even part of the tragic experience, but it is not an answer to the deep injustice of human society. It is a question asked time after time (if indirectly) throughout *Tess*—Why nature continues with such remorseless indifference in the midst of human evil and misery, reflecting "on the just and on the unjust alike." It is an unanswerable question, and what the tragedian shows by way of an answer is the human response it elicits. This weight of theodicy is placed solely on Tess in the novel, and her response is to endure with integrity. What she endures is both external privation and inner grief, until the sheer hopelessness of her situation, accentuated by Alec's insidious blandishments about helping her family and the unlikelihood of Angel's return, makes her give in.

In finally giving in to Alec, Tess represses a part of herself which comes alive again with Angel's reappearance. Her passional being both destroys Alec and herself as well, for her new life with Angel, though fully passionate and unrestrained, is short lived. Therein lies the tragic necessity of Tess's being. Her hatred is the obverse of her love; both are spontaneous and deep. And her murder of Alec is perhaps also her answer to the question of justice—she makes sure that the sun will no longer shine on the man who so crudely blighted her life. Thus, justice is undone when society consequently hangs Tess. In this sense *Tess* ends in untragic irony, for Tess has been rendered injustice, and the only force that offsets the injustice runs through the whole story: the unfolding of Tess's larger-than-life fineness and fullness of self. *Tess* is the story of a "pure woman," and that purity, that clear, strong substance of being, is the tragic answer to all the ugliness and injustice and violence in life and society. After all, what do these negative traits, staggering as they are, amount to when balanced against the deserted wife who can write the following letter to her husband:

> Angel, I live entirely for you. I love you too much to blame you for going away, and I know it was necessary you should find a farm. Do not think I shall say a word of sting or bitterness. Only come back to me. I am desolate without you, my darling, oh so desolate! I do not mind having to work, but if you will send me one little line and say, "I am coming soon," I will bide on, Angel—oh so cheerfully!
> It has been so much my religion ever since we were married to be faithful to you in every thought and look that even when a man speaks a compliment to me before I am aware, it seems wronging you. Have you never felt one little bit of what you used to feel when we were at the dairy? If you have, how can you keep away from me? I am the same woman, Angel, as you fell in love with . . . (p.356).

She is also the same person who stands apart in the tableau scene early in the novel when Angel first notices her, possibly disappointed that Angel didn't choose her as a dancing partner, and the same who later hangs for her love of Angel and for her final gesture against her sexual violation by Alec. Donald Hall says, "one's sense of this novel is one's sense of her"(p.430). My sense of Tess is of her tragic constancy, one of the important testaments in literature that a woman can have that constancy of self, the great steadfastness of being that we call integrity, that in Tess's case we should call tragic integrity. She is one of the few characters in modern literature to possess such a full beauty of self-continuity and inherence. Tess is all, tragically, one.

Notes

[1]Thomas Hardy, *Tess of the Durbervilles* (New York: New American Library, ᶜ1964), 245). All further references to this text are from this edition.
[2]Critics have differed on the nature of Tess's tragicness, and some have claimed that she is not tragic. D.H. Lawrence states the latter view as well as anyone: "They [several Hardy protagonists, including Tess] have naturally distinct individuality but, as it were, a weak life-flow, so that they cannot break away from the old adhesion, they cannot separate themselves from the mass which bore them, . . . Therefore they are pathetic rather than tragic figures." (*Study of Thomas Hardy*, in *Phoenix: The Posthumous Papers (1936)*. (New York: Viking Press, 1972), p.439). Dale Kramer, on the other hand, thinks that *Tess* is a tragedy, one "of the individual . . . there is no valid way to judge Tess according to an external standard of social necessity or duty." (*Thomas Hardy: the Forms of Tragedy* (Detroit: Wayne State University Press, 1975), p.114). What Lawrence regards as a weakness in tragic character, social dependence, Kramer rejects as even being a factor to consider. But if Tess cannot be judged by external standards, she judges herself by them more than once and significantly (such as agreeing with Angel's condemnation of her which represents for Lawrence a flaw in Tess). As for Lawrence's position, Tess may not be (to use his examples) an Oedipus or Clytemnestra of towering independence from conventional morality, but comparing her with powerful aristocrats steeped from birth in their own self-importance seems invidious. Put another way, Tess's tragic character is of a different order than that of the great Greek personnages. Perhaps one can compromise with Lawrence by saying

that Tess is less tragedic than the figures of classical tragedy, but is still tragic, not merely pathetic. Penny Boumelha has attacked the idea that Tess is a tragic figure from another perspective: " . . . the source of what is specifically *tragic* in her story remains at the level of nature." (*Thomas Hardy and Women: Sexual Ideology and Narrative Form* (Totowa, New Jersey: Barnes & Noble, 1982), 122). Boumelha broadens her criticism on the same page: "Tess is most herself—and that is, most women—at points where she is dumb and semi-conscious. The tragedy of Tess Durbeyfield . . . turns upon an ideological basis, projecting a polarity of sex and intellect, body and mind, upon an equally fixed polarity of gender. In this scheme, sex and nature are assigned to the female, intellect and culture to the male"(p.22). These seem like telling strictures until one reflects that with characters like Angel and Alec representing different aspects of mind and society, an identification with nature is, at least, in Hardy's eyes, a high commendation. Boumelha, however, is also objecting to Hardy's implied sexual chauvinism that women lack mind or learning, or are at their best when they are being instinctive or emotional (although Alec certainly is a *man* at the mercy of his instincts, and can lay no claim to earning his social and economic assets). Although Hardy in some respects idolizes both nature and the natural and thus his "naturing" of Tess possesses some worth and force, Boumelha's points have some force. They would have more force, however, if she could have found at least something attractive about *Tess*; that she does not makes her *Tess* chapter seem like an exercise in tendentious critical destructiveness rather than a balanced appraisal.

[3]If the tragic character of *Tess* is a subject of controversy among critics, so is the role of nature in the work. Peter J. Casagrande views nature as having an acceptably affirmative role: "In *Tess* he [Hardy] exhibited the regenerative power of nature for a tragic life lived in harmony with nature." (*Unity in Hardy's Novels: Repetitive Symmetries* (Lawrence, Kansas: Regents Press of Kansas, [c]1982), 199). When Casagrande goes on to assert that "Tess's death is not the end . . . because she has struggled valiantly to live, and because nature . . . will endure and prevail," (p.200), one must ask: *which* nature, that of the Froom valley or of Flintcomb-Ash, Tess's or Alec's? David Lodge regards the function of nature in Tess as being complex, indeed, as conflicted: "Hardy's undertaking to defend Tess as a pure woman by emphasizing her kinship with Nature perpetually drew him towards the Romantic view of Nature as a reservoir of benevolent impulses, a view which one side of his mind reflected as falsely sentimental. Many Victorian writers, struggling to reconcile the view of Nature inherited from the Romantics with the discoveries of Darwinian biology, exhibit the same conflict, but it is particularly noticeable in Hardy." (*Language of Fiction* (New York: Columbia University Press, 1967), 176). This observation suggests that if Tess is to be validated as a characterization, it must be done on the basis of her humanness, her qualities both of consciousness and unconsciousness that embody and project herself. Yet, it seems to me, nature, if seen as *both* dangerous as well as benevolent instinct in *Tess*, can to a certain extent be enlisted in defense of Tess as a meritable characterization.

[4]F. B. Pinion states that in Angel "the head has developed at the expense of the heart; . . . the springs of charity are blocked." (*Thomas Hardy: Art and Thought* (New York: MacMillan, 1977), 127). This remark suggests Angel's affinities as a type with some of the heartless characters of E. M. Forster's fiction, and thus Hardy's affinity not only with Lawrence but also with Forster.

[5]Perhaps too closely. Boumelha points out that "all the passionate commitment to exhibiting Tess as the subject of her own experience evokes an unusually overt maleness in the narrative voice. The narrator's erotic fantasies of penetration and engulfment enact a pursuit, violation, and persecution of Tess that is parallel with those she suffers at the hands of her two lovers." Op. cit., 120.

Conrad's *Lord Jim*: Courage, Cowardice, and the Self

I

If most people know what the fate worse than death is for females, they also know what it traditionally is for males. That male fate is cowardice, and it can be especially grim if it is publically exhibited or exposed. There are certain male authors who seem to have much at stake in the subject of courage and cowardice. Joseph Conrad, Ernest Hemingway, and Norman Mailer appear even sadomasochistically interested in testing fortitude or valor in their fiction, and there are times when for the two American writers such testing virtually resolves itself into a performance in a bull or boxing ring. The fact that all three authors have challenged themselves probably more mercilessly than they have anyone else, fictional or otherwise, is, I think, a significant consideration in any evaluation of their pressure on a reader's courage or fortitude.

The force of their probing a male's mettle seems all the more formidably relevant to modern concerns in view of the fact that all three have written in a period of either shifting, collapsing, or collapsed value systems, and unstable, destroyed, or post-war societies, so that it seems all the more essential to secure at least a few firm values by which to navigate the treacherous waters of the Twentieth century. Steering is of course a famous metaphor in Conrad's work. A complicity of manly silence about one's emotions represents a salient trait among Hemingway's heroes. And Mailer's work echoes something deeply and unpleasantly lurking in the fiction of Hemingway and Conrad as well—the keen sense that not only a protagonist, a Lord Jim or Jake Barnes or Stephen Rojack is being tested, but the reader as well.

This sense of the reader entering, or, perhaps being dragged into, the "ring" against the Forces of Darkness comes across as strongly in Conrad as it does in the two later authors, despite the fact that Conrad was not known as the literal pugilist that the two Americans were. Nevertheless, Conrad's life also was full of action and adventure in his capacity as a ship's captain on the high seas and up and down the Congo, and he undoubtedly underwent a test of courage which Hemingway and Mailer would envy. Thus, Conrad, himself put through ordeals psychological, social, nationalistic, and even filial in nature, in turn exposed many of his characters to severe pressure, humiliation, and even torture (such as the miserable Hirsch in *Nostromo*). If some of his characters come through looking very good, this is often attributed to their deficiency in imagination ("A coward dies a thousand deaths . . . "). Indeed, one implied tendency towards leniency in Conrad's outlook on cowardice is that to be a victim of one's imagination is to be in thralldom to demons and horrors that might frighten more courageous men, had they more imagination.

An example of this excessive imagination in action occurs in the pivotal scene in *Lord Jim* that generates in the rest of the novel endless ramifications of meditation and reaction in both its main narrator, Marlow, and its central subject, Jim: the ostensible sinking of the pilgrim ship *Patna* and its desertion by all of its officers, including Jim: "His [Jim's] confounded imagination had evoked for him all the horrors of panic, the trampling rush, the pitiful scream, boats swamped—all the appalling incidents of a disaster at sea he had ever heard of. He might have been resigned to die but I suspect he wanted to die without added terrors, quietly, in a sort of peaceful trance."[1]

This passage raises a fascinating consideration which we cannot take up: whether a person is courageous for being willing to accept death, or cowardly for not wanting to go through dying (at least, not violently, and we have the evidence of eminently brave individuals like Samuel Johnson being terrified at the thought of death). A more pressing question is urged on us by *Lord Jim* itself, and that is another aspect or role of imagination, that romantic drive to be heroic, the quixotic dream. Imagination in this regard also enthralls Jim, early in *Lord Jim* and throughout the novel: " . . . he would forget himself, and beforehand live in his mind the sea-life of light literature. He saw himself saving people from sinking ships, cutting away masts in a hurricane, swimming through a surf with a line . . . He confronted savages in tropical shores, quelled mutinies on the high seas, and in a small boat upon the ocean kept up the hearts of despairing men—always an example of devotion to duty, and as unflinching as a hero in a book"(p.11).

The contrast between illusion and reality is painfully clear in this passage. Less clear is the relation between two kinds of imagination in *Lord Jim:*   the imagination which makes one long for heroicism and noble deeds, and the imagination which "makes cowards of us all." Are they interrelated? The fact that Conrad's real or literal heroes also appear often to be unimaginative fellows, even dullards, seems to reinforce this idea.   Yet a noteworthy, though *not* crucial, character in *Lord Jim*, Stein, is himself a heroic man of action *and* contemplation. This fact supports Jim and his Imagination and indeed seems to support the type Jim represents when Stein says, with his generally overvalued crypticness, "That was the way. To follow the dream and again to follow the dream . . . "(p.161). Without trying my hand at unravelling the tough knots of Stein's Imponderables, I think that some region in Conrad supports Stein here in affirming value in the imaginative romantic outlook or temperament. It is improper to give too much force to a single quotation, but Ian Watt, in a discussion of romaticism in Conrad, exhibits a revealing sentiment from the "Author's Note" to Conrad's *Within The Tides:* "The romantic feeling of reality was in me an inborn faculty. . . . This in itself may be a curse but when disciplined by a sense of personal responsibility and a recognition of the hard facts of existence shared with the rest of mankind becomes but a point of view from which the very shadows of life appear endowed with an internal glow."[2]

As if this concentrated (if qualified) romanticism in Conrad and *Lord Jim* doesn't complicate matters sufficiently, there is also the substantial biographical and psychological evidence, presented by Conradians like Gustav Morf, Jocelyn Baines, Bernard C. Meyer, and Watt, that Conrad's own feelings about leaving Poland produced in him a profound guilt and a need for expiation:

> From one point of view the *Patna* corresponds to the *Vidar*, and Jim's 'jump' to Conrad's act of quitting that steamship, an act which he likened to 'a divorce—almost a desertion.' Just as this 'desertion' of the *Vidar* had been compared to Conrad's 'desertion' of Poland, so has Jim's jump from the doomed *Patna*. Morf has even suggested that the very name of that ship was chosen because of its resemblance to *Polska* (Poland), and that her rescue by a French vessel reflects the recurring historical expectation of the Polish people that it is to the French that they must ever look for deliverance.   It would seem plausible that Conrad too saw a parallel between his quitting Poland and Jim's 'jump'.[3]

Meyer sums up the etiology of Jim's cowardice (or, at least, shame) in Conrad's own guilt: "Conrad's recurring concern with the theme of desertion both in his personal life and in his fiction, arose not merely over his having left his native soil and exporting his literary genius, but over the gnawing conviction that he had perpetrated a perfidious reputation of the hopes, the ideals, and expectations of his martyred parents."[4]   Watt has added that Conrad's guilt might have been complicated by feeling responsible for the death of his mother, who died giving birth to him.

Yet readers with a tendency to identify Conrad with Jim should consider a crucial difference between them. Though Jim is motivated by shame, Conrad is mainly driven by guilt. Watt offers a useful distinction between shame and guilt: "It is usually agreed that shame is much more directly connected than guilt with the individual's failure to live up to his own ideal conception of himself."[5]

One result of Jim's shame is a very serious defect that has been detected by Watt: "Jim's sensitivity [to his honor, or dishonor, after the *Patna* 'jump'] . . . does not seem to extend to any internalized awareness of the intrinsic moral basis of solidarity.   He does not even seem to be aware that he has committed a crime, whose 'real significance,' Marlow explains, lies 'in its being a breach of faith with the community of mankind.'"[6]   Jim's feeling shame rather than guilt suggests not only his egoism but also his fate, and that is to be one who will "follow the dream" until it destroys him (and, by implication, some part of Stein's authority and wisdom).   The implication, which I shall elaborate later in the chapter, is that Jim's pursuit of his dream violates communal values.   His fantasizing about his heroicism makes him less capable of dealing with the forces of evil or the unexpected when it attacks, and his wanting and getting a second chance results in a slaughter of a part of the community of Patusan that has come to trust and honor him fully.

II

The question then about Jim is twofold: is he brave or is he a coward, and how does bravery and cowardice relate to the concept of self? I will consider the second question first. Bravery and cowardice are profound indices of self, for they test humans to the root of their being—they represent ontological properties in human character. How men and women respond to threat, pain, horror, violence, and death reveal the inner core of their character, definitively, according to the stark codes of simpler or more primitive societies, and perhaps, more obliquely, in more sophisticated societies as well. These conditions of extremity are also employed by certain novelists to compel male characters to prove what strikes them as most worth proving in any man: honor, valor, virility, pride—in *their* word, manhood. That qualities like compassion, empathy, serenity and magnanimity do not appear to rank very high in the work of Conrad, Hemingway, and Mailer is a point insufficiently considered.

What prevents Conrad's fiction from taking on a simplistic, "macho" character is the technical complexity and handling of his attitudes towards his principal ideas and characters, which are undoubtedly due to some extent to his own tendency to identify with people like Jim or like Razumov in *Under Western Eyes* who are, respectively, split in their ideals of loyalty to self or to a community. Both Conrad and Marlow are ambivalent towards Jim, but not in the same way. Marlow's involvement with Jim is calculated to involve the reader, by the very pressure of Marlow's agonized concern about Jim. Further, Marlow's attitudes towards Jim are rendered more complex by Jim's occasional accusative negativity towards Marlow, and, by implication, the reader. If Jim more than once asks Marlow (rather bullyingly) what *he* would have done during the *Patna* crisis, Marlow in turn obliquely asks the reader the same question. And if Marlow at one point insists to the rather wooden, allegorical Jewel that no one beyond the jungle wants Jim, because " 'he is not good enough' "(p.236), he follows this up by insisting that "Nobody, nobody is good enough.' "

But Conrad does not fully agree with Marlow here, nor does Marlow fully mean what he says. Is not the French Lieutenant who stays on board the ever-dangerous *Patna* for thirty-six hours while the ship is being towed to port *good* enough, or Bill Stanton, the little First Mate on another ship who drowns trying to rescue a large, hysterical Lady's maid? And what about Stein? What Marlow seems really to be saying is that *if* Jim isn't good enough, then no one is. We realize that Marlow harbors a kind of vested interest in suggesting that Jim's integrity is worth believing in or further testing, or, that if it is proven to fail, then most of us would also fail (and some would not even be worthy of the Test, like the thoughtless, pampered tourists in *Lord Jim* that Marlow loves to scorn). Jim's test and failure are sufficiently important to Marlow and Conrad to make the integrity of society and of human nature itself almost appear to be imperilled—such is the character of the gravity of Marlow's meditations and concerns throughout *Lord Jim*.

Are there other reasons for Marlow's closeness to Jim? I feel that on one significant level, Marlow and Jim are the same person, and when he says that it was "for my own sake that I wished to find some shadow of an excuse for that young fellow whom I had never met before," the proclivity to identify the two as one becomes pronounced. Marlow, in looking into Jim, admits he is also looking into himself, and few topics will goad especially a male into such scrutiny as the nagging fear that he is perhaps not sufficiently brave, or even not brave at all. If the word *"cabron"* rings in Spanish ears with a special quiver, so does the word "coward" in English. So powerful is it that Conrad asks us to believe that the dark sharing of Jim's weakness by the bold and experienced Captain Brierly was enough to drive the latter (a proven hero) to suicide.

As urged earlier, Marlow, on looking into himself, also looks into the reader, and when Jim asks him more than once whether in effect he, Marlow, would have done any better in the *Patna* situation, not only is Marlow put on the spot—so is the reader. Albert Guerard, discussing the formal innovative qualities of *Lord Jim*, describes it as the "first novel in a new form: a form bent on involving and implicating the reader in a psycho-moral drama which has no easy solution, and bent on engaging his sensibilities more strenuously and even more uncomfortably than ever before."[7] Marlow is the primary medium of reader-implication, and when he says to Jewel that " 'Nobody . . . is good enough,' " he means it to include the reader. If Jim in some way is part of Marlow, he and Marlow are also possibly a part of "us," and through Conrad-Marlow's "One-of-Us" Club, which (especially in the context of late 19th-century British imperialism) harbors social and even racial elitist connotations, takes on quite a different significance than is usually attributed to it. When Marlow (and even Conrad, in the last sentence of his "Preface" to *Lord Jim*) says that Jim is "one of us," he usually means that he is decent, reliable, honest, has the right sentiments, the right

impulses (although it was on impulse that Jim leaped from the
Patna), all those sterling qualities that most of "us" like to think
we possess. In view of the marked racial contexts in *Lord Jim* in
which Conrad's One-of-Us is located, however, this cliquish
phrase also seems to designate people of European (even North
European) descent, fair-skinned, even fairhaired and preferably
blue-eyed like Jim.

Yet some evidence in the novel suggests that when Jim
lands in the lifeboat already containing the Captain of the *Patna*
and the other two ship's officers, he has joined his true community, one of unpardonable cowards. Which community does
Jim belong to—is he "one of us" or is he "one of *them*"? And if
the reader, indeed, if all human beings (Marlow claims, partly to
vindicate Jim) are not good enough, it ultimately makes little
difference whether one is "one of us" or "one of them," as both
groups appear almost identical—and *Lord Jim* would seem to
lurch into nihilism.

Yet this argument is not foolproof, just as it is unsound to
consider Marlow always reliable. There is an amazing distance
and difference between the French lieutenant (or Stein) and the
Captain of the *Patna*. It is typically revealing and obfuscating of
Conrad that he gives the Frenchman little insight into cowardice, beyond the seemingly humane attitude that we are all
born with fear, born cowards. When Marlow almost thanks the
Frenchman for "taking a lenient view," he gets a rude shock in
one of the most unforgettable passages of vivid character
description in *Lord Jim:*

> The shuffle of his feet under the table interrupted me. He drew
> up his heavy eyelids. . . . I was confronted by two narrow grey cir-
> clets, like two tiny steel rings around the profound blackness of the
> pupils. The sharp glance, coming from that massive body, gave a no-
> tion of extreme efficiency, like a razor-edge on a battle-axe. 'Par-
> don,' he said, punctiliously. . . . 'I contended that one may get on
> knowing very well that one's courage does not come of itself. . . .
> There's nothing much in that to get upset about. One truth the more
> ought not to make life impossible. . . . But the honour—the honour,
> monsieur: . . . . The honour . . . that is real—that is: And what life
> may be worth when' . . . he got on his feet with a ponderous impetu-
> osity, 'when the honour is gone . . . I can offer no opinion . . . be-
> cause—monsieur—I know nothing of it.'(p.113)

I cite this passage at length partly because, though offering
one of the most impressive character vignettes in Conrad's no-

vel, it is seldom quoted.   The passage of course is a shocker.
After Marlow has seemed to get Jim, the reader, and "us" off the
hook, we are suddenly confronted with his massive display of
austere devotion to high courage and oblique horror towards the
dishonor of cowardice.   The Lieutenant is neither arrogant nor
haughty.   He even seems rather human in declaring that courage doesn't come easily—one has to work at it (" 'It would be too
easy otherwise . . . ' "p.112).   But if one has behaved cowardly, if
the potential for it has somehow been actualized, that is an utterly different matter.   The Frenchman can offer no opinion about
it because he has never experienced it, but his sentiments on
honor indicate that life without it, lived in cowardice, would not
be worth living.   This position is re-enforced by some brilliant
descriptive writing, the slow clumsy rising to his feet of the
heavy Frenchman in instinctual protest to his basically strict
ideas of courage and cowardice being misunderstood, the keenly
narrowed gray eyes ("like two tiny steel rings"), the "razor-edge"
sharp glance, the excessively restrained politeness—all of it
suggests a formidable, if heavy and rigid, sense and presence of
courage.   Stein may see and accommodate Jim as a romantic, but
such would hardly be the Frenchman's definition of Jim, and I
would suggest that the Lieutenant's implied perspective on Jim
is no less important than that of Stein (who is a blurred characterization).   The only real leniency implied by Conrad about
the Frenchman's position on courage and cowardice is that he
might well be lacking in imagination.   A more attractive way of
putting it is that certain kinds of brave individuals *control* their
imagination under pressure.   Less attractively, some would say
today that the Frenchman is deficient in right-brain thinking.

Now Conrad cannot entirely approve of that lack (or that
control) without discrediting the creativity that led to writing
Lord Jim in the first place.   Conrad, as a man of imagination himself, would be likely to respect a courage tested by a formidable
imagination.   Thus Marlow's place in the novel as the principal
agent of the creative moral imagination, and as a meditative second self to Jim.   Himself—judging by *Heart of Darkness*—a
brave man, Marlow still possesses enough sensitivity (and imagination) to empathize with Jim in his terrible plight.   He ex-
cuses and justifies Jim, sometimes, and condemns him (and the
reader) at others.   So, again I will ask, how brave, how cowardly,
is Jim?   Let us look at a number of incidents and passages to see

if we can make an assessment, keeping the big Frenchman's steely-gray eyes and 48-hour *Patna* watch in mind, yet not being daunted by them.

III

The *Patna* incident, and, specifically, Jim's jump, are the catalytic events in the plot of *Lord Jim,* and thus deserve pride of place in my investigation. Van Ghent offers what amounts to a concept of self in regard both to Jim and to *Lord Jim*: "Jim repudiates the other self that has been revealed to him; at no time does he consciously acknowledge that it *was* himself who jumped from the *Patna*—it was only his body that had jumped, and his career thenceforth is an attempt to prove before man that the gross fact of the jump belied his identity."[8] Jim, in partly trying to defend himself from the damnation of *complete* cowardice, divides, as Van Ghent states, his being into two, impulsive body and conscientious mind or soul. Now, even if we accept this view of self and its operations, the fact remains that the body won out over the mind, and took the latter with it on the fateful descent. Jim may have jumped on impulse as soon as he felt the ship move (it had not moved for days, he claims), and thus such a movement might well have signified the beginning of the Patna's fatal sinking. Yet he himself condemns his act or physical response in terms that suggest that another part of his mind feels that the jump was integral to, even definitive of, his being: " 'There was no going back. It was as if I had jumped into . . . an everlasting deep hole . . . ' "(p.87). This frightening figure of the almost bottomless hole implies both moral death and self-damnation. Some part of Jim's self is, like the unimaginative Frenchman, or like the too imaginative suicide, Captain Brierly, passing judgement on Jim. It would be neat formulaically to say that Jim is judged by his own Superego were it not for the fact, perceived by Watt, that the remorse motivating Jim is based not on potentially disastrous irresponsibility towards other people, but on a failure to live up to his own romantic ideals.

Engrossed in his solipsistic dream heroics, Jim fails to be fully alive to the moral (or immoral) reality of his failure of character on the *Patna*. Watt claims that "Jim's personal moral code is stricter than Marlow's; Jim is egocentric, but his ego sets the highest possible standards for its dealing with others."[9] Although this last point may be so, it might well be compensatory for some sense of his inadequate courage, his "failure of nerve." Watt also states that "He [Jim] does not even seem to be aware that he has committed a crime, whose real significance, Marlow explains, lies "in its being a breach of faith with the community of mankind"(p.157). This is a crucial failure of awareness. Jim's stricter moral code means little if it cannot expand to accomodate a sense of the Other and the principle of community. One can even say that Jim's inability to socialize his act of cowardice, to realize, that is, that the way to make the best of it is precisely by seeing his moral flaw in terms of others rather than only in terms of himself, is what damns him, rather than the jump itself. His understanding of his cowardice, whether an act only of his body or of more, is egotistic; had it been more altruistic, had it been centered on a real sense of those abandoned and almost doomed 800 non-European pilgrims, he might perhaps have laid the groundwork for a valid, humane self-redemption. Instead, Jim will go on in life, shamed to the roots by his act, but not penetrated by his lapse in one's obligation to the Other as society, whether one's vulnerable and dependent passengers or the maritime community. No one can blame him for wanting a second chance; most of us want another chance for a collapse of our courage. But Jim wants to redeem an essentially Romantic self-image; his goal of self-redemption is essentially narcissistic. Rather than accepting his own cowardice and integrating this acceptance with an awareness of the Other and with the attempt to be braver (and, perhaps, less self-important) in the future, he burns to be the Hero. His failure to mature, to draw conclusions from his terrible suffering, leads if not to his being responsible for the disaster of Patusan and the massacre of his friend Dain Waris, at least to his own death through his somewhat quixotic interpretation of these events.

Thus, I contend that Jim's sense or concept of self is radically faulty; schizoid, solipsistic, hyperegoistic, he dissolves the Other into the obsessively fanciful machinery of his psyche. As a consequence, no one is really *out there* for Jim. The world of sea and ship life, or of hinterland Malayan feuds and politics, merely comprise the backdrop against which he performs his rituals of romance fantasy, until his fantasy collides with the reality of evil in the form of the vicious desperado Gentleman Brown and shatters. If this contention is true, what does it mean when weighed against another point I will now develop—that Jim, if cowardly, is also brave, even if his bravery after the *Patna* incident is goaded by his leap?

For indeed Jim is brave, too. As Marlow says, talking to the arrogant, conceited but also brave Brierly: " 'There is a kind of courage in facing it out, knowing very well that if he went away nobody would trouble to run after him . . . ' "(p.55). (Jim is willing to face a maritime court to explain why he deserted the *Patna*.) However, Brierly's response has to be weighed, too: " ' That sort of courage is of no use to keep a man straight . . . ' ". What Brierly implies here is that "facing-the-music" courage perhaps makes it too easy to succumb to a more formidable challenge to one's bravery, the kind the buckling in to which makes one fall back on the more passive "facing-the-music" variety of stoic endurance. Brierly even goes on to suggest that Jim's facing it out is a kind of cowardice. The truth lies between, surely. Facing it out is a lower kind of courage, or at least less sensational or dramatic, than staying on the *Patna*. Conversely, it is more courageous, obviously, than jumping from his ship. But if the truth lies between Marlow and Brierly's position, it is a truth the reader must define himself, as happens so often in *Lord Jim*, and as Conrad, coercing our participation, intends.

Further, Jim doesn't resolve to leave the *Patna* as soon as he finds out that it almost certainly will sink. The other ship's officers do, and behave basely both in the immediacy of their decision and in the hysterical, curiously comic, clumsy haste with which they try to salvage a lifeboat for themselves. Jim stands aloof from all this indecent frenzy, and "protests" that he had not thought of saving himself; rather, he had thought only of the appalling fact of eight-hundred people and seven boats (p.69). He also asks Marlow intensely, almost bullyingly, "Do you think I was afraid of death?' " Though he is probably sincere in thinking he was not, his jump indicates that some part of himself, perhaps distinct from his "I" self, *was* afraid.

But the courage or faith behind that sentiment and that part of himself, the ego-subject represented by his "I", is perhaps what emerges in the subsequent six hours of the night when, on the lifeboat with the three ship's officers he has repudiated for taking the boat, he has to guard against their murderous hatred. As the one dissident to their conspiratorial lie that the ship sank,

Jim endangers their vicious story. Further, he has made his disapproval of their desertion emphatic, and has made his own high idealism hellishly compromised by his Jump. Thus, if they could kill him, it would have secured their own false version of the event, and no one would have known of the murder. Jim's contending with this murderous situation possibly shows bravery. Yet, as Marlow asks, " 'Firmness of courage or effort of fear?' "(p.95). It is not easy to be sure, and we begin to realize that in any metaphysics of courage and cowardice, the paths, the truths, the answers are murkier than might at first be thought.

Jim, trying to shake off his *Patna* experience, leaves one part of the Southeastern Pacific after another. At one point he has a humble job as a "runner" for two merchants named Egström and Blake, one of whom says about Jim: " 'Can't get a man like that everyday . . . ; a regular devil for sailing a boat, ready to go out miles to sea to meet ships in any sort of weather'"(p.145). This sounds like bravery, certainly, but the recklessness of it seems suspiciously compensatory. Jim is of course making up for something, and so this daring is a "kind" of courage, hardly despicable, yet not of the highest order. It should not be overlooked, incidentally, that in exhibiting this valor, Jim endangers the lives of "two frightened niggers" in his perilous manner of almost colliding with a ship in mist just in order to make the first commercial contact for his firm. Again, the violation of the "Other" in the form here of racially scorned natives must be considered in testing the quality of the courage Jim enacts.

When in Patusan, sent there by Stein to represent his commercial interests as a trader, Jim exhibits many acts of valor, from escaping from the Rajah's stockade where he had been imprisoned, to, after he is free and has been accepted as a leader among the rival communities of Patusan, drinking the Rajah's potentially dangerous coffee on his monthly diplomatic visits. Jim becomes so admired by the Patusans that he becomes "Lord" Jim, a person in whom they repose their trust. Thus, Jim has his symbolic "Patna pilgrims" at his mercy again, and has his second chance as well.

Yet despite his eminence in Patusan, Jim remains haunted by his First Chance and its results. " 'If you ask them (in Patusan), who is braver—who is true—who is just—who is it they would trust with their lives?—They would say, Tuan Jim. And yet they can never know the real, real truth. . . . ' "(p.226)

Shortly after, when Jim asserts that he hasn't done so badly, and Marlow concurs, Jim says, " 'But all the same, you wouldn't like to have me aboard your own ship—hey?' "(p.227). Clearly, Jim has not gotten over the *Patna* incident, nor has Marlow, whose answer to that question, though he wouldn't admit it to Jim, would be *no*. It preys on Jim's mind, and one recalls the sinister implications of his jumping into his "deep hole." Indeed, it is a common interpretation to blame his remembrance of the *Patna* jump for his fatal giving in to Brown. According to this viewpoint, Jim senses a "dark brotherhood" with Brown, who elicits Jim's guilt by his random and desperate remarks. Surrounded, exhausted, without food, Brown admits to Jim that he would just as soon give up or be killed, " 'But there are my men in the same boat—and, by God, I am not the sort to jump out of trouble and leave them in a d—d lurch' "(p.283). Brown, further, asks Jim " 'whether he himself . . . didn't understand that when it came to saving one's life in the dark, one didn't care who else went—three, thirty, three hundred people,' . . . , I made him wince' "(p.286). In such exchanges as these, Brown not only accidentally implies a capacity for ruthlessly selfish behavior in Jim, but also that in one respect, not deserting one's men or charge, he is *superior* to Jim.

Watt has argued that Jim is *not* psychologically paralyzed, that he does not grant Brown and his men liberty to leave Patusan out of guilt, or even "That any other decision was possible"(p.341), in Jim's handling of Brown. He states, further, that "In practical, moral, and in psychological terms . . . Jim had no real alternative but to let Brown go, and whatever he may—consciously or unconsciously—have thought or felt about Brown could hardly have changed this."[10] More concretely, according to Watt, fighting Brown, given Brown's desperation and viciousness, would have possibly meant a lot of deaths among Patusans. Further, Jim's own moral upbringing would make the cold-blooded annihilation of any human being (including Brown) repugnant to him.

First, it seems to me that Watt dismisses the psychological criticisms of Jim's behavior towards Brown too readily. Jim's own failings, as I have indicated, still lie heavily on his mind. Moreover, the narrative itself indicates how affected Jim is by Brown's random thrusts into Jim's continuing sense of his own shame and worthlessness. It is indeed possible that in excusing Brown he is also excusing himself, because, as Robert E. Kuehn has observed, "unconsciously it is the kind of response he would like to evoke from the world for his own act of cowardice."[11]

I feel that Watt endows Jim with more coolness than Jim, under the impact of his "dark brother" Gentleman Brown, always possesses during this confrontation. Whether or not it is correct to deny, as Watt does, that Jim's errors regarding Brown are "the result of unconscious guilt," Jim definitely shows some befuddlement, which is caused by Brown's touching on the sensitive areas of his shame. But Watt is on stronger ground when he claims that Jim is not essentially to blame for letting Brown go, for, as Watt says, no one could have anticipated Brown's demonical revengefulness.[12]

Yet all the discussions of this crux in the novel overlook one significant point, which is that Jim does *generally* behave with attractive calmness in dealing with Brown. One can argue about whether it would have been more moral or immoral of Jim to have tried to attack Brown and his men; moreover, there is the undeniable fact that Brown, probing the weakness of Jim's past, disturbs him. These points notwithstanding, Jim generally acts intrepidly during a tense and even dangerous confrontation with a trapped psychopath. That he didn't save all of the community and live up to his excessive self-ideal makes us realize that only one way remained to him, given his character structure, for responding "honorably" to Brown's surprise massacre, and that is sacrificial self-dramatization before the father of Dain Waris. The question to be posed, then, is whether this self-sacrifice is an act of redemptive bravery or an act of folly and self-delusion.

Jim, states Watt, approvingly, "dies for his honor."[13] Such conduct of course has traditionally appeared attractive; it is conduct perhaps from nobler, simpler, or more romantic ages. But Watt's point demands a closer look. The impressive if rather unimaginative French lieutenant thinks that once honor is gone, life is inconceivable. Yet Van Ghent has asserted that the Frenchman "is above Jim's failings by virtue of his mediocrity . . . ,"[14] a deft insight that ignores an important consideration in Jim's favor. The Frenchman is blessed (or undercut) by a lack of the kind of imagination that both fuels Jim's dream and triggers his fears. The two, Conrad implies, are interrelated, perhaps even one. Yet Jim's imagination also creates a kind of moral sensibility that, unlike the Frenchman's, suffers profoundly from the disastrous results of one's deepest, strongest dreams,

and that makes ideals out of dreams. However, even more than Don Quixote, Jim fails his dream-ideals, because he cannot accept, or doesn't realize, a crucial lesson that Guerard defines:
. . . nearly everyone has jumped off some *Patna* and most of us have been compelled to live on, desperately or quietly engaged in reconciling what we are with what we would like to be."15

This sounds like the "adult" acceptance of one's mediocrity, or, at least, limitations, the very opposite of Stein's "following-the-dream" advice. To make matters more difficult, modern society gives mixed signals on the matter of being realistic or idealistic. On the one hand, people are told by psychiatrists to "grow up, accept one's limitations and become a functioning member of society," but, on the other, it is obvious that both high and mass culture is rife with examples, both exquisite and vulgar, of attaching one's "real" to one's "ideal" self. I am suggesting here that there is no easy solution to Jim's plight: Jim is the Romantic Egoist who wants to sacrifice all, including himself, to be worthy of his dream of noble, heroic selfhood, yet finds the other self (or selves) of his instinctual or impulsive being betraying him. Jim is too hard on himself in some ways and too soft on himself in others.

Conrad, tortured, according to his fine psychoanalytical biographer, Bernard C. Meyer, by a merciless guilt about the betrayal of country and parents, could vicariously relieve his guilt in the creation (and destruction) of Jim. Jim, assaulted by a demanding yet ethically flawed conscience, a conscience, that is, that badly undervalued the social character of his maritime cowardice, can only assuage his sense of disgrace by lusting for the Second Chance. In this quest, he is all too humanly like many of us, for many people can bear themselves for past weakness in loyalty or honor and bravery only by vowing to make good the *next* time. The individual reader has to decide whether in fact Jim is his (or her) double, and, if so, experience Conrad's acute pessimism and disapproval like the moisture on one's own tongue.

However, the crucial consideration often is not only what we do on the first chance but how we live with it. Such self-reconciliation can be one of the harshest states to experience. It is internal and decidedly unromantic, it demands we inspect our ideals and our strengths and weaknesses in the glare of our actual or experienced qualities, and, perhaps most important, it demands that we integrate the Other into our idealism.

Does Jim fail in Patusan? I agree with Watt that he does not. His definitive failure lies in the *Patna* leap. When he says he feels as if he had fallen into a deep hole, he has because he feels or thinks he has. If this inflexibility expresses his ego-ideal of honor, it also represents a rigid determinism that will destroy him.

A moral force that lifts Jim's plight above melodrama is Marlow's empathetic brooding over him. Marlow's identification with Jim is so intense, sustained, and deep that symbolically he *is* Jim, a wiser, surviving Jim who is intimating within Conrad's maze of discontinuous narrative and shifting and multiple narrator viewpoints that when *we* face the forces of menace so sharp and sudden and dark they take our breath away, we might do even worse than Jim. That gloomy possibility is for Marlow and even more for Conrad the true repository of his profound pessimism in *Lord Jim*, rather than that such a fine-looking, blue-eyed, blond youth could be so rottenly untrustworthy.

The question finally is not whether Jim is "one of us," but whether *we* are, in a sense different from Conrad's British Club of Gentlemen Imperialists that "we" ourselves must define. Conrad's definition of Jim's ultimate merit is ambiguous in part because of his uncertainty about Everyman's valor, as well as about his own filial and nationalist fidelity. This definition is also ambiguous because courage and cowardice, like death and rebirth, are deep mysteries of human experience, unpredictable, irrational, numinous. " 'It is always the unexpected that happens,' " says Marlow, talking about events that test courage. But more often than we like, it is also the unexpected in behavior that results, and this plays havoc with all our codes of rationality, stoicism, and preparation. Indeed, D. H. Lawrence's metaphor from his *Studies in Classic American Literature* of "strange gods" who go back and forth from our consciousness to the unconscious, is relevant here. Patently an idea akin to early 20th-century psychoanalytical theory, Lawrence's figure suggests a way for Jim to have more realistically come to terms with his weakness or cowardice of "dark gods" of self-terrorization and ideality, and that would be to accept the existence of cowardice—as well as of courage—within one. Even the brave French Lieutenant grants that shortcoming as natural, even congenital. The Frenchman's inability to accept the cost of actual cowardice (loss of honor), represents a position Conrad himself clearly supports in his "Preface" to *Lord Jim*. Today, however, we would not generally feel as strongly about it. Though the modern era may be riddled with pessimistic doubts about the ultimate character of human nature and society, it has made us realize that our failure to unify reality with ideality, self with dream, our daily selves with our best selves are failures we can live with if we accept them as a basis for realistic effort towards self-enlargement or creative change. This lenient practicality is not meant to condone disgraceful conduct, but to place it within a humanizing context. If Jim had lived in our age, he might have survived. On the other hand, if Conrad had lived in our era, he might not have written *Lord Jim*.

Lord Jim may not illuminate courage and cowardice definitively, but it does show unforgettably how penetrated our deepest roots of being are by courage and cowardice, and how, if we undergo a kind of death in cowardice, we can experience a new life in courage, or even in the hope of courage. In this moderate offering of life's real possibilities as well as in his metaphysical ambiguity about courage and cowardice, Conrad embodies the modern temper; here, he is "one of us."

Notes

[1]Conrad, Joseph. *Lord Jim*. (New York: NAL, 1961), 70. All further references to this text in this chapter are to this edition.

[2]Watt, Ian. *Conrad in the 19th Century*. (Berkeley: University of California Press, 1979), 324.

[3]Meyer, Bernard C. *Joseph Conrad: A Psychoanalytical Biography*. (Princeton, New Jersey: Princeton University Press, 1967), 63.

[4]Meyer, 68.

[5]Watt, 343.

[6]Watt, 318.

[7]Moser, Thomas, ed. *Joseph Conrad, Lord Jim: An Authoritative Text, Backgrounds ... Essays in Criticism*. (New York: Norton, 1968), 390.

[8]Van Ghent, Dorothy. *The English Novel: Form and Function*. (New York: Harper & Row, 1953), 233-34.

[9]Watt, 318.

[10]Watt, 341.

[11]Kuehn, Robert E., ed. *Lord Jim: A Collection of Critical Essays.* (Englewood Cliffs, N.J.: Prentice Hall, Inc., 1969), 12.

[12]Watt, 342-43.

[13]Watt, 356.

[14]Van Ghent, 242.

[15]Moser, ed., 391.

Henry James' *The Beast in the Jungle:*
The Ego as Self-Devourer

I

Although the self can be regarded as a neutral term in it-self, it is of basic importance that, as Gordon Allport has observed, "the commonest compound of self is *selfish*. . . . "[1] It is not, at least in the 20th century, considered "selfish" to want to realize one's self.[2]   Indeed, in the place of traditional religious sublimations or consolidations of the self, some individuals even consider it an ethical duty to "actualize" the self.   Many of the great Classical Modernist authors, such as Conrad, Lawrence, Joyce, Kafka, Hemingway, and Faulkner have investigated and dramatized the image of the self so intensely as to create a modern myth counterpoising the self against an accumulated weight of societal opposition and oppression seldom known in past lit-eratures.   The self of modern literature is in fact often a char-acterization and a symbol so deeply invested with value that it runs the danger either of being overvalued or of being insuf-ficiently related to mediative social standards.

A grave danger the self faces is that one's investigating or developing it might engender or embody acute selfishness.   Our pursuit of the self might violate others.   Certainly it is a great par-adox of literature, religion, and mysticism that one realizes the self in helping to realize or relate to another.   There is always the irreducible presence of another human being, another human significance, in an individual's achievement or self-accom-plishment, and when this other presence is missing or ignored, then one's achievement, particularly the consolidation or apoth-eosis of the self, can be dangerous.   Such is the fate of John Marcher, the protagonist of Henry James' novella *The Beast in the Jungle.*   Marcher's pursuit of his self is expounded in terms that ambiguously appeal to the reader, and that even suggest an appeal to identify that the reader sooner or later is expected to reject.[3]

Midway through the story, the "situation" is put in the

ironically violent and melodramatic terms of the title:
"Something or other lay in wait for him, amid the twists and the
turns of the months and the years, like a crouching beast in the
jungle. It signified little whether the crouching beast were destined to slay him or to be slain. The definite point was the inevitable spring of the animal, and the definite lesson from that
was that a man of feeling didn't cause himself to be accompanied
by a lady on a tiger-hunt."[4]

The last sentiment, as we shall see, compromises one of
the governing ironies of the entire narrative. At this point the
metaphors in the title need consideration. The peculiarly violent and savage character of the terms in which Marcher couches
his sense of his personal destiny are conspicuously melodramatic, like the basic conditions of a dangerous adventure
story. A certain vanity resides here, but also a symbolic pertinence, in view of what does materialize. There indeed is a
beast in this story. Marcher does occupy a sort of jungle, or
maze—he certainly inhabits a realm of confusion and darkness
of his own making. But there is a serious self-deception here in
his terms for the dangerous glamour, the "adventure-story"
stature, of his metaphors which will turn against him, both in
suggesting that he has not too much, but too little, heart, for his
"adventure", and too little rather than too much insight into
what the true nature of his "fate" is.

Another famous and ambiguous passage of Marcher's self-
definition occurs later in the story, shortly after it is revealed that
his close friend and the companion of his fate, May Bartram, has
a "deep disorder of the blood," and may even die: "It wouldn't
have been failure to have been bankrupt, dishonored, pilloried,
hanged; it was failure not to be anything"(p.778). The fact that
these different forms of punishment not only imply different
kinds of offense, but strongly indicate a social frame, a public or
societal judge and judgement, suggests the nature and even the
cause of Marcher's offense. What, after all, does one do to a person who has not done *anything*, has not even *been* anything,
anything, that is, that relates to another human being in some
tangibly or legally offensive way? But there is one thing that
Marcher does do; it is perhaps not a hanging offense, yet it is
subtly offensive. He violates love and the Other, by violating
May Bertram as a potential beloved. He does so in effect because
he doesn't think love, and thus May, is important enough to his
quest of self. His "fate" is too "big" for both love and May, and,

in his self-infatuation with the unrealistic urgency of a grand destiny, commits the "crime" of disregarding the old idea that nothing of value is durably accomplished for one's own sake alone. Thus the themes of spurned love and vanity or selfishness are tightly integrated in *Beast*, and by following the track of one theme, one is dealing with both. Vanity suggests altruism by the pressure of antithesis, as selfishness connotes generosity. If we have a selfish person in Marcher, we have a generous, very self-denying, one in May.

May is one of those sibylline females that haunt James' fiction. Like Alice Staverton in *The Jolly Corner*, she is willing to extend her confused male friend or beloved a helping thread—but the onus is placed on him to find his way out through the labyrinth. As James says early in *Beast*: "she had not lost it [the thread], but she wouldn't give it back to him, he saw, without some putting forth of his hand for it . . . "(p.754). If Spencer Brydon, does, with the help of *his* Ariadne, find his way out, John Marcher does not. His companion, in fact, is helpful to the point of a self-abnegation so extreme as to make one feel that its best artistic justification is to highlight by contrast Marcher's abysmal self-centeredness or blindness.[5]   And part of James' main point in *Beast* is that ultimately blindness and selfishness can be the same thing, as certain kinds of foolishness can be a form of evil.

May, on the other hand, is anything but selfish or blind. A woman who has experienced, who has suffered, she is taken with Marcher's presentiment of a fate, *his* fate: " 'You said,' says May, 'you had had from your earlier time, as the deepest thing within you, the sense of being kept for something rare and strange, possibly prodigious and terrible, that was sooner or later to happen to you . . . ' "(p.760). Being "kept for" something also suggests being kept *from* something, from many things, including some of importance. This May realizes, and, as we discover, even embodies, for she occupies the peculiarly strategic position in Marcher's vain quest of being both a witness and a participant. She watches the drama in which she also participates, which makes her both object and subject in this epistemological theatre. May is objective witness, guide, adviser, and seer, but is also subjectively involved as only a person who wants to be the "subject" of another person's deepest quest can be. Part of Marcher's failure will lie in his treatment of May as a virtual object.

But that May has an uphill battle is apparent from
Marcher's invincible self-centeredness, which in a way she, as
tester, abets:

> 'It hasn't yet come. *Only,* you know, it isn't anything I'm to *do,* to a-
> chieve in the world . . . ' 'It's to be something you're merely to
> suffer?' 'Well, say to wait for—to have to meet, to face, to see sud-
> denly break out in my life; possibly destroying all further conscious-
> ness, possibly annihilating me; possibly, on the other hand, only
> altering everything. . . ' (pp.760-61).

The implicit passivity here on Marcher's part (not to mention the sly Jamesian comic effect of Marcher's doltish "only's")
is revealing, and dangerous. " 'It isn't anything I'm to *do,*' " he
claims, but that's a decision Marcher has made. He doesn't *want*
to do anything; rather, he wants something to happen, to happen to him. It might be a psychological devastation—and in a
sense it is that, though within a radically different structure of
meanings than Marcher anticipates.

May, in both her "object" and "subject" roles, decides almost to show—or give—her hand: " 'Isn't what you describe
perhaps but the expectation—or . . . danger . . . of falling in love?'
"(p.761). Marcher's response is both smug and self-damning: "
'Of course what's in store for me may be no more than that'
"(p.761). When May asks and Marcher confirms that he *has* been
in love, and he goes on to say that " 'It hasn't been overwhelming,' " May offers another one of her clues: " 'Then it
hasn't been love!' "(p.761). Marcher wants something more
"special" than love, not realizing, through the sheer ubiquity of
his vanity, that nothing is more "special" than love. Whatever
he awaits, it fills him with what he calls apprehension, a kind of
numinous fear. This question of fear leads to the agreement of
May to watch together with Marcher for this "thing," this visitation, this Beast, to arrive. Catastrophe, annihilation, obsession,
danger—such are the overcharged terms of Marcher's sense of
his special destiny. One would think that Hamlet or Macbeth
were on stage.

James however knows who's on stage, and at one point, a
bit sadistically, he shows *his* tragic hero to be short on courage.
Developing the sense that whatever he (or he and May) awaits is
portentous and thus possibly even perilous, he understandably
has a sense of exposure. Still, he has to be assured by May that he
isn't afraid or fearful, a fine comic touch by James. Yet, as she re-
joins, in the elaborate network of progressing qualifications and

pronominal reflexivities constituting a James' fiction, " 'it isn't the end of our watch' "(p.272). He senses a certain presence in May, and realizes that she *knows* what the end of the watch is or will lead to. Thus, in keeping it to herself, Marcher assumes that it is something for him bad enough to compel her to keep it to herself. Her answer to this developing fear in a man who had just timidly asked whether he might be a man of courage elicits the *sphinx-like* response, "You'll never find out' "(p.772).

II

Marcher does find out of course what is to happen to him, but the fact that he finds out too late is the ironic and appropriate form that the happening takes. Instead of learning more with time and with the "partnership" of May Bartram, he seems to learn less. Even the idea of losing May by " 'some catastrophe . . . yet wouldn't at all be *the* catastrophe . . . ' "(p.775). Almost as a consequence of this particularly gross self-centeredness, May indeed does become seriously ill—a "deep disorder in her blood," James calls it—and the sense of an illness related to a starved need for reciprocity with Marcher urges itself on one. The hopelessness of the situation—for *both* people—is underlined by Marcher's converting even May's grave illness into a "direct menace for himself"(p.776)—everything, even his good friend and crucial confidant, seems to pivot on his need for self-realization. His quest is insatiable.

Marcher resembles an Elizabethan Character, an Overbury portrait of Vanity, or a monster who could rival Moliere's Tartuffe or Miser in the accentuated development or persistence of a vice. When May is virtually on her death bed, Marcher is more concerned that she "would die without giving him light" than he is about her possible death itself. May is dying, and the meaning of Marcher's apprehension, if connected in her mind with her dying, is not so connected in Marcher's. Reducing this significant passage to its essential meanings, one has this sequence:

> 'I'm afraid I'm too ill.'
> . . .
> 'Too ill to tell me?' [a question he thinks but doesn't utter]

...
'Don't you know—now?' [now that she is dying],
...
'Now'?
...
'What then has happened?'
...
'What was to, she said.' (p.785)

Part of James' narrative method in his work generally is a tantalizing (and aggravating) gift for pushing his ulterior meanings ahead cumulatively, holding one with a carefully controlled entelechy of dialogue, ambiguities, and character perplexities, as protagonists roam the labyrinthine corridors of their opacities to a final realization. This kind of patterning is sometimes developed by a Sophia figure (such as Alice Staverton in *The Jolly Corner*) who, usually wiser than her Theseus, drops hints and clues along the way, or, like May, hand in hand, watches and waits for the revelation, knowing all the time the answer to the riddle. May possesses the special art of disclosing and not disclosing the answer; the insights she offers require considerable insight to understand, as in the following exchange:

> 'What I long ago said is true. You'll never know now, and I think you ought to be content.'
>
> 'You've *had* it,' said May Bartram.
>
> 'But had what?'
>
> 'Why, what was to have marked you out—I'm too glad,' she then bravely added, 'to have been able to see what it's not'(p.788).

We realize sooner or later why she is "brave" to say this, but Marcher does not until it is too late. Shortly after, May tells her fellow "watcher" this: " 'You were to suffer your fate. That was not necessarily to know it.' "(p.790).

Beast begins to look like a travesty of tragedy, and Marcher a grotesque mockery of the tragic hero, a figure who traditionally not only finally realizes his fate, but whose realization affirms himself, and, through his heightened if burdened status, all humanity. Marcher, in contrast, looks almost like a buffoon from low comedy when his Destiny, his Experience, occurs, for he feels, sees, and understands nothing until it is too late. May goes to the grave with the "secret." It is only at the grave at May's funeral, and thus in a pronounced context of death, that Marcher finally has his realization. It is devastating, for it amounts to an annihilation of self.[6]

Marcher's relationship with May is so little known to her family that Marcher is not even invited to the funeral ceremonies—a large slight in itself, and a hint of his marked solipsistic condition. Marcher visits May's grave by himself, recalling that "the creature beneath the sod *knew* of his rare experience, so that strangely now the place had lost for him its mere blankness of expression"(p.795). Even when his dear friend is dead, her prime value for him is her exploitability for his self-esteem.

While at the cemetery, Marcher encounters another mourner, a middle-aged man whose grief is very sharp, at least compared to Marcher's: "The stranger passed, but the raw glare of his grief remained, making our friend wonder in pity what wrong, what wound it expressed. . . . What had the man *had* to make him, by the loss of it, so bleed yet live?' "(p.798).

Although this mourner is a nameless minor character in the story, he is nevertheless the agent that triggers Marcher's ultimate recognition of his destiny. What did this other man—Marcher's double—once have that he could "so bleed yet live"? " 'Something . . . that *he*, John Marcher, hadn't; the proof of which was precisely John Marcher's arid end. No passion had ever touched him, for this was what passion meant . . . where had been *his* deep ravage?' "(p.798).

Where indeed? One usually does not suffer grief for another if little or no feeling had been directed towards that person in the past. A great grief bespeaks a great attachment, a large sense of another human being, that helps one to come out of one's shell, and, in relating to another, expand one's self. The expansion carries a serious risk, for loss of the other person threatens or even destroys part of oneself. But in the loving and losing of another (person), and of thus losing part of oneself, one has certainly lived. As Lambert Strether says so famously in *The Ambassadors,* " 'It doesn't so much matter what you do in particular so long as you have lived your life. . . . Live, live!' "

That, however, is Marcher's flaw; he hasn't lived, if living means significant relation to another person substantially free of exploitation or selfishness.

But James' indictment becomes far more specific than this. This specificity is brought home to Marcher again by his mourning double: " 'He had seen *outside* of his life, not learned it within, the way a woman was mourned when she had been loved for herself . . . ' "(p.758). As a result, what Marcher confronts, in one of James' most terse and stunning judgements, is "the sounded void of his life." Marcher has finally reached bottom, and with this descent into "the desolation of reality," Marcher arrives at the definition, not of his destiny, but of its cause, and its condition: " 'she [May] was what he had missed.' "(p.798). And this dark realization leads to his destiny, his punishment: " 'He had been the man of his time, *the* man, to whom nothing on earth was to have happened"(p.798). This is his "visitation"; May had "seen" it, we are told, and "served at this hour to drive the truth home"(p.798), "served" here being a heavily weighted word, suggesting her sacrifice to, and exploitation by, Marcher, and, unintentionally, the manner in which her sacrifice and manipulation "serve" to vindicate her by embodying the final devastating awareness for Marcher in words climaxing the whole story:

> The escape would have been to love her; then, *then,* he would have lived. *She* had lived . . . since she had loved him for himself; whereas he had never thought of her (ah! how it hugely glared at him!) but in the chill of his egotism and the light of her use.(p.799)

Is it a salvation of sorts that Marcher finally recognizes his vanity and its savage inhumanity? Not only is his vanity or egotism savage; it is figured by the beast in the title, in the dark, menacing presence which romantically usurps Marcher's mind, and finally in the beast references in the final paragraph of the novella: "The beast had lurked indeed, and the beast, at its hour, had sprung . . . "(p.799). The narrator is alluding here to a time earlier in the year, when, seriously ailing, May hopes Marcher will finally see that she (and love) is the rare experience to be his if he turns to May with love. But he is insensitive to her, to the offer of the situation. May, with almost unbelievable kindness, even prays he might never realize what he has missed out on—not only her or a love relationship, but an opportunity for engaging himself in passional experience that might have given Marcher's life authenticity.

What in the way of savagery that Marcher finally sees now—the beast of his vanity and the attack of his self-punishment—leaps in the final beast metaphor and words of the story:

> He saw the jungle of his life and saw the lurking Beast; then,
> while he looked, perceived it, as by a stir of the air, rise, huge and
> hideous, for the leap that was to settle him. His eyes darkened—
> it was close; and instinctively turning, in his hallucination, to a-
> void it, he flung himself, on his face, on the tomb (p.799).

This beast is the sort of deadly creature that springs from
the "jungle" of the unconscious (or the Freudian Superego),
rather than from the romance land of Marcher's imagined destiny. *Beast* is often regarded as a story about a man to whom
nothing happens, and that is true enough. But the ending of
Beast suggests more. According to F. W. Dupee, "[Marcher] was
to have had no experience beyond the searing knowledge of his
inexperience."[7]   Leon Edel puts it differently: "Marcher at last
had had his vision. He had learned the meaning of egotism."[8]
Yet one might ask if Marcher really learns anything here.   He
certainly does have an experience, but rather in the way one
might experience his car going off the edge of a precipice.   Even
this sufficiently authentic experience Marcher tries to dodge, and
James conveys the resultant meaning with both stern force and
subtlety.   Marcher falls on May's tomb, as if trying to reach her
through the impenetrable wall of death.   However, in trying,
understandably, to flee his own darkness, he symbolically kills
himself.   In either event, Marcher seems to have no real choice
by this point.   Confrontation with the beast here would seem to
imply psychic destruction.   Rather than being crippled by a mega-
lomaniacal vanity, he now is on the verge of being destroyed by
its consequences.

Even that late gesture of self-punishment would provide
a glimmer of redemptive consciousness, could Marcher bear being pounced on by the inner beast.   But he cannot, and, in a
heartbreaking ignominy of despair, he faces finally towards May
in a direction that, once meaning enhanced life through self-
transcending love, now, in a final, resolving irony, means an in-
eluctable death in life.   Marcher's egoism, swallowing his self,
has not so much destroyed the inner reserves that nurture the
self, as it has instead converted them into a fury that almost literally flings him towards despair and death.   Burdened during
his life with a viciously self-deluded vanity, Marcher ends up
with scarcely an ego. *Beast* is a gothic story of the self unselving
itself.   This process occurs, paradoxically enough, through the
very resourcefulness of the self to vindicate an ideal of selfhood
by savagely punishing one's betrayal and belittlement of genuine

self in its crucial form as relation to other human beings.

Beast harbors a certain numinosity, because it speaks so intimately to everyone about the strong proclivity of the self to feel that it is meant for a special destiny. By the unique nature of our individuality, we are so destined indeed. The cravings inspired by the mass-media "world" of fantasy, romance, and glamour make it clear that it is not Marcher alone who feels that the common run of life experiences is not enough, and that one needs or is reserved for something more. In so waiting, one waits for Nothing to attack one's undeveloped self—and destroy it. *Beast,* a parable of vanity, ranks prominently among James' harsh judgements against the individual who places self-centeredness before relation to others.

Notes

[1]Gordon Allport, "Is The Concept of Self Necessary," in *The Self in Social Interaction,* eds., Chad Gordon and Kenneth S. Gergen (New York: Wiley & Sons, 1968), 28.

[2]Anthony Channell Hilfer points out that in the English Victorian novel attention to one's self was considered not only selfish but a vice. (See *The Ethics of Intensity in American Fiction* (Austin, Texas: University of Texas Press, 1981, 12, 13). Thus, Hilfer claims that Hardy's Alex Durberville can be regarded as a Victorian villain of "self," a "selfish seducer"(p.76).

[3]Wayne C. Booth contends that point of view in *Beast* plays a large role in eliciting our sympathy towards Marcher: "By seeing the whole thing through the isolated sufferer's vision we are forced to feel it through his heart. And it is our sense of his isolation, of vulnerability in a world where no one can set him straight, that contributes most to this sympathy." (*The Rhetoric of Fiction* (Chicago: University of Chicago Press, 1961), 281).

[4]Henry James, *The Great Short Novels of Henry James,* ed., Philip Rahv (New York: Dial Press, 1944), 766. All further references to this work are from this text.

[5]According to Hilfer, genteel convention of the time would be another factor in restraining May from making her ardent feelings towards Marcher more overt. Hilfer also thinks that what May wants of Marcher goes beyond substantive expression (Op. cit., 78).

[6]It is one thing to claim, as Booth does, that Marcher elicits some sympathy from the reader. Others have made stronger claims for Marcher. According to Krishna Balder Vaid, "The anti-hero [Marcher], instead of remaining a mere pathetic figure, becomes a tragic hero, arousing pity and terror because of the single-mindedness with which he has looked forward to his destiny and the intensity with which he experiences his doom" (*Technique in the Tales of Henry James* (Cambridge, Massachusetts: Harvard University Press, 1964), 231).   I feel that this status overvalues Marcher.   There is nothing affirmative in his final realization of his folly, nor does he bear the stature throughout the narrative of the noble or high qualities traditionally associated with tragic character.   Yet I agree with Vaid that Marcher is more than pathetic.   His ending is too grim and overwhelming for him to be lightly dismissed, however much we may be revulsed (or perhaps made uneasy) by his monomaniacal egotism.

[7]F. W. Dupee, *Henry James: His Life and Writings* (Garden City, New York: Doubleday & Company, 1956), 156.

[8]Leon Edel, *Henry James: The Master, 1901-16* (New York: Avon Books, 1978), 139.

... note the danger signals which mark all the murderous hypocrisies of our society, and never again let it pass you by without fully grasping its importance. . . . I tell you, worthy little people, life's riffraff, forever, beaten, fleeced, and sweating, I warn you that when the great people of this world start loving you, it means that they are going to make sausage meat of you . . .

Ferdinand-Louis Céline, *Journey to the End of the Night*

Céline's *Journey to the End of the Night*: Moral Nihilism and the Self-Degrading Society

I

During one of the most vicious scenes in Louis-Ferdinand Céline's novel *Journey to the End of the Night* (and in modern fiction as well), the narrator-protagonist makes a pivotal statement about himself (and his *self*):

> Bit by bit, while this humiliating trial lasted I felt my self-repect, which was about to leave me anyway, slipping still further from me, then going completely and at last definitely gone. . . . Say what you like, it's a very pleasant sensation. After the incident I've always felt infinitely free and light; morally, I mean, of course. Perhaps fear is what you need most often in life to get you out of a hole. Personally, since that day I've never myself wanted any other weapon or any other virtues. [1]

Ferdinand Bardamu, the narrator and protagonist in *Journey*, is in a frightening and degrading situation on a French ship full of colonialists bound for long term service in Africa. It has become recognized that Bardamu is a paying passenger, an overt sign of dubious status on this kind of ship where "respectable" passengers travel free through bureaucratic or military connections. As malicious rumors multiply about Bardamu, he is gradually converted into a diabolic figure of total infamy. Even the ship's captain himself, in a typically violent Céline metaphor, asks whether Bardamu has been " 'flung overboard yet. Like a lump of dirty phlegm.' "(p.105). Although innocent of any actual offense, Bardamu is finally confronted a few days before the ship reaches Africa by the leading officials and men on the ship. A severe, even dangerous, beating is very likely (the narrator even fears execution). This fate he avoids by an hysterical and abject display (and parody) of patriotism. His desperate ruse works and the men, including the scapegoat narrator, go off to the bar to get drunk (as "the females on board watched us silently and in slowly growing disappointment"(p.112). The long quote above follows.

That quote deserves a consideration in any study of fiction from the perspective of the self, for it is a striking revelation of being. First, we see the central character in the novel badly degrading himself in order to avoid grave danger, admitting that he has lost his self-respect in the process of surviving. He goes further, and says he enjoys losing it, because, in effect, it makes life easier to live from this point on. In what almost amounts to a travesty of Dr. Johnson's apothegm about courage being the first of the virtues because without it all the others are hard to acquire, Céline's anti-hero turns Johnson's dictum on its head, at least in dealing with very dangerous situations. Moreover, unlike Dostoyevsky's Underground Man, who has the peculiar luxury of making his desperation and concocting his degradations, Céline's Underground Man is forced into his degradations, which also are remorselessly and unavoidably social. If Dostoyevsky's mouse-man describes Everyman's instinctinal and intellectual unregeneracy within himself, Céline's Bardamu finds disgusting behavior both within and all around him.

Further, he says at one point in the novel that he has the morals of a stoat (p.213), and that "I don't care a hoot about human morality myself—just like anyone else"(p.286). And near the end of *Journey*, he even admits that it would give him pleasure to strike an angry woman's face—and does so (a woman, granted, that he has been arguing with, and who ends up murdering her lover, Leon Robinson, a major character in the novel).

This should be enough evidence to indicate that this novel possibly harbors major problems of interpretation and reader identification. In a section of *The Rhetoric of Fiction* entitled "Morality of Narration," Wayne Booth raises some considerations about the relationship of Céline to his "vicious hero" (as Booth calls him): "Céline is never undeniably there, even in the long-winded commentary. But he is never undeniably dissociated, either, and therein lies the problem. The reader cannot help wondering whether Ferdinand's [Bardamu] moralizing, of which there is a great deal, is to be taken seriously or not. Is this Céline's view? Should it be mine . . . ?"[2]

One feels tempted to answer these questions in this order: yes, obviously, yes obviously, obviously, it isn't. Such questions are not suitable for a novel like *Journey* which functions transvaluatively, operating on an inverted or subversive set of values. As Kingsley Widmer, in an acute reading of *Journey*, points out, Bardamu's "journey into the darkness" is "a will to truth."[3] The inversion of the customary direction of truth and enlightenment suggests Joseph Conrad's *Heart of Darkness*, a work with which *Journey* has more than titular affinities (such as a morally dubious and ambiguous narrator).

I don't want to imply that Bardamu is some kind of Nietzschean tough who lives by his own rules, braving society's fierce disapproval; the ship scene and speech (and the war sequences) should indicate the opposite. Nor can one accomodate Bardamu to Booth's narrator expectations by recognizing in him the prestige of a Sancho Panza or even a Falstaff. The Spaniard after all possesses a lot of fine qualities, including a profoundly human and winning sense of reality, and Falstaff is too richly, explosively comic to be seriously stigmatized by his battlefield discretion. Although *Journey* is not lacking in humor, Bardamu lacks the substantial, winning traits of these two comedic titans; for some, his main source of strength might be some identifiability with the author. Yet, for Booth, at least, such an identification would also be an insufficient guarantee of value, for so loathsome is Bardamu to Booth that such an identification, rather than elevating Bardamu, would stigmatize Céline. And if no such identification exists, then how, to repeat Booth's query, do we take Bardamu?

Widmer, whose essay posits a transvaluative approach to *Journey*, exemplifies it in his remark that *"Journey* amply demonstrates cynical self-disgust as the most useful morality. But as long as he keeps journeying, Céline's hero never finds himself to be an adequate sod, despite the knowledge that this is what the world demands"(p.89). This is a position on the narrator different from Booth's indeed! Whereas Booth finds the novel virtually unacceptable—"It is *not* an honest picture, it is not a realized picture at all . . . the central intent is morally questionable"(pp.383,385)—Widmer sees Bardamu's "sodhood" as part of a dramatic or dialectic context, in which through contrast with the more heroic (or "darker") Robinson, Bardamu is seen as insufficiently heroic, an inadequate Existentialist, which thus does indeed distance Céline from Bardamu, as well as suggesting authorical objectivity and thus a measure of control.

Put another way, Booth and Widmer regard the nihilism in *Journey* differently. For Booth, *Journey* is a book which "if taken seriously, . . . would make life itself meaningless except as a series of self-centered forays into the lives of others"(p.384). He finds *Journey* a corrupting book, whose sense of the sordidness of the modern world in not sufficient (or sufficiently artistic) to justify the moral turpitude of the narrator or the novel.

Widmer's position, as I take it, is that Céline's sense of the sordidness of the modern world *is* presented with sufficient authority to justify the moral inadequacy of the narrator, a thesis I will enlarge on later in the chapter. Céline regards the world itself as nihilistic, certainly as brutal, vicious, and rapacious: " . . . since modern society is simply war by other means, any journey through it is irrational violation of meaning and self"(p.87). As Widmer states in his monograph *Edges of Extremity: Some Problems of Literary Modernism*: "Everywhere he [Bardamu] discovers a world that has no meaning."[4] For Widmer nihilism is not a value-neuter ideological stance, but a form of dark wisdom; *Journey* is "inverted wisdom literature"(p.61), and "the way down reveals its wisdom only when it does not pretend to be the way up"(p.62).

I wish to look at *Journey's* "dark descent" in terms of what it reveals about the self in modern experience. More particularly, I will try to show that Céline's treatment of the self is basically or ultimately concerned with dramatizing a negative image of modern society itself. If the protagonist of the novel is in some respects reprehensible, perhaps even disgusting, he is less so than the society that partly makes him disgusting, and which he is rightly trying to survive. Further, any man as alienated as Bardamu obviously is inevitably embodies censure of the alienating society.

II

Somewhat like the protagonist of *Notes from Underground*, Bardamu is a degraded being. And, like Dostoyevsky's character, the degradation of being depicted reflects on society. Yet this reflection significantly qualifies the degradation, however self-deluded or repulsive the protagonists in the two fictions may be. Dostoyevsky's character, by the sheer intensity of awareness of his profound self-degradation, effects a radical and satiric critique of his society and of Utopist, rationalist values as well. He knows that he is damned, yet his damnation by its very nature implies salvation through suggesting an idea of the harmony and wholeness possible for human beings only if they acknowledge and assimilate the ineradicability of human will and instinct.

Céline, in contrast, does not offer an ontology of degraded being as profound, sustained, or substantial as Dostoyevsky's. His character's humiliations and cynicism reflect the author's sense of the bankruptcy of values in early 20th-century experience more directly than *Notes from Underground* reflects that of 19th-century life. *Notes* is far more ironic, its author and narrator more distanced than is the case in Céline's *Journey*. This is one reason why Céline early in *Journey* places his protagonist in the savagely chaotic milieu of World War One. The war is presented as a senseless havoc in which enlisted men—also carefully placed in civilian society throughout the novel as lower class or socially powerless—are virtually seen as the "enemy" by their officers. This inversion of "standard" values is so basic to Bardamu's (and Céline's) understanding of modern war and the class structure of society as to generate a powerful symbolic image of modern life as a nihilistic darkness:

> In all this solid blackness, which you felt would never give you back your arm, if you stuck it out in front of your face, there was only one thing that was clear to me, which was—and it at least was very clear indeed—that the desire to kill was lurking within it, vast, and multiform.
>
> This brute of a brigade major busied himself when evening came sending us to our death, and often he'd get like that as soon as the sun set. (p.22)

. . . .

> Everyone queued up to go and get killed. Even the general couldn't find any place that wasn't full of soldiers . . . Those who still had a little courage left lost even that. It was from that month on that they began to shoot troopers by squads, so as to improve their morale. (p.28)

Passages like these should be related to Bardamu's dramatic loss-of-self-esteem speech on the colonialist ship to Africa, for it suggests the crucial interrelation in Bardamu's mind between war and peace in the modern world—one is the extension of the other. War, as we have painfully learned since the "end" of World War II, goes on in peacetime, and it takes two forms both of which at first *seem* misanthropic or pessimistic in *Journey*. The first, which appears early in the novel, is conveyed through a slave-ship metaphor that extends across the entire novel:

> we are all galley slaves together, rowing like the devil—you certainly can't deny that. . . . And what do we get out of it? Not a thing. A big stick across our backs, that's all, and a great deal of misery, and a hell of a lot of stinking lies poured into our ears! A fellow must work, is what they say. It's the lousiest part of the whole business, this work of theirs. You're stuck down in the hold, puffing and panting, all of a mucksweat and stinking like polecats . . . And up on the bridge, not giving a damn, the masters of the ship are enjoying God's fresh air with lovely pink ladies drenched in perfume sitting on their knees. They have you up on deck. Then they put on their top-hats and let fly at you as follows:
> 'See here, you set of sods!' they say. 'War's declared. You're going to board the bastards on Country Number 2 yonder and you're going to smash them to bits . . . And if there's any of you who don't want to die at sea, of course, you can go and die on land, where it takes even less time than it does here.'[5]

"Normal" society, the peace-time world, is seen as a crudely oppressive class order. The "masters" are on top, the "galley-slave" proletarians on bottom, keeping the ship of society going and getting lashed for their efforts. Sex, one of the continuing energies of life and thus of society, is presented as an upper-class erotic preserve.

In itself, this ship metaphor, partly satirical in its heavy farcical accents, is not exactly original, nor is the idea that soldiers are hostages to their own commanders. Both concepts and images are conventional stock-in-trade of Communists and radical propaganda. What gives these symbolic images force in *Journey* is that they are used to project an image of societal corruption that will justify Bardamu-Céline's going beyond the socio-economic conditions for a "solution" or response. A society that so swindles and even crucifies those at the bottom of necessity evokes a transvaluation of values as the only sensible morality, a point Bardamu will insist on more than once. This helps *Journey* to rise above the drab or lurid fate respectively of being a superficial proletarian novel or Booth's evil fiction.

Céline of course will suggest through Bardamu the necessity of a sense of what is really going on (thus giving his narrator at least one firm base of the reliability that Booth seeks and cannot find). Tiresome as Bardamu's preaching may be to Booth, some of this material, such as the following injunction, is essential to the moral structure of *Journey*:

> The greatest defeat, in anything, is to forget, and above all to forget what it is that has smashed you, and to let yourself be smashed without ever realizing how thoroughly devilish men can be. When our time is up, we people mustn't bear malice, but neither must we forget; we must tell the whole thing, without altering one word,—everything that we have seen of man's viciousness. . . . That is enough of a job for a whole lifetime (p.23).

"Everything we have seen of man's viciousness"—this includes class brutalization, and though one can question whether Céline tells *his* story without malice, he definitely gives convincing material of men's (and women's) baseness, greed, brutality, and exploitativeness.

Journey is full of attitudes, actions, and material of the sort in the above quotes, from the frustrated vigilantes on the ship of Africa and the briefly-presented brutal de-individualization practised in a Detroit auto-manufacturing factory, to the greedy murderousness of the Henrouille family in Toulouse towards a member of their family and the parents who tie up and viciously beat their young daughter to excite themselves into sexual intercourse. Indeed, such material permeates Céline's novel, embodying the novelistic substance behind what is too readily seen as Céline's cynical misanthropy:

> . . . one saw [on the ship bound for Africa] the whole of the white man's revolting nature displayed in freedom from all constraint, under provocation and untrammelled; his real self as you saw it in war. This tropic stove brought out human instincts in the same way as the heat of August induces toads and vipers to come out and flatten themselves against the fissured walls of prison buildings . . . their [human] rottenness rises to the surface as soon as they are tickled by the hideous fevers of the tropics. It's then that the wild unbuttoning process begins, and degradation triumphs, taking hold of us entirely. (p.103)

. . . .

It never entered the heads of the antique school to give the slave a 'Mister' before his name, to get him to vote now and again, to buy him his newspaper; above all, to put him in the front line so as to rid him of his baser passions! (p.128)

. . . .

The people I could see through my window, who looked so ordinary walking about in the street like that, even they made me think of *him* [Robinson], standing there in doorways talking, cuddling each other. . . . Oh, I knew perfectly well what they were after, what they were hiding under that nothing-in-particular look of theirs. To kill others and to kill themselves, that's what they wanted; not right off, of course, but bit by bit, like Robinson, with anything that came to hand,—old sorrow, fresh griefs, still nameless hatred. . . . Unless there is a war on, a war in full blast, and then the job takes only half the time. (p.246)

. . . .

There was a crowd outside a butcher's shop. You had to squeeze your way into the circle to see what was going on. It was a pig, large. . . . He was grunting away in the middle of the circle like a man who's been disturbed. . . . He was being damnably treated all the time. People were tweaking his ears to make him squeal. He twisted and turned, trying to escape, tugging at the rope which held him; other people teased him and he squealed all the louder in pain. And everyone laughed all the more.
    The fat old beast didn't know how to hide himself in the little straw he'd been given and, grunting and snorting, he kept scattering it all the time. He didn't know how to get away from these humans. . . . There *was* no way out. . . . The butcher behind in his shop made signs and jokes to his customers and waved a great knife in the air. (p.264)

It is shortsighted to view these attitudes and situations merely as Céline's or Bardamu's misanthropy. They project all too recognizable actualities in human experience. These actualities, moreover, are fleshed out in one form or another in *Journey*. The pig is a symbolic pig indeed. It should immediately carry the reader back to the colonialist-ship scene of Bardamu's degradation (a pivotal episode for the entire novel). Clearly, Bardamu is that pig in that nightmarishly humiliating colonialist-ship situation. But, in view of all the stress in *Journey* on the sheer abasement and manipulation of the lower classes, the pig also represents them at the mercy of the governing and butchering class. The symbol broadens beyond these two applications to stand for any helpless victims of a ruthless social order, whether it is enlisted men in wartime or the unchanging misery and squalor of the poor. Finally, the pig is an accurate symbol of human instinctuality goaded by "civilization" into a frenzy of desperation, Freud's Civilization caricatured as tormentor and destroyer of the helpless "id."

The fact that some of the passages above contain pessimistic, even cynical, attitudes about human baseness and cruelty does not rule out the reality and horrror of the baseness and cruelty. Wars—and not just the first World War—are, by Bardamu's outlook, innately and utterly vicious in their making cannon fodder of the "underlings" of society for no genuine or valuable end. And though a paranoiac outlook is projected by both Bardamu and Robinson, it is an objective paranoia similar to Leon Trotsky's prescient sense that Stalinist assassins lurked in the bushes ready to gun him down—as indeed they did. The *self* implied in Céline's violent flattened-toad-and-viper metaphor validly represents an area of real human sensibility and conduct; it is an authentic vision of human beings at their worst. Although this is only part of the totality of human nature, the fact that it is part—and thus a significant part—of it lends force to Céline's pessimism, and lifts it above mere scurrilous or even immoral cynicism.

III

Although Céline-Bardamu reveals sympathy towards the poor, he also makes it clear that the poor can be as vicious as the rich, if in a different way. In a suburb of Paris where he works as a doctor, his kindness in charging his poor patients little or nothing is repaid in malicious slander:

> Sometimes I would overhear them talking among themselves when they did not know I was there, as they sat awaiting their turn. They said the most awful things about me and told lies about me that absolutely made one gasp. It obviously braced them up a lot to go for me in this way; it gave them some mysterious courage which they needed so as to be really pitiless and tough and swinish, so as to keep going, and last out. Yet I had done my best to make myself pleasant to them in every way; I espoused their cause, I tried to help them... (p.304)

Besides pointing up some impressive decency and consistency of attitude in Bardamu, this passage depicts the lower class as something less than the noble proletariat of Stalinist rhetoric. Bardamu also points out (and not unsympathetically) how the poor people of his area would rather have a government pension than work:

> They spent whole afternoons and weeks, while outside the rain came down, waiting on the threshold and in the entrance to my wretched dispensary, working out hoped-for percentages, longing for the definite, tested presence of bacillae in their sputum, for real hundred-per-cent tubercular spittle. Relief from their illness lagged far behind the government pension in their hopes; it is true, of course, that they did hope to be cured—but they only just hoped for it, whereas their desire for a regular income, however tiny, dazzled them completely. (p.303)

This is balanced judgement indeed, no sentimentalization on the one hand, no condescension or harsh censure on the other. With this sense of the reality, of the climate and texture, or poverty, Bardamu can even offer this homely truth against the hypocritical condescension of the well-off: " 'When you've no money to offer the poor, you might as well shut up. If you start talking to them about anything else but money, you are almost invariably tricking them, lying to them"(p.303). At one point (and at others) our narrator, so harshly viewed by critics like Booth, can even sound like some downtrodden hero out of a B. Traven or early Steinbeck novel crying for elemental human rights: " 'The rest of what exists on earth is not for them! It's no concern of theirs. Their job, their only job, is to overcome that feeling of obedience, to spew it out. If they can manage that before they're altogether dead, then they can boast of not having lived in vain' "(p.343).

Thus, evidence can be found of the decency and compassion of Bardamu; if he is in some ways a figurative "sodomite," he is also a man with some virtues . Despite the harsh or even nihilistic things he sometimes says about himself, his virtues and vices almost average out. He may have lost self-respect in the ship scene (probably few lose it permanently or entirely), but it is hard to believe that only a few people would have behaved similarly, or even worse. He may not have self-respect for a while after the African-ship sequence, but he does later in the novel behave at times with self-respect, and during his phase in Africa as a colonialist, his clear-sighted, non-approving description of the brutalities of European imperialism suggests a moral recorder. Having nihilistic attitudes does not necessarily make one a swine.

As mentioned earlier, Widmer sees the role of Robinson as crucial to *Journey*; he is a kind of double to Bardamu who "enforces the awareness of Bardamu's failure."[6] "Robinson," Widmer continues, "did have what the narrator finally lacked: a single good solid idea to die with. That idea is simply negation, the certitude of 'no.' . . . Robinson will not accept the rotten world"(p.90). Widmer's thesis of the courage of refusal, as represented by Robinson, is a significant perception into the structure of *Journey*. For one thing, it gives a moral context to the problem of Bardamu's moral inadequacies, and thus lends esthetic stability to the novel. Bardamu becomes the "Sod" whose darkness or weakness makes Robinson's gestures of refusal all the more compelling.

Robinson does commit a villainy that shouldn't be overlooked. He tries to carry out the murder of the Henrouille's old mother for a large sum of money. Yet he is put up to this deed by the Henrouilles themselves, and bungles the job, creating one of the many deliberate distortions effected by the important vein of black comedy often overlooked in *Journey* by critics. He is indeed superior to Bardamu in his unyielding, as Bardamu admits shortly after Robinson dies in resisting the assault of society in the form of the increasingly threatening love-suit of Madelon: " '. . . I hadn't gone as far in life as Robinson had . . . I hadn't made a success of it; that much was certain. I hadn't acquired one single good solid idea . . . ' "(p.457). Robinson had developed an idea one could die by, indeed, a "really superb idea that was definitely stronger than death"(p.458). Robinson had said No to what Kenneth Rexroth has called the Social Lie.

Our narrator couldn't do this. But does this disqualify him? It does for Booth: "The world he [Céline] portrays as reality contains no conceivable explanation of how anyone in that world could bring himself to write such a book—even this book."[7] Part of what Booth seems to be implying here is how such a scoundrel as Bardamu could narrate the world of *Journey*, a remark that seems to overlook the entire sub-genre of picaresque literature.

However, my basic objection to Booth's strictures of Céline and *Journey* is that his strictures are morally fastidious and unrealistic. Granted, Bardamu is at times vicious or weak or conniving; he even partly condones Robinson's plan to murder the old Henrouille woman. However, he also feels badly about the plot and about his condoning, or a least, not preventing it, and certainly doesn't encourage or participate in it. Earlier in the novel, Bardamu also refuses to certify that grandmother Henrouille is insane, to get her off her family's hands. When in America, Bardamu lives for a while with (and off) a tender-hearted American prostitute named Molly. Molly wants him to keep on with her, but he decides against it, partly in terms of the recurring (and, as Booth rightly says, heavy-handed) dark-journey metaphor. He is generous towards the poor in his capacity as a doctor. Certainly he is not a war hero, but then, this could be said of many men. On the other hand, his depiction of the sheer irrationality of World War I (and thus of all wars) is so authentic and vivid that one feels sympathy for all victims of the voracity of war, including the school teacher Princhard, who Bardamu meets in a mental asylum for war-shattered soldiers.

Bardamu, then, as suggested earlier, possesses virtues as well as vices. He is not simply Booth's "vicious hero"—that is a simplification. Bardamu instead is, despite his iconoclasm, unpleasantly close to being the average man on the street. Rexroth has said that Henry Miller is Robinson, and enjoying it.[8] Bardamu also in not unlike Miller, and Miller in turn is rather close, as again Rexroth has observed, to the average American business man.[9]

What I am suggesting is that the man who has struck an angry woman's face partly out of curiosity is unattractive but not necessarily uncommon. The complex truth is that a moral *sod* can also create a work of art (or many—one thinks of Picasso extinguishing a cigarette on the face of his future wife, or of Kenneth Rexroth's Pacifica radio-broadcasted opinion that of the 100 worst people in the world, the top fifty or so are poets). A moral sod or neuter can also be manipulated by an author so as to communicate a vision of life that is ultimately moral, as Ford Madox Ford does masterfully with the narrator of *The Good Soldier*. This is evident in the metaphor of the journey not only into a darkness of the heart or self, but into a darkness of the body social as well. The novelistic morality is embodied in the figure of a journey to an End, *the* End. There is a suggestion of the apocalyptic in *Journey*, one way of dramatizing the potential and actual nihilism of 20th-century society. Booth claims that Céline and his protagonist are nihilistic; the latter two in turn assert that the *modern world* is nihilistic, that it is a chaos to which they bear witness.   If their claim is true and their witnessing adequately presented, and I think they are, then *Journey* harbors a genuine moral dimension.

Widmer views *Journey* as inverted wisdom literature, and Robinson as hero of the dark road of disaffiliation from society.   But if Robinson is the agent of heroic action, Bardamu is his bard, the intelligent registrar of Robinson's toils and exploits. He (and of course "Céline") conveys the *meaning* of Robinson. Granted, Bardamu also performs the Dostoyevskian confessional role of a self-deprecating foil to Robinson, ultimately revealing in himself what not to be.   Yet he too tries to make the "journey," and realizes its value.   Does not this sort of awareness and definition of purpose embody worth too?

> Even back in New York that time, when I wasn't sleeping well, I had begun wondering whether I couldn't go along a bit further with Robinson, and further yet.   You delve deeper into the night at first and start to panic, but you want to *know* all the same, and after that you don't come out of the depths of the darkness.   But there are too many things to understand at one fell swoop.   Life's much too short.   You don't want to do anyone an injustice.   You have your scruples, you don't want to jump to conclusions, and above all you are afraid of having to die before you have done hesitating, because then you would have come into the world for no purpose whatsoever.   And that really would be hell. (p.345)

Bardamu hesitates, Robinson finally does not.   But Bardamu had to live that Robinson, his sacrificial double, could die, and in dying as he does, consummate his character.   The two men are doubles, so much so that they at times almost appear to be one character split into two roles and purposes.   Without absolving Bardamu of his ugly qualities, I am contending that Bardamu had to live, had to draw back, had to compromise, in order that his alter ego could realize his "big idea," but also so that Bardamu could tell a story and in his telling lend purpose to the world.

This is one way of dealing with Booth's moral problem of the unacceptable narrator.   Bardamu's very unacceptability morally is, in this light, the basis of his integrity, or, at least, reliability, as a narrative.   Like Dostoyevsky's Underground Man, Bardamu is in some respects unsavory, reprehensible, "stoatish"—but he is also intelligent, sociable, generous, more victim than victimizer.   He is a picaresque rogue in a world in

which the societies wherein the "adventures" occur are appallingly vicious or oppressive. One has to go far before finding a
writer who can exhibit social or class privilege reverberating so
flagrantly on the backs of the "down-trodden." Céline not only
makes one feel the very sensation of the "treading," but
identifies it with sexual sensibility, thus creating a
comprehensive ontology of degraded being. The degradation in
Journey is ultimately not individualistic—it is not Bardamu's;
his is only, unlike Dostoyevsky's narrator, incidental, though
not unimportant. The ultimate self being judged is the one
inherent in all the people who "forget what it is that has
smashed you, and . . . let yourself be smashed without even
realizing how thoroughly devilish men can be"(p.23), and even
more those doing the smashing. Beside this credo of the
integrity of remembering one's exploitation or oppression,
Bardamu's discretion or cowardice about war seems excusable,
even almost moral. And beside the following hallucinated
reality of the chaos, innate purposelessness, and madness of war,
his opting out of it becomes a gesture of legitimate selfhood:

> Could it be that I was the only coward on earth, I wondered. The
> thought was terrifying. Lost in the midst of two million madmen,
> all of them heroes, at large and armed to the teeth! With or with-
> out helmets, without horses, on motor bicycles, screeching, in cars,
> whistling, sniping, plotting, flying, kneeling, digging, taking cover,
> wheeling, detonating, shut in on earth as in an asylum cell; intend-
> ing to wreck everything in it, Germany, France, the whole world,
> every breathing thing; destroying, more ferocious than a pack of
> mad dogs and admiring their own madness (which no dog does), a
> hundred, a thousand times fiercer than a thousand dogs and so infi-
> nitely more vicious! What a mess we were in! Clearly it seemed to
> me that I had embarked on a crusade that was nothing short of an
> apocalypse.(p.13)

Merely registering this sort of war ferocity as madness, as
society in a state of disintegration, is a testament to the self and
its survival. Bardamu may be a coward, but if so, he is a coward
in a way that any ethic justifying war must confront, yet would
have trouble confronting honestly. For if military dedication to
one's country is or can be a form of social survival, the self in
Bardamu asserting its right to life within the modern stresses of
war, nationalism, and patriotism is as central to one's being as
breathing and the circulation of blood. And within the brutally

arrogant class context of war as emphasized in *Journey*, self survival becomes downright Panzaic good sense, basic respect for one's self and its continuousness.

When Bardamu's patriotic American girl friend, the Red-Cross nurse named Lola, tells him that he is a coward because he is afraid to die in battle, he has a response worth citing: " 'I simply reject it, absolutely refuse to have anything to do with it and all its soldiers. If they were nine hundred and ninety-five million and I were only one alone, they would still be wrong, Lola, and I right, because I am the only one who knows what I want. I want not to die' "(p.59). This is perhaps a brave coward; it, also, in some ways, is the Robinson side of Bardamu. Bardamu's insistence on the survival of the self has force in an age when war is senselessly destructive and peacetime society a facade for ruthless privilege and brutal greed and mechanization. *Journey* implies that the self—however craven, anarchic or unrealized—is today the only significant reality, and must make its own terms with life. This is perhaps not the way it should be, but it is, *Journey* insists, the way it is in our time. A nearly solipsistic universe emerges from Céline's nihilism, but it is paradoxically a nihilism one feels urged to confront not only to make modern human experiences meaningful, but even, as Céline suggests, to make survival of the self and thus of the human race possible. That is the "truth," the vision, at the journey-end of Céline's *Night*; it is a vision which if anything seems even more terrifyingly relevant at this end of the 20th-century than at Céline's end, in the middle of two world wars.

Notes

[1]Ferdinand-Louis Céline, *Journey to the End of the Night* (New York: Avon Books, ©1934), 111. All further references to this book are from this edition.

[2]Wayne Booth, *The Rhetoric of Fiction* (Chicago, University of Chicago Press, ©1961), 380.

[3]Kingsley Widmer, "The Way Down to Wisdom of Louis-Ferdinand Céline," *The Minnesota Review*, VIII (Winter 1968), 88.

[4]Kingsley Widmer, *Edges of Extremity: Some Problems of Literary Modernism* (Tulsa, Oklahoma: University of Tulsa, 1980), 60.

[5]Anyone who regards this quote and other war-passages in *Journey* as merely demented anti-war hysteria on Céline's part should recall and ponder some of the statistics about the "Great War" presented by Paul Fussell in his memorable study of the First World War. Describing the disastrous Somme offensive planned by General Douglas Haig, Fussell informs us that "Out of 110,000 British troops, who attacked, 60,000 were killed or wounded on this day, the record so far, "(*The Great War and Modern Memory* (New York: Oxford University Press, 1975), 13.) In a British attack on the Ypres salient in 1917, Fussell adds that 7000 yards were gained "at a cost of 160,000 killed and wounded" (14). Bardamu-Céline's attitude that soldiers were cannon-fodder in a purposeless slaughter hardly seems cynical or nihilistic, furthermore, in view of this climactic statistic: the war "cost the allies over five million men" (Fussell, 19), which evoked Edmund Blunden's horrifyingly profound *mot* after the Battle of the Somme that "the war had won, and would go on winning" (Fussell, 13).

[6]Widmer, "The Way Down to Wisdom of Louis-Ferdinand Céline," p.89. A strikingly different interpretation of the role and value of Bardamu and Robinson can be found in David O'Connell's *Louis-Ferdinand Céline* (Boston: Twayne, 1976); 'The use of Robinson as a foil, the reminder that there are two ways to face up to society—in a civilized way which, after all, is Bardamu's way; or Robinson's way, the way of blind self-interest—is a successful device. Robinson's way cannot lead very far, and for this reason he must die before the end of the novel. In contrast, Bardamu, for all his failure and failings, is still alive and struggling when the book comes to an end . . ." (69).

[7]Booth, Op cit., 383-84. Booth has since described the section in *The Rhetoric of Fiction* on *Journey* as "clumsy" in 'The Rhetoric of Fiction and the Poetics of Fiction" (in *Towards a Poetics of Fiction*), ed., Mark Spilka (Bloomington, Indiana: Indiana University Press, 1977), 77. He also suggests in the same section that he could rewrite the Céline Section, but to my knowledge he has not done so. Another foe of *Journey* is Irving Howe: "One comes to suspect that Céline writes from a total emptiness, that his show of energy hides a void, that he is really without any genuine attitude or values," a surprising statement in an individual as conversant in Modernist literature, esthetics, and strategies as Howe is (*A World More Attractive: A View of Modern Literature and Politics.* (New York: Horizon Press, 1963), 204). A Céline scholar with an emphatic sense of Céline's *moral* authority in *Journey* is Allen Thiher, who describes Bardamu as "a *moralistic*, a descendant in that long French tradition of disabused observers of human folly," which, Thiher states, includes a La Rochefoucauld, Pascal, and La Bruyère (*Céline: The Novel as Delirium* (New Brunswick, New Jersey: Rutgers University Press, 1972), 16).

[8]Kenneth Rexroth, *Bird in the Bush* (New York: New Directions, ©1959), 161.

[9]Ibid, p.160.

Saul Bellow's *Leaving The Yellow House*:
The Elderly Self Against Dying

The idea that life is mainly a preparation for death has possessed the authority or backing of some religious and ethical phi-
losophies. Yet this does not of course make it acceptable to everyone. Indeed, it is only one aspect of a concern that *is* almost
universal: that one must die, and therefore should address oneself to this basic fact. If one accepts it, *how* does he or she do so?
And if one does not, what form does one's resistance or refusal
take?

In a long story from Saul Bellow's fiction collection
Mosby's Memoirs called "Leaving the Yellow House," an elderly
woman named Hattie Waggoner, stuck in a desolate setting,
more or less alone, decides that she will *not* accept death, or, a
crucial difference, the *idea* of death. Her one possession—a
yellow house—helps her keep her hold on life and decide to go
on living. It does this by becoming a symbol as self of immortality in Hattie.[1]

During a personal crisis and climax in the story, Hattie
decides to will her house to herself. She knows this is not
"right," "Yet it is the only thing I really wish to do. . . . "[2] This act
about her will is a perverse and yet glorious gesture and assertion of self; it is wrong-headed but "right-hearted." What makes
Bellow's novella relevant to a study of the self is that his protagonist at first seems like a "bundle" of perceptions almost in
that Humean sense that has for some seemed like the final word
in refutation of the philosophical validity of the self. Yet part of
the considerable force of "Leaving the Yellow House" derives
from Bellow's ability to create and realize in Hattie a character
with such a fierce hold on life that despite all her contradictory
selves (or "bundles"), she has enough self to sustain her life and
give it value in the midst of an increasingly desolate existence.

The setting is dramatically important in "LYH": the West,
the desert, somewhere very isolated in Nevada (as one character
puts it, "Five hundred and some miles to San Francisco and 200
to Salt Lake City. Who wants to live out here but a few ec-

centrics like you and India?   And me?"(p.73).   This paradise is
called Sego Desert Lake and has a total population of "six white
people"(p.65).   Forty miles away is a small town, but otherwise
the area consists of desert and mountains, and Sego Lake.   Described as a "barren place" by the narrator (p.66), it seems like a
kind of limbo, a last outpost before entering either total desert or
despair or death.[3]

Hattie herself is ambivalent about the area.   She describes
it at one point as "one of the most beautiful places in the
world"(p.63).   This however is part of a fantasy she creates to
make Sego Desert Lake and environs endurable, for later, in one
of her more truthful moments, she admits to herself that it's a
place that "burned you out . . . and turned you to ash"(p.91).
Further, in a rage with one of her neighbors named Pace who is
trying to swindle Hattie out of her house, Hattie, speaking of the
area, says again: " 'I keep saying that this is my only home in all
the world, this is where my friends are, and the weather is always perfect and the lake is beautiful.   But . . . it's not human
and neither are you' "(p.85).   Further, "the mountains were as
red as furnace clinkers."   Although the lake does possess some
beauty, it is apparent that its environment is extremely isolated
and inhospitable to human beings.   It has a "few trees, cotton-
woods, and box elders.   Everything else, down to the shores, was
sagebrush and juniper"(p.66).

In such austere surroundings, one can become very dependent on other people.   These people, minor characters compared to Hattie, are worth considering.   Furthermore, because of
the retrospective character of this story and its use of a film metaphor whereby Hattie evokes her past life, a number of "off-
stage" characters also have importance.   But whether the characters are visible or invisible, their chief importance derives
from how they bear on Hattie and her quest for survival.   One of
them, Darly, a ranch hand for a dude ranch run by the man
named Pace, commits an act that has major significance for
Hattie.   One night when Hattie is driving home from the house
of some friends with whom she has had too many drinks, her
only car gets stuck on the railroad tracks.   Near Pace's place, she
walks there to get Darly's help to remove the car from the tracks
before her only mode of transportation connecting her residence
with the town is destroyed.   She has the bad luck of approaching
Darly as he is in the process of swindling two customers out of
their money through gambling.   Thus she prevents the swindle

and incurs Darly's keen annoyance, which leads him to handle the car-towing in a hasty, angry way. His anger results in a chain slipping off the stuck car, and hitting Hattie in the knee, which causes her to fall and break her arm.

Having her arm broken is one of the conditions intensifying the desperation of Hattie's Sego-Desert-Lake life. Yet a deeper cause of Hattie's car accident and injury lies in her alcoholism. Hattie has been an alcoholic or at least a heavy drinker for many years, even before she was bequeathed the yellow house by another woman named India, for whom Hattie, down on her luck and divorced, served as a companion and servant. Both women drank, spending days wandering around the house in an alcoholic daze.

Hattie's drinking, then, is a problem and a deep-seated cause of her car accident, and thus a factor driving her towards the point reached by some people somewhere in their lives when they decide whether or not they are going to fight for life, or sink under the pressure of adversity or vice of one kind or another. Her alcoholism also partly contributes to her life-force. Her love of drinking is one with her love of life, her joy in being with people she likes or who are convivial like the Rolfes, her memories, happy and sad, of past spouses and lovers, her beaming, good-natured energy.

The Rolfes are key characters in the narrative. Hattie depends heavily on them, and when they indicate (by leaving for Seattle on a visit) that she cannot rely on them completely, the story moves a large step towards its climactic concern: whether Hattie should let herself die, or struggle to live. Jerry serves as a kind of Reality Principle for Hattie, testing and confronting her in her fantasies and self-delusions. He proves to her that she has little money and thus small means for financial survival. She thinks her house is worth $20,000.00; Jerry says $8,000.00 is a more likely estimate (p.75). She thinks or pretends that the house is located in a beautiful place; Jerry points out that Sego Desert Lake is a very isolated place. Hattie assumes that she possesses valuables (rugs, and so on); Jerry proves that they are worth little. At the end of this sequence, after Jerry has removed some of Hattie's superficial and self-deceiving optimism about her future security, and has tried to get her to admit that she was drunk during the accident, Hattie says this:

'I've driven drunk for forty years. It was the sneeze (that caused the accident). Oh, Jerry, I feel wrung out,' said Hattie, haggard, sitting forward in bed. But her face was cleft by her nonsensically happy grin. She was not one to be miserable for long; she had the expression of a perennial survivor (p.74).

Hattie harbors a sizable life-force, although it is not always at her command. Clearly, such a force is essential to a person her age, who has "no husband, no child, no skill, no savings"(p.76), and who, had she not inherited the yellow house from her friend India, would also have had no roof over her head. A pious brother named Angus would have taken her in but his heavy piety would have made the food and keep stick in her throat. Residing with her brother Angus would have been a living death for Hattie.

Her desperate condition is implied not far into the story when we overhear one of her delusions: " 'People will help me out. It never did me any good to worry. At the last minute something turned up, when I wasn't looking for it. . . . Helen and Jerry love me. Half Pint loves me. They would never let me go to the ground' "(p.75). Nor would she, Hattie thinks, let her good friends down. Whether this is so or not, Hattie *is*, in her terms, let down even by her best friends. Put another way, she discovers that life offers no absolute guarantees. As she learns this late in life, it makes her confrontation with age and death all the more stark. As a key double character, Amy Walters, says about Hattie, when asked by Jerry Rolfe whether Amy would look after Hattie, " 'She doesn't know how to take care of herself' "(p.83). Amy, who also lives by herself, surviving her husband and living completely alone in the desert, twenty miles away from even the small Sego Lake Community, successfully lives a Spartan existence, taking winter baths in the lake, making vegetable soups for herself, playing waltzes on her piano for herself.

Amy too is a survivor, in some key ways a far hardier one than Hattie. But she lacks Hattie's joy of life and exuberance of spirits. Amy wants money for taking care of Hattie. When Jerry tells her that Hattie hasn't much money, Amy next says she would take care of Hattie if Hattie left the yellow house to her. As the narrator says at the beginning of the story, "Amy was crazy about money, and knew how to manage it, as Hattie did not"(p.65). Part of the purpose of the doubles characterization here is to mirror each woman's strengths and weaknesses, virtues and flaws. If Amy is self reliant, Hattie's cheerfulness and love of a good time imply that Amy is lacking in other ways. Though Amy is a survivor, she begrudges life to others; her self-dependence suggests, ironically, a deeper paucity of self, and implies that even survival is not an absolute value in this story. Like alcoholism, its deeper significance depends on other contexts. But as Jerry reflects, during the visit to Amy about helping Hattie, "He couldn't speak to Amy of the solitary death in store for her"(p.84). Nevertheless, seen from another perspective, Amy's self-dependent hardiness and abstemiousness makes Hattie's fun-loving sociability also look like irresponsible self-satisfaction and aimlessness. Even for the tough-grained Amy, death will be death, a mystery of suffering and, perhaps, of desolating loneliness and fear.

II

Having presented the foreground of Bellow's story, we can now examine it in terms of the self. As Hattie is the towering figure in this story, it is *her* self, or selves, that concern us. She is full of them. They are all self-conceptions by which she keeps herself together under pressure or adversity. This is not to say that these conceptions are superficial or dishonest. As with most of such projections, though, they are only part of the truth, and indeed, considering the resourcefulness of personality and character, could become a deep part of the self, even if only a persona to begin with. Hattie has too much versatility and disunity in her nature to allow any one persona to take over. Indeed, her variety of personae function to lend her even more versatility, and, ultimately, greater capacity to survive. In the long run, though, they prevent her from experiencing, until near the end of the narrative, what could be called a transcendent self, a self, that is, that either rises above her more fragmental self-interpretations or that unites her with some larger polarized opposite, such as nature, deity, or other human beings.

To begin with, although Hattie is not a native Westerner, it is understandable that she comes to think of herself as one, a Western Gal. One of her lovers, Wicks, is a cowboy that she lives with for a while. Though he is not a gentleman, and thus gives Hattie as the East Coast Lady a social reason for not marrying him, she reflects that "There was nobody like him in the sack; he was brought up in a whorehouse and the girls had taught him everything, said Hattie. She didn't really understand what she was saying but believed that she was being Western. More than anything else she wanted to be thought of as a rough, experienced woman of the west. Still, she was a lady too"(p.67). These two selves—tough Western Gal and Lady—need not be a contradiction, yet her Lady side, connected with her earlier marriage to a wealthy Philadelphian named Waggoner (who later divorced her) contains too much snobbery to fit in with the rough-hewn equalitarianism one might expect from a Western Gal: "She too had been a snob about her Philadelphia connections. Give up the name of Waggoner? How could she? For this reason she had never married Wicks"(p.87). Yet, she had loved Waggoner for himself, it seems, not, or not mainly, for being from an old Eastern family. And though she doesn't marry Wicks, she does live with him. Indeed, she even shows remorse near the end of the story for having with just violence kicked him out during a hard phase of her life when she was running a hamburger stand near Bishop, California, and Wicks was freeloading on her. In a moving memory that exhibits what she would identify as her *Christian* remorse, she remembers that Wicks was basically a good friend, and also says, " 'Wicks, dear . . . Please! I'm sorry. Don't condemn me in your heart. Forgive me. . . . I hurt myself in my evil' "(p.91). This forgiveness, which is genuine, is important as well because it will make her rejection of Wicks as an heir to her house all the more sincere and unvindictive.

Hattie's Christian self and capacity for forgiving meet a different kind of test with her mistress-friend India who, when they were living together, sometimes treated Hattie badly. India afterwards would beg for forgiveness: "Hattie would keep a stiff bearing. She would lift up her face with its uncurved nose and puffy eyes and say, 'I'm a Christian person. I never bear a grudge.' And by repeating this she actually brought herself to forgive India"(p.76).

Thus Hattie the Christian has its authentic side, though this self doesn't quite jibe with the Philadelphia Lady. This Christian aspect is also connected with a mystic dimension in Hattie which I will consider later. Suffice it to say now that it presents a religious motif central to the significance of the story.

Hattie is also a Woman of the World and an old divorcée. Driving, as she herself puts it, drunk in the desert for 40 years coalesces several selves which can be put compositely as the Tough Western Woman of the World. This also dramatizes her alcoholic self. She also keeps special supplies both in her car and in her house for tippling. And her roles as Drinker and Divorcée blend in her habit of driving to town occasionally, having martinis with lunch at a favorite hotel, then spending the rest of the afternoon "gossiping and drinking with her cronies, old divorcées like herself who had settled in the West"(p.66).

She has some right to the compound Western-Woman-of-the-World, though, for besides trying to survive in the West with little to sustain her ("no husband, no child, no skill, no savings"), she has known men intimately from both East and West. And though she is in a panic about her car when it is stuck on the train tracks, she can stick up for herself when she has to. After Darly, from bad temper due to his fear of Pace, has inexcusably broken her arm, and tells her that she can't take care of herself, she gives it right back to him: " 'You're old yourself,' she said, 'Look what you did to me. You can't hold your liquor' " (p.70).

Her pride, which is the other side of her Christian forgiveness, also puts Pace down when he crudely offers to pay her fifty dollars a month for the rest of her life if she would take in lodgers and bequeath the yellow house to him in her will. Her distrust of him emerges, and she explodes: " 'Everybody wants to push me out. You're a cheater, Pace. God! I know you. . . . You'd let me go away and never send me a cent. You never pay anyone. You can't even buy wholesale in town any more because nobody trusts you' "(p.84). From what one recalls of Pace's using Darly to cheat his customers, this would seem to be an accurate indictment. It also shows something of Hattie's temper, and the temper of her self-respect. And it also brings us back to the issues of survival, Hattie's will, and her deepest or ultimate being, the transcendent self.

The run-in with Pace determines Hattie to make her will so that Pace will never get her house. This forces her to confront not only the insuperable factuality of wills but of what makes wills necessary—death, one's own death, *her* own death. She now is, or thinks she is, not only threatened by the unscrupulous Pace, but feels that she no longer can rely on anyone. Drunk, she has some basic reflections on her present situation:

It was strange. . . . I used to wish for death more than I do now. Because I didn't have anything at all. I changed when I got a roof of my own over me. And now? Do I have to go? . . . I thought Helen and Jerry would never desert me, but they've beat it. And now Pace has insulted me. They think I'm not going to make it'(p.86).

"They think I'm not going to make it"—"They" now include her two very good friends the Rolfes who did more for her than most friends would, but who have finally made it clear, by leaving the area for a while, that friendship has limits. As suggested earlier Bellow implies here that life is conditioned, that one cannot depend on anything or anyone absolutely. Yet Hattie on another level already realizes this, even if she has not fully absorbed or accepted it, for shortly before the passage above, she says: " 'I was never one single thing anyway. . . . Never my own. I was only loaned to myself' " This is a pregnant remark. First, it helps her to accept the heavy fact of her old age ("She no longer even smelled to herself like a woman. Her face with its much-slept-upon skin was only faintly like her own"—p.86). One transcends the ego and the body by seeing oneself both more impersonally and by accepting the fact that one is not *one* self or entity or personality, but several, or even many. One of these selves, the *current* one, is that of old age, a sad time when "you swell up with tears and fat" (p.86). But the implication of the insight is that time and that self will also pass, and though it ultimately passes into death, it might pass through other kinds of selfdom too.

Actually, Hattie has had a mystical experience here, an idea with the intensity and depth of a vision. If one is only loaned to oneself, one belongs to something or someone else. The Christian Hattie would say God, but it need not be anything that religiously personified. The point is that Hattie's idea of the loaned self makes both age and death more acceptable. If this is so, one must ask why she wills herself the yellow house, for this is what she does at the end of the novella. Put another way, one should ask why Hattie, after having a powerful insight that makes her life and death more acceptable, resists death by commiting an act that attempts to bestow upon herself a kind of immortality?

These antithetical propositions are not necessarily opposed. But before attempting to prove that contention, it is best to consider the concluding portion of the story, for its stress on Hattie's capacity for survival is important. In the process—now quite drunk—of determining her will, Hattie "replays" her past. Bellow employs the metaphor of a film to indicate Hattie's self-consciousness; it is a psychic reflexiveness that allows her to review her life and pass judgement on it, a power that only age and the releasing liberation of whiskey can give her. The "film" thus is a mechanism by which she composes her soul by examining her past self, or selves. Thus she will think of Wicks and Wagonner, of others, of acts she now repents. She also thinks of the present and the future, who she could live with (relatives come to mind, only to be dropped for one reason or another), who she could, accepting mortality, transfer her house to. One terrible event for her on the film is the killing of her pet Doberman Pinscher "Richie."

    This event is one of the repressed horrors of Hattie's life. It is made all the more painful by her Christian morality about taking life in any form, as well by her love for horses, birds, and dogs, especially dogs. Yet the story, replayed on her psychic film, does not really do her discredit, especially from the perspective of survival. A Doberman she had adopted when he was already fully grown turns on her one day. Her alternatives are either to kill the dog or be savagely killed by it. The dog had already fastened his teeth into Hattie's thigh, and her presentiment that it would next go for her throat once she fell is sound.

    Grabbing a nearby hatchet, she strikes and kills the dangerous, crazed dog in one blow, thus saving her own life. Although she is ashamed of this event, it also exhibits her ability to survive under extreme conditions. Yet an attack by a dog named "Richie," a male, seems somehow typical of her bad times with other males, whether being abandoned by her wealthy Philadelphia husband or kicking Wicks out of her hamburger joint at gunpoint. It is in the light of her vicissitudes with the canine and human males in her life that Hattie's sympathy for a trapped coyote that Wicks kills with a kick (to save bullets) becomes significant. It is hard times, and Hattie and Wicks are living by trapping coyotes. But the one trapped is white, " 'White as a polar bear,' exclaims Hattie, " 'You're not going to kill him, are you?' "(p.87). Wicks does kill him, and the narrator says "What else could he have done?"

    A white coyote is not only rare, but is a beautiful creature. It is also a wild animal, and this anecdote about it just preceding the one about Richie suggests both an idea about primitivism and about survival or biological necessity as well. The coyote, despite its possibly sacred or preferential whiteness, must die for Hattie and Wicks to survive. Richie too must die, if Hattie is to live. Yet something is lost to her in the death of these animals, a kind of pristine, wild life, a sense of male energy and freedom which Hattie possibly feels to be a symbol of *her* desire for freedom, for untrammelled "Western" existence. The deaths of these animals, like the loss of her friends or the use of her arm and her car, also represent the loss of appendages of power and beauty and freedom in her own life and person. More and more, the narrative centers on the yellow house, its used furniture, its scrawny garden, its bleak yet curiously beautiful vistas as the remaining and shrinking resources of Hattie's existence.

Hattie loses her car (and thus her trips to town for groceries and martinis at her favorite hotel) by being unable to drive it, due to her broken arm. She then begins to consider all the candidates for inheriting the house. For one reason or another none of them will do: brothers, cousins, a scholar niece, Wicks. Wicks would be ill-at-ease in such a house, and the niece would rot here, perhaps start to drink.

Hattie's "head" tells her that she will have to live with her pious (and non-drinking) brother Angus, but her "heart" tells her that she should remain in the yellow house: " 'it is for somebody like me . . . only I fit here. It was made for my old age' " (p.91). This extraordinary self-acceptability initiates another mystical opening and heightening in Hattie's consciousness:

"She was now very drunk, and she said to herself, *'Take what God Brings. He gives no gifts unmixed. He makes loans'* " (p. 91).

The yellow house is one of these godly loans. It is also a "mixed" gift. It represents life for Hattie, survival with dignity (if in solitude). But, as the "yellow" suggests, the house also implies the area, the desert, and thus, death. The yellow house is a mixed gift indeed, but it is also the best thing that Hattie can acquire, her circumstances being what they are. Thus because Hattie doesn't want to depend on anyone else, and feels, as she says, " 'cast off and lonely,' "she decides to will her house (including water rights, so crucial and symbolic in the West) to herself. God may make only loans, but this realization won't prevent Hattie from making the most of what is loaned to her. I asked earlier why Hattie has a vision that seems to accept death, then makes out a will that seems to reject her death, and had asserted that the two ideas are complementary rather than opposed. Life and the potential of self may be loans, conditioned gifts, but that is no reason not to make the most of them. By clinging to a self that accepts the changing of oneself, by accepting mutability, one transcends one's "normal" or customary selves, and achieves enlightenment, even a kind of salvation.

This salvation or self-transcendence will not obviate the desperation of Hattie's condition. She is now more cut off from friends and youth and (her favorite word) succour than ever before. But something in her, typically abetted by liquor, has broken through the skin and limitations of her usual self or selves, and she feels and thinks like a seer.

But not like a philosopher,[4] or a least, like an Aristotelian. For, her final thought, she can't remember or accept the idea of an End, of *her* ending:

> 'Then she thought that there was a beginning, and a middle. She shrank from the last term. She began once more—a beginning. After that, there was the early middle, then middle middle, late middle middle, quite late middle. In fact the middle is all I know. The rest is just a rumor' (p.92)

Her last words, realizing she is drunk, are, " 'I'll think again. I'll work it out for sure' "(p.92).

This ignorance of an end is of course not really ignorance; it is a credo. If there is an ending, death, she won't give into it, but will fight it one way or another. Rather than giving in, she will fight for herself and thus for *her self*, the new self emerging amidst an isolation and desperation probably unparallelled in her life.

Life is a loan, but one fights for it, even if one's once fine hair is frizzled and "old, like onion roots" (p.74). "Let the dead bury the dead," she says, thinking both of *Luke* in the *Bible* and of her dead friend and benefactor India—"but go thou and preach the kingdom of God." Bottle of whiskey in hand, yellow house hers (at least until her death), nearby Sego Desert Lake and her house the only symbols of renewal, Hattie will do all she can to keep alive, despite, and because of, the new self deriving from her new knowledge that all her selves are not really hers. The "loan" nature of life makes her selves and her new self all the more precious. Hattie's new self rises above both age and self to a kind of ravaged glory of being. This mystery of transcendent selfhood she has earned by confronting the waste of her life, and thus is possibly more prepared for the end than she realizes.

Hattie's new self will perhaps compose an end that she won't shrink from.

Notes

[1]Constance Rooke makes a general point about houses in Bellow's fiction as well as about "Leaving the Yellow House": "Houses . . . of symbolic importance appear with great frequency in Bellow's work. Usually the house is an extension of the occupant's heritage, physical circumstances, or spiritual well being, and always it requires his attention . . . Hattie's yellow house is a complex symbol; it is as precious to her as life itself (which it represents . . .)." See "Leaving the Yellow House: The Trouble With Women," *Studies in Short Fiction*, 14, 1 (Spring, 1977), 185.

[2]R. V. Casill, ed., *The Norton Anthology of Short Fiction* (New York: Norton & Co., 1981), 92. All further quotations from "Leaving the Yellow House" are from this edition.

[3]Norike M. Lippit, who regards "Leaving the Yellow House" as depicting "the wreck of the American dream comically and pathetically," feels that "Sego Desert Lake is a sarcastic symbol of America's Eden" ("A Perennial Survivor: Saul Bellow's Heroine in the Desert," *Studies in Short Fiction*, v. 12 (Summer), 1975), 281.

[4]Constance Rooke contends that Bellow gives Hattie no intellectual gifts, and claims that this is generally true of the women in his fiction. Op. cit., p.181. She asserts further that "Hattie is a victim of Bellow's sexual chauvinism—she is allowed no real intellectual intelligence, no life plan or training (Henderson becoming a doctor in old age, or Charles Citrine's journey near the end of *Humbold's Gift* towards mysticism)" (pp.186-87). Bellow's characterization of women in novels like *Herzog* and *Humboldt's Gift* certainly strikes me as pushing the stereotypes of the Bitch and the Sex Goddess unduly far. In "Leaving the Yellow House," though, Bellow, if he does not give Hattie much of an intellect, does, as I argue in the chapter, bestow a mystical dimension upon her.

Ralph Ellison's *Invisible Man*: The Self as Black

I

Probably few works of modern fiction are so weighted with an overt sense of self—and selves—as Ralph Ellison's novel *Invisible Man*. Indeed, the metaphor of invisibility—basic to the entire narrative—generates and climaxes the narrator's experience both of 20th century America and of his own deepest being as a Black. His realization, first announced in the post-narrative "Prologue" and consummated, through the experience of the narrative, in the "Epilogue," is precisely of his invisibility. What this means in terms of self is partly rendered in the first paragraph of the novel:

> I am invisible . . . simply because people refuse to see me . . . When they approach me they see only my surroundings, themselves, or figments of their imagination—indeed, everything and anything except me.[1]

The scope of this awareness dovetails into the final sentence of *Invisible Man* in a powerfully reverberative insight: "who knows but that, on the lower frequencies, I speak for you?"(p.503). "You" is first the reader of course, but more deeply it designates the White race and indeed all the groups polarized by racism and its dehumanization, as well as every tangent and orbit of modern alienation. As Jonathan Baumbach observes, "Though the protagonist of *Invisible Man* is a Southern Negro, he is, in Ellison's rendering, profoundly all of us."[2] Ellison's narrator not only speaks to all of us (and this narrator is a speaker, orator, public and private man of exhortative words), but in a crucial sense, *is* us in the sheer intensity of his pursuit of his true being. An authoritative sense in which he might not be his readers could be one which derogates us: he seems to live at a higher pitch of purpose, crisis, and significant pain than the average person could stand or would dare to invite.

Reflexiveness of identity designates the real symbolic

thrust of *Invisible Man*. Ellison's novel presents a search not only for a Black man's racial self, but for his (and our) most human self. That these latter two selves are the same does not make the human self investigated in *Invisible Man* superficial; rather, this subtle blending lends considerable penetrative force to the *human* definition being attempted in the work. In a crucial sense, then, *Invisible Man* is not only a "Black novel"; it is a novel in which Black humanness is converted into a violent inquiry into the self that, as Ellison subtly intends, inexorably reflects *any* human self. He is not saying that we are all Blacks, but that to the extent we don't see human beings (Black and others), we don't see or relate to reality, at least the reality of true or essential being.[3] Thus, the literal story level about a Black person's experiences can in one sense be viewed as a metaphor for an ontological inquiry into 20th-century American existence, accelerated by its literal aspects as Black experience, and thus racism, exploitation, and dehumanization, into a powerfully hallucinated projection of the modern condition.

Like most quests for the self, that of *Invisible Man* must focus on one's central *social* identity. For a Black American, this is likely to be embodied in his race. Accordingly, on one level *Invisible Man* is the story of a Black youth's "pilgrim's progress" from the South, youth, and illusion to the North, young adulthood, and realization. We are familiar with Northrop Frye's conception of a character in literature moving from reality to realization. Such is the narrative pace and the pressure of the prose in *Invisible Man* that this novel can be described as moving from nightmare and illusion to realization, the realization, again, taking the revelatory form of the awareness of one's invisibility as both a Black and thus as a human being as well.

In the journey towards this vision, the narrator (significantly nameless in the Modernist Kafkaesque tradition of faceless and virtually nameless questers) takes on and discards a series of selves. Some he temporarily accepts, others he finds imposed on him by the force and shape of events. As a Black, he finds it common to be seen as one kind of Black or another, depending on the social context and the observer. Down South a "nigger" boy, he also sees himself at one point as another Booker T. Washington, educator of Blacks who will lead the way towards Black survival—and adjustment—in a White-dominated society. At his high school graduation, he presents a speech in which he indicates that "humility was the secret, indeed, the very essence of progress"(p.20). He does not really believe this, but "believed that it worked"(p.21). A person, he thinks then, can get ahead by making clear one's sense of his subordinateness to the governing and threatening White world. This means of course a shrinking of one's self, a limitation of one's autonomy and self-respect. That such opportunistic submission is a very high price to pay for self-advancement he learns in various ways.

One way to view *Invisible Man* is through Freudian allegory, as a confrontation or dialectic between Superego and Id. The narrator, molded in the South and thus in a context of overt racist pressures, tell himself he should placate the White man. But another region of his consciousness, surely with roots in the Id, wars with his "humble" persona. Taking his cue (as he does throughout the novel) from his "yea-saying" grandfather, who, on his deathbed, first reveals that he used humility and a posture of subservience towards White society as weapons of irony and veiled hostility, the narrator is often aware of a "dark" side in himself the development of which would be beneficial to him. It is often, especially early in the narrative, so in abeyance that it functions virtually as a creed from the unconscious. But as Baumbach implies,[4] it emerges when the narrator takes a powerful Northern trustee of a small Black Southern college on a car trip into the poor section of the area around the college where the trustee, an elderly, genteel man named Norton, comes across a Black family in which the Father has committed incest with his daughter during his sleep. The hypocrisy or, at least, superficiality of the trustee's concern for Black "improvement" is shown by his obsessed desire to hear the sharecropper's story. This account not so much revulses as fascinates him, as if confirming his own latent racist sense of Blacks' inferiority and his resentful envy of their supposed greater sexual "license."[5]

The result of this revelation—harmful to the trustee but ostensibly disastrous to the narrator's career as a Bledsoe-type Black educator—is the expulsion of the latter from his genteel Black college and his betrayal by its President, Dr. Bledsoe, who fawns on powerful white supporters of the school, but also manipulates them for his own ends. Both Bledsoe and the narrator destroy the latter's Booker-T.-Washington ideals and self-realization; Bledsoe sends him North with venomous letters of non-recommendation, and the narrator, perhaps following an unconscious impulse to threaten his role of humble, self-advancing

Black, conducts a powerful White man into one region of Black Unconsciousness made possible by the history of American slavery and racism.

Thus the forced trip North represents an expulsion from a fraudulent Eden. It also marks the beginning of the experience of a number of other "selves," all illusionary to one degree or another, yet all or most essential in the narrator's descent into a more authentic being embodied in the realization of his invisibility as an individual and unique human being.

During the course of the narrative, the protagonist is taken for a number of different types of people, ranging from an ignorant Southern rural Black to a hip Harlem pimp, numbers runner, lover, cop-briber, and preacher named Rinehart. Perhaps the most crucial and precipitative identity, though, is his party self, his role as a member of the American Communist Party (called in the novel, with effective generality and increasing irony, the Brotherhood). In an exchange with Brother Jack, the New York director of the Party and the person who proselytizes the narrator, he is told that he is wrong to think he is still a Southern Black. That side of himself is now dead; his new self is in step with History, this new comrade claims. Brother Jack, fascinated by the narrator's impromptu speech-making and his ability to arouse a crowd during a Harlem eviction, wants to use him for the party's own ends. At a high-toned Party party in *downtown* Manhattan, the narrator overhears a hard-bitten, attractive woman he has just met ask Jack whether he is Black enough. This is a hint of his new role of self as an instrument to be used for the Party's own interests. The sheer opportunism of the Party becomes evident to the narrator only after he realizes late in the novel that the "Brotherhood" is not really interested in helping Blacks, but in accomodating social or racial unrest to its own selfish interests. Or, more accurately, the Party is following the dictates of the Party line laid down by Moscow, so that local needs or conditions are brutally ignored for the sake of an international ploy. This makes one consider why Ellison didn't make the actual character of the Brotherhood more obvious. He might indeed have done so, in view of other realistic segments in the novel (not to mention the Party sequences themselves).

Yet I think more is gained than lost by not making the depiction of the American CP too literal. As a "Brotherhood," it gains dimensions of mystery and of a universality beyond political connotations, so that instead of only representing the CP, the Brotherhood represents as well any heuristic, ideological organization that attempts to impose a false social label on one's intrinsic being. "Brother" Jack (another of a number of betrayers of the narrator in *Invisible Man*, Black as well as White), tells him that his health is important, because it (and thus he) belongs to the Party. As a Brother Hambro, the narrator's instructor in "doctrine," puts it, " 'it's impossible *not* to take advantage of the people' "(p.436). And Jack too states that " 'such crowds are only our raw materials, *one* of the raw materials to be shaped to our program' "(p.408).[6]

This novel is full of people who deceive others by pretending to do their bidding, while actually carrying out their own wishes: Bledsoe, Norton (in his vain, self-deluded way), the Brotherhood, which in Jack's words makes the Black masses (to the Party all masses are Blacks) do what the Party wants. Exploitation, trickery deception, manipulation—all are maneuvers and attitudes calculated to deprive a person of his true self or deepest being for organizational and ideological ends.

In a rather crude symbolic gesture late in the novel, Ellison implies that Jack (and the Party) is blind by having Jack accidentally dislocate a false eye from its socket during a heated exchange with the narrator about the nature of the Party's obligation to the people. This participates in the fundamental motif of blindness running throughout the work. People don't see others; rather, they see what they are constrained by upbringing or prejudice or vested interest to see. It produces a world less of the blind leading the blind than of the blind attacking the blind, whether in the battle royals in chapters one, twenty-four, and twenty-five, or of a predominantly White-run political organization like the Brotherhood, which never really sees the American Black because it does not want to.

II

As a Southern Black, the narrator has presumably had his share of intimidating and oppressive experiences. But if, as Aldous Huxley claims, experience is not simply what happens to one, but what one does with what happens to one, then it becomes clear that the protagonist of *Invisible Man* is bent on

108 Ralph Ellison's *Invisible Man*: The Self as Black

doing something significant with his experience. Accordingly, I want to suggest that the narrator is in some ways heroic, because of the significant resistance he makes to various forms of disintegration or enslavement of his self.[7] But this strength—symbolically derived from his Grandfather—emerges gradually at first. Some of the protagonist's experiences would crush anyone's aspiration to selfhood, or a least scarify it badly. An example of the sort of archetypal experience of racism that would imprint itself on anyone like a red-hot branding iron is the Smoker sequence following the "Prologue." Though deservedly famous, this sequence has not been scrutinized in detail. It is a brilliant combination of compacted racist terrorization and first-person narrator sensitivity and interiority. It is also a microcosm of Southern society. As the narrator tells us, in sharply evocative prose, "All of the town's big shots were there in their tuxedoes, wolfing down the buffet foods, drinking beer and whiskey and smoking black cigars"(p.21). A number of Black boys have been rounded up to put on a battle royal for the benefit of the White men, but just before the fights, they are put in a vicious double bind by, while in their boxing trunks, suddenly being exposed to a gorgeous naked blond dancer. That Southern Black youths have already learned what it means to be in any kind of erotic context with a white woman, (particularly an attractive, let alone naked, one, especially when surrounded by a lot of half-drunken White males), makes this scene particularly vicious.

The youths are forced into a kind of lynch-mob psychodrama in which the make-believe element threatens to dissolve at any moment and leave the young Blacks face to face with raw Southern-White racist violence. Just before the "boxing" begins, one of the White men (one of the town's "big shots") has to be restrained by the others: " 'Let me at those black sonabitches!,' someone yelled. 'No, Jackson, no!' another voice yelled. 'Here, somebody, help me hold Jack!' 'I want to get that ginger-colored nigger. Tear him limb from limb," the first voice yelled' "(p.24). Considering that all of the boys, including the narrator, are blindfolded, that Jackson is so strong or big and violent that it takes more than one man to restrain him, and that the "ginger-colored nigger" refers to the narrator, the horror of the situation is overwhelming—one has to be a Black or other minority or, as a White, have had the extreme bad luck to be in an analogous or similar situation to fully experience the visceral terror of this moment. The sexual double-binding of the boys in regard to the nude blonde is evident in some men threatening them "if we looked and others if we did not"(p.23). One boy faints. The men, who have hired the blonde to dance erotically, and force the boys to watch, thus wedge the youths into the traditional Southern horror-zone for Blacks of exhibiting desire for a White woman (made more blatant by their wearing only boxing trunks). This scene also suggests that the most flagrant promoters of racial violence and stereotyping of women into erotic entertainers or whores and, by implication, frigid "good" women are adult White males.

The fight or battle royal sequence begins. "Everyone fought hysterically. It was complete anarchy"(pp.25-26). They are egged on by the brutal support of the white men: " 'Slug him, black boy! Knock his guts out! . . . Kill him!' "(p.26). All the youths are blindfolded with white cloth. The symbolic material here seems to be more authentically generated by the plot than that of Brother Jack's false eye. Indeed, it is white bullying and duplicity that is setting Blacks blindly against one another, a point that the Back-to-Africa primitivist Ras the Destroyer makes later in the novel when he accuses the Brotherhood of blinding the Blacks to their true brothers and interests.

The level of violence in *Invisible Man*, high even for an era of considerable violence in serious fiction, is controlled by the clarity and vigor of the prose and by the underlying design of the narrative. But just barely; a little more brutality, and one would find himself in the drugged or extreme physical violence, respectively, of William Burroughs' *Naked Lunch* or Hubert Selby, Junior's *Last Exit in Brooklyn*. Ellison's prose sustains a traumatic narrative authenticity through cinematic rapidity of action and a precision of images of description and sensation typical of *Invisible Man*:

> Blindfolded, I could no longer control my motions. I had no dignity. I stumbled about like a baby or a drunken man. The smoke had become thicker and with each new blow it seemed to sear and further restrict my lungs. My saliva became like hot bitter glue. A glove connected with my head, filling my mouth with warm blood. It was everywhere. I could not tell if the moisture I felt upon my body was sweat or blood. A blow landed hard against the nape of my neck. I felt myself going over, my head hitting the floor. . . . I . . . felt myself seized by hands and yanked to my feet. Get going, black boy! Mix it up! My arms were like lead, my head smarting from blows. . . . A glove landed in my midsection and I went over again . . . (p.25)

"I had no dignity," says the protagonist; who could blame
him? This is one of the humiliations that he will look back to in
a climactic realization late in the story. He ends up here being
beaten and almost knocked out by the remaining, larger
survivor. A culminating irony behind all of this evening of
violence, shock, and brutality is that the narrator at the end of it
is supposed to repeat his popular, self-degrading graduation
speech on Black humility, non-resistance, and self-subordi-
nation. It strains his young sense of self almost to the breaking
point to have to accomodate his Booker-T. role to the brutalization through fear and violence forced upon him by the
"cream" of Southern White society. It also suggests his naiveté,
and his tenacity early in life to realize himself in White terms,
an ambition that he suddenly and finally drops one-third
through the novel when Bledsoe's vicious betrayal is exposed to
him by a comically pathetic white liberal.

But the horrors of the evening are not over. When the
battle royal concludes, the youths are to be rewarded. Their
reward, a pile of coins, lays on an electrified rug. The shock that
the boys receive, already wet from their exertions, is all the more
intense. Yet, this pain, and the involuted evil that designed it,
does not prevent them from trying to pick up as many coins as
they can bear. The recollection of this different kind of degradation is possibly what in part makes an image of a cast-iron
Black that the hero discovers in his Harlem boarding-house
room later so infuriating to him. It is a bank, " . . . the kind of
bank which, if a coin is placed in the hand and a lever pressed
upon the back, will raise its arm and flip the coin into the grin-
ning mouth"(p.277). The figure is a "very black, red-lipped and
wide-mouthed Negro, . . . his face an enormous grin." This
stunning image of the mocked and unselved Black, like other
images and actions in *Invisible Man*, towers above its immediate narrative context, emitting a kind of violent, numinous authority, so powerful is its symbolic reverberancy. It is a "self" to
be overcome by a dedication to accepting and pursuing the deepest or darkest essence of one's being.

During the Smoker, one White man announces that it is
"good hard American cash" that the boys are scrambling for in a
scene as revealing and prophetic as it is debasing of both Blacks
and Whites (but particularly debasing of the Whites, for they are
adults and hold the power in this situation). Something of the
mettle of the narrator comes across when at one point in the

melee of greed, sweat, electrified pain, and sadistic pleasure, he tries covertly to topple one of the white men onto the rug, only to get savagely kicked in the chest for his efforts and propelled onto the deadly rug.

More of the spirit of the hero's grandfather looms in the final event of the smoker, a school speech which, by this point in the evening, is a humiliatingly ironic event. The speech, cast in the stilted rhetoric of a blind idealism, says in effect that Blacks should both help themselves and keep their place. It is put in the figure of a ship at sea without water, and includes a "friendly" vessel that comes into sight and says to "cast down your bucket where you are!"(p.31). This is also meant as advice to be friendly to the Southern White Man. So far, the worst bigot in the room could not object to this ornamentalizing passivity towards the racist status quo. At one point, badgered by the drunks to repeat his big words, the narrator shifts from the phrase "social responsibility" to "social equality." "Equality" immediately quiets the room down, and one of the more sober men politely if menacingly makes the youth eat his words: "'You sure that about 'equality' was a mistake?' 'Oh, yes, sir,' I said. 'I was swallowing blood'"(p.33). The cross-cutting images of opportunistic, self-advancing words uttered while swallowed blood is going where the words come from exemplifies the powerful, almost at times, electrical, ironies of *Invisible Man*. The protagonist has not yet learned to confront reality in terms that won't undercut his integrity; he is still too oriented towards making good, and, like some minority people, understandably feels that that's the chief goal, despite whatever mishaps or humiliations occur along the way. The only problem is that making good is posited or achieved in White terms, within a "benevolent" paternalism the acceptance of which is also an acceptance of racism and of one's consequent dehumanization. "'We mean to do right by you,'" says his Graduation-Speech critic, " 'but you got to know your place at all times' "(p.33). Ellison in the Smoker sequence conveys what the price of acquiescence is in its most naked terms: Black children coerced into brutalizing entertainment the pay for which is a beating, a shock, and a profound debasement.

Why does the narrator even give the speech, after such gross evidence of being cynically manipulated? Perhaps he couldn't have gotten out of it anyway, but the deeper motive is a blind idealism impelling him to realize some noble concept of self, if even within racist terms. He could become a leader of his people, and help to ameliorate their condition while not offending White society.

Later that night he has a dream which shows how the unconscious can see what consciousness, blinded by illusion, idealism, or vanity, cannot. If his gift from the White town leaders is a scholarship to a *Black* state college, the real gift is of a different character. Told by his Grandfather, who represents both a Superego and an Id figure, to open envelope within envelope, he finally finds an engraved message that says, "To Whomever It May Concern—Keep this Nigger-Boy Running"(p.35). The hero will understand this dream after Bledsoe's betrayal which consists of seven letters of strong disrecommendation for a summer job in New York with various important White businessmen. Just before the young liberal Emerson, himself in revolt against an oppressive father, shows him the letter and the shattering truth, the hero even admits that he would like to become Bledsoe's assistant; in other words, he would like to be Bledsoe's double, another ambitious Black educator and "leader" who subtly manipulates White power for his own ends. Young Emerson allows the hero to read the letter which with fawning tact and hypocrisy makes it clear that the narrator has committed a terrible but unspecified offense, that he can't ever return to the school, and that he must not know of his decision. He is in effect being written off in a vile collusion between White and Black power, and only through the good luck of an alienated son's rebellion does the truth emerge. Rather than being in the dark, the hero now sees the light, but it is the dark light of Joseph Conrad's better fiction, in which revelation is disillusioning, and everything, as William York Tindall once said about *Heart of Darkness*, looks gray. Ellison continually works with the metaphorical ironies of light and white, darkness and blackness.[8] The revelation of Bledsoe's treachery is so blinding and so dark that the narrator's life is radically changed: he will move, if gradually, from a fraudulent ascent to light downward to a liberating darkness.

III

The main narrative action in the latter half of the book

concerns the narrator's involvement in the Brotherhood or the Party. But rather than deal with that large phase in any detail, a phase that is given too much space by Ellison, I wish instead to focus on a few of the more important paradigms of the self and what one might call the anti-self in *Invisible Man* with regard to Whites and Blacks. Whatever the individual self of a Southern or Northern Black person may be, it is obvious that his anti-self, projected primarily by Whites (and to a lesser extent by some Blacks), is represented by the epithet "nigger." Whether one is a poor sharecropper like the incestuous Trueblood or a powerful, cunning, and ambitious Black educator like Bledsoe, to racists one is still a "nigger." The category of insult in the term covers everyone in the crude generality of race. Thus, race in a racist society stigmatizes and shrivels both one's humanity and individuality.

I venture these platitudes about American race relations to suggest why the problem of self takes the form it does in a race-conflicted society like ours. According to Ellison, members of *both* races don't see each other; as the traditionally oppressed group, Blacks have more excuse for their blindness, hatred, or projection than do Whites. But the horror of racism anywhere, not only in America, is that it projects a sense of the anti-self of each racial group onto the other group. If a Black, by his mere skin color, embodies a stimulus to all sorts of negative associations, such as Rapist, Mugger, Thief, Drug Addict, etc., his self is dissolved in this bile fantasy of fear and/or hatred. Early in the "Prologue" the narrator has a violent encounter with a White man because of a collision on a dark street. The White man insults him, and the hero, responding from his instinctual *self* to this anti-self insult, bangs the man's chin on the crown of his head, infuriatedly demanding an apology, but getting only continued curses from the weakening if larger man. The narrator is so angry that, having rendered the man helpless, he is ready to slit the latter's throat, only to realize in the nick of time that the White man was not insulting *him*—he was insulting a shadow, an evil projection of his own possibly called "nigger" (though Ellison doesn't specify the word); "the man," claims the narrator, "had not *seen* me, actually"(p.8). He could also stress the "me" here for they mean related if distinct things. He sees the narrator as a derogated *type*, and, following the collision, responds to that image of type and anti-self out of the blindness of his own evil temper or anti-self. The narrator sees him as another White asserting oppressive White social power through "personal" and haughty insolence.

Thus the encounter is frightening and nearly disastrous, because it involves a collision of shadows in the general, American darkness. The self in our hero, emotionally mutilated by the Smoker males and Norton and Bledsoe and all the Emerson Seniors and Brother Jacks and countless other whites, is sullied by a White stranger who not only is ignorant of this personal history of humiliations, betrayals, and manipulations, but assumes in effect that this one Black individual is indeed a "nigger" (or whatever other scurrility he flings at him), and deserves the insult because his type, his race, is for this White man his basic trait. The narrator's race is also a human trait, but that seemingly inalienable fact is what the evil madness of racist projection ignores and severs because the "projector's" own self is flawed, corrupted, or unbalanced and to relieve this pressured sense of self-dislike or disequilibrium insults one's own anti-self in another person, thus perniciously "objectifying" one's own alienation. Fantasy or not, projection or not, the "social" results are vividly real: the blind White man, maligning another's self, almost loses his own life.

The irony of Ellison's little parable of course is the fact that the projective mechanisms here have traditionally resulted in the Black being threatened, terrorized, tortured, and/or killed. In American race relations, the Black, not the White, has been the customary victim of human blindness and exorcism of one's own self-dehumanization. Jungians would say the Black is the White's shadow, but that formula is too neat. It might be more accurate to say that the Black is the White man's fate (to copy and mock Norton's conceited notion), but the very pith of self of the Black male and female has too often been at the mercy of the White man and woman's reading—or misreading—of his or her fate. He or she sees not; as a consequence, the Black has suffered for what the White person imagines he sees in him. If the White's projection is self-alienating, its serious result for his Black opposite is the brutalization and dehumanization of the Black who bears the White person's inner devils on his skin like a disease. Ellison has a key passage near the end of *Invisible Man* in which the hero thinks of the Brotherhood's ignorance and manipulation of Blacks, and his sense of his humiliation and exploitation by Whites expands to include his whole race. It is one of the great climaxes of the book, and deserves quoting at length:

> And now all past humiliations became precious parts of my experi-
> ence, and for the first time . . . I began to accept my past and, as I ac-
> cepted it, I felt memories welling up within me . . . images of past
> humiliations flickered through my head and I saw that they were
> more than separate experiences. They were me; they defined me. I
> was my experiences, and my experiences were me, and no blind men,
> no matter how powerful they became, even if they conquered the
> world, could take that . . . They were blind. . . . And because they
> were blind they would destroy themselves and I'd help them. Here
> I had thought they accepted me because I felt that color made no
> difference because they didn't see either color or men . . . we were so
> many names scribbled on fake ballots, to be used at their conven-
> ience . . . (p.439).

One highlight of this important "peroration" is the hero's
realization through his "dream vision," that Jack and Norton
and Emerson are symbolically one individual. This is not necessarily an intimation that all *Whites* are the real enemy, but
that areas of sizable White power—in business, education, and
(radical) politics—are embodied in people who want to exploit
Blacks and are totally indifferent to the reality of the Black self as
an order of human existence possessed of or deserving com-
pleteness or individuality of being. Thus the narrator and all
Blacks are "invisible" even to political pseudo-radical organizations like the CP, making a mockery of their name, the
Brotherhood. White acceptance, he now sees, is a confidence
game, because it is not on terms that respect, let alone accept, a
Black's real humanity. The only viable (if formidable) and true
acceptance for the Black is of his whole past: "I was my experiences, and my experiences were me," he says—they *were him*,
and define him.

This realization is tantamount to the acceptance of and
responsibility for Black experience that includes all of its pain
and anguish, fear and rage, as well as its distinctive strengths and
joys and wisdom. It is a great gesture of recognition of one's enduring humanity and its capacity to assimilate and develop from
suffering. This acceptance of one's experience will also mean
that, like the idinal figures of Dostoyevsky and Céline, Ellison's
protagonist will go underground, although, significantly, only
for a while. However, more than that of those two underearth-
lings, *his* underground sojourn is a metaphor for what one
might call an integrity of alienation from a White power struc-

ture whose very existence and any cooperation with which would deny his apprehension of his own essence as a Black and *thus* as a human being.

The hero "goes underground" by literally falling into it. Chased by some White rioters down a street, he falls into an open manhole and lands on a coalheap in darkness. The black-on-black symbolism would be heavy were not the naturalness of the whole sequence of events so compelling. Mocked by one of the Whites as a "nigger in the coalpile," he is indeed returned to the elements and to his racial and human elementality by the whole thrust of his "pilgrimage" from naiveté, opportunism, and "White" idealism to a tough acceptance of his racially un-assimilable self. In his new darkness he destroys all the credentials of his compromised self-identifications, such as his high-school diploma and his Party name. Being "run" into his dark hole, he decides not to run anymore—" 'You're through with them at last,' "(p.402), he claims, in an internal dialogue in-dicative of a new self.

This Fortunate Fall can be seen as a variation of the an-thropological symbol and literary mechanism of the dark des-cent, a process which usually initiates a series of developmental or revelatory experiences, from Alice's drop into "Wonderland" to Conrad Jim's *Patna*-plunge into the metaphysics of his own cowardice. In *Invisible Man*, the descent evaluates the exper-iences of an individual and implies censure of an entire nation. But the depth and finality of the disaffiliation is most empha-sized by a dream in the narrator's new unconscious world in which not only Jack and Emerson and Norton but also Bledsoe and Ras castrate him. One's final emasculation of self is per-formed by people representative of or addicted to power for the self in *both* races. Mockingly informed by comrade Jack that he is now free of his illusions, the symbolic castration suggests his transcendence through rebellion and extreme suffering of the values and ideals of any conceptions of humanity—whether Marxian History, the American High Standard of Living, Black Africanism, or Booker-T.-Washington genteel racial gradu-alism—that in any way invalidates one's Black, and thus fun-damental, self.

That this "Black" self is also ours is made clear in the final words of the novel:

Being invisible and without substance, a disembodied voice, as it were, what else could I do? What else but try to tell you what was really happening when your eyes were looking through? And it is this which frightens me: Who knows but that, on the lower frequencies I speak for you?(p.503).

Can one be or have a self by oneself? This ontological and trans-racial enigma is the ultimate implicit question of this novel, and partly explains why the narrator on the last page of the work states that he will surface again; he will do so in order to participate in some larger social reality and responsibility. This re-emergence signals the difficulty of the Black person's goal of self-realization. But, just as important, it underlines the difficulty of *any* person's journey towards self-realization.[9] If the narrator speaks for his opposite, the White, the symbolic Other, this is "frightening" because one's opposite doesn't realize he is blind, cannot recognize the reality of other human beings, and projects a mis-identity of Blacks. What perhaps is worse, the White person does not realize that he or she is invisible too, and thus leads a life of compounded self-delusion. In *Invisible Man* Ellison has unforgettably registered the terrible fact that racism is ultimately a blinding destructiveness towards all selves and every self, a hallucination of false being for racist and victim alike. Spring, hopes the narrator, might come if we do assimilate and grow within our darkness—but "death waits," he insists, "for both of us if you don't," if you don't, that is, recognize the phenomena of human invisibility and illusion, and the hatred and fear that they create. The universality of this "underground" observation has hardly dated in any dialectic of the contemporary self.

IV

Yet is it too easy or facile to say that we need to accept the darkness to achieve some kind of redemption or renewal? Accepting the darkness, whether inner or outer, one can also be overwhelmed by it. It is possible for darkness to become so visible, so overpowering, that a hell from which there seems to be no retreat descends on one.

This sort of darkness a more recent novelist, Diane Johnson, attempts to explore in psychological and feminine terms as a contemporary Gothic chiller in which the monsters of the genre are translated, frighteningly, into friends, neighbors, domestics, husbands, lovers—the elbow-close humanity of our routine lives.   In fact, Johnson's novel *The Shadow Knows*, which I will examine in the next chapter, extends the sensationalistic terror of Gothic romance into the racy vein of comtemporary, sophisticated first-person narrative realism to effect a darkness that seems ubiquitous and inescapable.   If Ellison invites us to look beyond our invisibility into our inevitable darkness, Johnson reveals a darkness not only in the other but also in the self that, like the eternity of time during a panicking, makes us despair of where to turn next, or what other self to produce in order to survive a sinister reality both pervasive and encroaching.

Notes

[1]Ralph Ellison, *Invisible Man* (New York: NAL, 1947), 7. All further page references in this chapter to this text are from this edition.

[2]Jonathan Baumbach, *The Landscape of Nightmare* (New York: New York University Press, 1965), 68. Other critics have also been sensitive to the broad implications of *Invisible Man*. According to Tony Tanner, " . . . *Invisible Man*, so far from being limited to an expression of an anguish and injustice experienced peculiarly by Negroes, is quite simple the most profound novel about American identity written since the war," ("The Music of Invisibility," in John Hersey, ed., *Ralph Ellison: A Collection of Critical Essays* (Englewood Cliffs, New Jersey: Prentice Hall, 1974), 81). William J. Schafer contends that "Ellison's novel is above all an American novel about us all, black and white together." (Hersey, ed. *Ralph Ellison*, 115).   Thomas A. Vogler suggests another dimension of the novel, a subtle literary one: "If Ellison has entered the mainstream of modern art, it is through his fusion of the problems of his Black protagonist with those of the writer." (Hersey, ed., *Ralph Ellison*, 113).

[3]Thus I think that Norman Mailer is wrong to say that "*Invisible Man* insists on a thesis which could not be more absurd, for the Negro is the least invisible of all people in America. (That the White does not see each Negro as an individual is not so significant as Ellison makes it—most Whites can no longer see each other at all." (*Advertisements for Myself* (New York: NAL, 1959), 42). I will attempt to show later in this chapter that Ellison's treatment

of invisibility in *Invisible Man* is quite significant in terms of ideas of the self about both Blacks and Whites.

[4]Baumbach, Op. cit., 72.

[5]According to Houston A. Baker, Jr., " . . . the entire episode [of Trueblood's narration] constitutes a brief drama of slavery." (*Singers of Daybreak: Studies in Black American literature* (Washington, D. C.: Howard University Press, 1974), 29.

[6]Irving Howe raises an objection at this point worth citing: "Ellison makes his Stalinist figures so vicious and stupid that one cannot understand how they could have attracted him or any other Negro" ("Black Boys and Native Sons," John Hersey, ed. *Ralph Ellison*, 38.)

[7]William J. Schafer calls the narrator an anti-hero because he is "invisible, nameless, and dispossessed . . . " ("Ralph Ellison and the Birth of the Anti-Hero," John Hersey, ed., *Ralph Ellison*, 122). This strikes me as very severe treatment both of Ellison's protagonist and of all invisible, nameless, and dispossessed people. Alfred Kazin also regards the narrator as a non-hero or anti-hero (*Bright Book of Life: American Novelists and Storytellers from Hemingway to Mailer*. (New York: Dell Publishing Company, 1971), 250. In fact, Kazin seems to regard Ellison's narrator as being little short of a fool or grim clown, which fails to explain how the novel could register the enormous charge it unquestionably possesses through so weak a conductor. Ellison himself refers to his narrator as a hero, and, despite D. H. Lawrence's famous mot "Trust the Art, not the Artist," this fact should carry weight. (*Shadow and Act* New York: Random House, 1964), 177.

[8]According to William J. Schafer, ". . . Ellison, like Melville, has used the black and white of Manichaeism ambiguously so that the "power of black" is a moral consideration . . . " Ibid., 123.

[9]Irving Howe has accused Ellison of indulging in self-liberation to escape the tougher task of relating individualism to social reality and pressures: self-liberation, he asserts, "violates . . . the interplay between external conditions and personal will. . . . The unfortunate fact remains that to define one's individuality is to stumble upon social barriers which stand in the way . . . of 'infinite possibilities.' Freedom can be fought for, but it cannot always be willed or asserted into existence." (Op. cit., 38). It seems to me that Howe is demanding of a novel what he wants it to be, rather than accepting the intrinsic character or goals of the work. In the case of *Invisible Man*, the goal is to exhibit the experiential maze of racism the assimilation of which leads to the "exit" of what the narrator calls "infinite possibilities." Of course the narrator "exits" at the point where life will be difficult, but he got there by a substantially evoked experience of racism and social nightmare that designates the darkness and illusion he had to encounter before realizing what, for him, is life's true scope and character, and thus, within *those* limits, as well as those of his social appearance and personal nature, the character of life's "infinite possibilities." Enlightenment, even a dark one, offers a sense of liberativeness and thus expansion. This sense in turn might be self-deceiving, but at least it gives Ellison's narrator the energy to confront life on his own terms rather than on those dictated to him by social and racial authority. We know from the ending that he will now confront society. Howe's implication that *Invisible Man* ends solipsistically reveals his own tendentiousness, rather than an artistic shortcoming in Ellison's novel. Ellison has peppery views of his own about

Howe (which he recorded in a long essay in *Shadow and Act* entitled "The World and the Jug"): "I fear the implications of Howe's ideas concerning the Negro writer's role as a actionist more than I do the state of Mississippi."(135).

Diane Johnson's *The Shadow Knows:*
Domestic Terror and Female Liberation

I

Diane Johnson's novel *The Shadow Knows*, published in 1974, is supposedly about the early Seventies. In a 1983 interview, Johnson says that *Shadow* is "about how things were between Blacks and Whites in the 1970s . . ."[1] Just before that, she also says that *Shadow* is "a novel about fear." These two points are true, but I think the real authority of Johnson's powerful novel is that besides being concerned with Blacks and Whites and fear in the Seventies, it presents something more permanent about both races in America, as well as about love and hatred in relation to fear, and does so precisely through the form or sub-genre of the detective-story thriller. In this regard, the 1983 interview again merits mention: "instead of clarity being created out of ambiguity and mystery, quite the opposite occurs—the possibilities seem to proliferate as the book goes on"(p.211), an idea with which Johnson agrees in the interview. She should, for *Shadow* significantly inducts the detective story as an ordering form for not only Gothic fears, but for terrors and anguish that are overwhelming because they are so integral to everyday life. The point about the place of ambiguity in *Shadow* also suggests that if, on one level, this novel is a detective thriller, on a deeper level, it is a narrative of psychological realism concerned with the texture of contemporary domestic life as experienced by a highly intelligent and responsive young woman.

One intent in this chapter, then, will be to try to understand why Johnson uses two contrastive narrative designs, what she gains from such narrative complexity. More deeply, I will probe the terror and fear and hatred and love themselves to see how Johnson's almost hallucinated vision of these states of mind define something essential about contemporary marital, love, and racial experience. I will examine as well the key theme of justice in *Shadow*, and the outlook of an intellectual woman on a male-dominated institutional world. Though other women novelists have confronted the latter condition, Johnson has memorably related it to sex, physical and psychological terror, love and hatred. If the resultant condemnation of men as fractured, hypocritical, or out of control is not "Feminist," it nevertheless represents a strong womanly judgement on male power and inadequacy, and a moving depiction of the plight of women striving for personal and professional self-realization.

II

With a title like *The Shadow Knows*, questions about the form or forms of the work are worth considering first.[2] Does *Shadow* indulge the melodrama of the Thriller's cause-and-effect structure, despite its deeper novelistic intentions, or do the two narrative levels converge into a sophisticated significance? If Johnson's own admission that she is herself not a good detective might give heart to those of us who like Edmund Wilson don't care who killed Roger Ackroyd,[3] and if thinking of *Crime and Punishment* reminds us, without permitting us to beg the question, that distinguished novels can be written in the detective-story mode, still, our most authoritative gloss on the matter of narrative forms might come from the narrator in *Shadow* itself: "'For a while I gave up all reading but detective stories, where sameness comforted me, whose morality assured me of order outside of my own disorder.' "[4] Although this is the narrator, N. Hexam, speaking, it suggests something about the form of *Shadow* as well. Detective stories generally possess a firm, rather simple-minded morality, a rigorous ratiocinator, and an ultimate assurance of order. They solve problems and mysteries, set right from wrong, protect society and the individual from evil and madness, or, when evil has struck, strike back definitively, imposing tidiness, light, cause-and-effect order on any darkness and disorder in the world.

All this offers comfort of sorts to the protagonist, an intellectual woman with four small children, and with a husband she dislikes more every day. But the larger reason N. needs solace from the fantasy worlds of detective mysteries with their progression towards achievable clarity and moral resolution is because, as she all too well knows, she inhabits a world full of mysterious and sudden violence, hatred, disorder, insanity, and increasing darkness. Her world is full of unexpected and savage violence, and it bespeaks the force of *Shadow* that this violence implies a condition endemic to America that is beyond time and place, even though virtually all of the setting is located in a Northern Sacramento, lower-class public-housing site during the first eight days of January.

Right at the start, one is introduced to incidents of both external and internal violence in the world at large about which the narrator, N., is revealingly knowledgeable: "There was that man in Carmichael who walked into the beauty shop and murdered all the women by tying them to the dryers and pulling plastic bags over their heads"(p.31). She next mentions a neighbor's wife who, seemingly content, slashes her wrists one day ("People get sudden notions").

But Johnson opens *Shadow*, significantly, by blending the mystery element with an important modern philosophic concern, when she says, "You never know, that's all. There's no way of knowing"(p.3). Of knowing what? There's no way of knowing what will happen next, what shocking evil some *normal* person might suddenly perpetrate, where violence or ugly emotion will next rear its head from—or *why* it will. To the old epistemological mystery about whether humans really know what they know—a problem fundamental to *Shadow*—Johnson adds the questioning of our knowledge about the darknesses lurking in *anyone's* heart, that potentially dangerous and terrifying area of ignorance. And to bring this urgent philosophic concern closer to the bone, *Shadow* scrutinizes not only the evil or insanity in another person or even in the mystical or beloved Other, but also in oneself. Johnson, in other words, really utilizes the detective form to pose two forms of life extremity, one threatening large physical danger on the one hand, and radical self scrutiny on the other. Thus, at one point, at the tip-end of terrorization, when N. whispers for help in her bedroom phone around three in the morning, possibly talking to a demented phone harrasser, and pleads that "The murderer is in the house . . ." (p.248), the statement rings with richly philosophical and psychological irony.

Thus, the detective form is not an artistic limitation in *Shadow*, but a pathetic yet shrewd attempt by the protagonist, and an adroit maneuver by the author, to introduce some order, no matter how superficial or melodramatic, into a mysteriously

menacing world. For that "outside" world of gratuitous homicide and rape and raging, brutal wars (the Vietnam War is in
progress) is also part of N's life; in fact, it exists inside her house.
Her own family, house, and property are threatened by acts of
mysterious violence: first, her front door is attacked—"hacked
and slashed . . . with an axe or knife, and smeared . . . with some
disgusting substance like a mixture of blood and vomit and
crankcase oil"(p.5). If doors are viewed as representing our outside self, our persona, then this action can be seen as an initial
stripping of the narrator that will continue until a climax of the
novel when her naked soul, tortured by a series of appalling
events, is confronted by the revealed inner being of another person in true, non-melodramatic terror.   By this point, N. *does*
know something, and just in time possibly to save her life.

The novel, in its title and its allusions to knowing and not
knowing throughout, thus possesses a fundamental epistemological dimension. In taking its title from the old radio thriller
and thus suggesting its introductory words—"Who knows what
evil lurks in the hearts of men?   The Shadow knows"—*Shadow*
effectively combines traditional mass-media mystery with the
labyrinthine character of the self by suggesting an alternate
"logic" for that old program: "Who knows what self lurks in the
hearts of men—*and women*?   The Shadow knows."   *Shadow* basically concerns a quest of the selves within the individual
through the "night journey" of adulterous love, racial animosity
and identification, deeply emotional self-confrontation, insanity,
stalking, revenge, abandonment, and one of the most startlingly
ironic resolutions in contemporary fiction.   This is another way
of saying that *Shadow* is an important novel about the self in
extremity, and about an "Everywoman" self registered with such
inner revelatory immediacy and authenticity as to represent
both sexes.   The novel centers on the experience of a small,
frightened, attractive young woman who finally transcends the
chauvinistic convention of the genre: being "done in" brutally,
her only or final statement a dehumanizing scream at impending horror. No small portion of the attraction of *Shadow* is that
its heroine survives by and large with intelligence and integrity.

III

The self material can be readily located in *Shadow*, though the mystery of the self, underlying the Who-Will-Do-It and Who-Done-It level, is everywhere. N. admits at one point that she has always been afraid of her huge Black domestic, Osella, and drifts towards wondering where in the immensity of flesh that is Osella resides her self, and "Where do I feel my self? Inside, behind my nose, and along my lower spine most particularly"(p.50). This latter identification of self with her spine means that N. relies on her instinctual areas of being. This trust saves her life later in the narrative, but it also locates some of the energy generating her erotic rebelliousness. For one of N's selves is really that of a rebel of "true" passion in the ideological yet visceral, non-conformist sense of D. H. Lawrence's *Lady Chatterley's Lover*. N. goes for love, for the truths of the heart and the "gut," rather than for the safety of superficially ordered and loveless marital life, which is one reason why women like Cookie Mason, wife of N's lover Andrew, and N's "good" friend, Bess Harvill, really hate her.

A major theme in *Shadow* is that of the self pursuing genuine and passionate love, even at the cost of marriage, respectability, position—perhaps even of life. N. finds this pursuit exciting, but it also creates fear and guilt, and thus partly accounts for her state of "objective paranoia." N. feels menaced by terrorists, and there is evidence that she *is* threatened by dangerous or malicious people. Her fear is, understandably, so intense that it evokes fantasies of danger that, going beyond any retribution the accusative, superegoistic self in her would impose, become part of the horror latent in the modern age itself. One of these fantasies is worth quoting in full:

> Sometimes I scare myself with this idea: you are alone with someone you love and trust, whom you have always known, whom you were a child with, maybe, and have seen each other cry, and are known to one another's mothers. Now you are grown and it is a cloudless day, as blue as the eyes of your friend. The two of you are away in the country, I imagine lying under a pasture tree surrounded by innumerable pleasures of exquisite days—fragrance, the grass to lie on, blue flies singing, your picnic lunch in a basket and the friend smiles over you at this moment of perfect repose, of perfect rapport; leans toward you smiling, and then his hands are around your neck, but *even when you are dying still you cannot see anything in the blue eyes that you had not seen before, they are the last thing you see, illimitably familiar and strange.* (p.72)

This passage is central to *Shadow*, because it presages N's betrayal by her lover Andrew, who will turn out not to be an outlaw lover and liver after all, no Mellors. But it also looks forward to her friend Bess who, late in the story (where it best belongs), will also lean over the vulnerable person of her friend N. It is not accidental, too, that Bess's name is mentioned in the very next paragraph.

But more deeply the passage suggests the mystery-epistemology dimension of the novel, "who knows what evil. . . ." If one can't even trust one's best friends, people one has known well for many years, if one cannot trust or does not really *know* one's lover (who one *knew* so well), who or what can one trust? Can one even trust oneself? And what *can* one know? If only the back of one's spine knows the most essential or urgent truths, knows when one should not turn one's back on an old friend, that means that one must indeed grope in a dark labyrinth for the truth, for reality. One is in the dark, it is universal, ubiquitous, and one must learn to see with eyes of darkness. Such insight into Andrew is lacking in N. Andrew's cowardly retreat to entrenched respectability, an unloved and vulgar wife, and an attractive San Francisco home threatens to destroy N. far more than the real ghosts and shadows of her guilty and libertarian mind. The mystery story that is *Shadow* is really the deeper, philosophical mystery of epistemology—what does one know, and what part does knowledge or ignorance of one's self and the Other play both in safeguarding one's physical existence from serious human menace and hatred, and in establishing for one the Good Life that derives from a realization of self? These are the structural questions embedded in Johnson's "mystery thriller."

Sex, of course, has always been a vast mystery in itself. N's sexual being breaks readily into two sides or selves. A "wanton woman," she says in her guilt phase, "is her own murderer, having first slain womanliness, delicacy, virtue, isn't that so?"(p.19). The implicit questioner here, the voices or selves of conscience, is less the essential N. than a reflection of Bess (a big reader of psychology who has also been psychoanalyzed), of the despised and victorious Cookie Mason, and of the mad, threatening, sex-obsessed and elephantine Osella. In opposition to these accusers is an ecstatically happy passage like the following which stands out vividly against the prevailing fear and anguish of N's experience:

> I guess what I mean by love, besides desire, is confidence, a
> confident state of mind, a clear and reliable feeling. Your heart
> is clear, knowing that when it thinks about the person it loves
> it won't surprise itself by stumbling unaware on some ugly reser-
> vation, some knowledge that must be suppressed or excused.
> The heart is glad just to think about its lover, is suffused in glad-
> ness.(p. 112)

A beautiful passage, to be sure, almost a mystical bliss, and
part of the reality of N's experience of love for and with Andrew.
Yet is is also appallingly ironic, because of the knowledge N.
stumbles on later.

N's self as erotic rebel is a deeply significant aspect of
Shadow. Johnson has indicated in the McCaffrey interview that
she is not a feminist, that "my works are not feminist
works"(p.20). However, she also says that she is "not at all trying
to disavow feminism," but that "most of my books have been
about other things." This latter point may be true generally, but
Shadow is in effect a feminist novel in the authoritative sense
that it defends in novelistic terms the right of a woman to a free,
open life that permits self-development both in love and career.

One of the leading clues in the novel about Andrew is
that he works in a law firm, the same one that N's husband
Gavin and Bess Harvill's husband work in. (Another significant
detail that Johnson does little with is the fact that N's lover is a
corporation lawyer, surely material for rich development about
massive male power and identifications).   Thus, Gavin and
Andrew are doubles in significant ways.   Both know N. intimately, both are lawyers, and both virtually identify with sexually chauvinistic values as members of the law firm of Briggs,
Harvill, & Mason.   When the divorce between N. and Gavin is
being adjudicated, N's ambition to continue in Graduate school,
study for her Master's exams, and ultimately get a doctorate is
obliquely disapproved of, both by lawyer Briggs and the judge.
Rather than Gavin giving N. money so that she could finish *her*
education (as he had finished his while she cared for the home
and the family) and enter a profession, both men suggest that
she should be content with being "a typist, a telephone operator,
or a nursery-school teacher:"   "Mrs. Hexam should be more
practical"(p.212). In other words, the male-ranked world of law
and authority is forcing this intelligent and sensitive woman
into a low-paying, non-prestigious, non- or semi-professional
job—such is her place in society, her status in life, they decree.

She is already educated enough (with a B.A. degree), states the judge. It is revealing that Andrew, despite being furious with Brigg's legalistic sexual chauvinism, says nothing to Briggs about his role in suppressing N's self-development.

This male alignment is extended by Bess, who, psycho-analyzed and thus liberated into conformity and self-sacrifice, functions throughout the novel as an agent arguing reconciliation by N. in terms that would subordinate, even kill, N's energies as a free lover, intellectual, and professional. In one exchange, she urges on N. that "you have *children*, you'd get some kind of job"(p.122). Though perhaps N. really would get a job, even a miserable one, she insists that she wouldn't, or that if she did, that she would hate her kids. In view of the concern N. shows for her children through *Shadow* , the reader can't write her off as an irresponsible Mother (as Bess and the lawyers certainly would). N's candor here is actually part of a larger point, or campaign, that provides us with one opportunity to introduce the racial element in *Shadow*, material which broadens this novel impressively.

Bess attacks N. for harboring intellectual pride, but is actually assaulting N. for exercising a free and independent intelligence; if she didn't have a scholarship, her academic pride would not exist, argues Bess, and N. would be just as willing to go out on a sordid 9-to-5 job as . . . As who? N. (as well as the sold-out Bess) knows that the dreary semi-slave jobs are done largely by women, and by minority women at that. This work status is merely part of a larger slave existence: "Though I couldn't convince Bess of it, I know I would become like the other welfare mothers in this unit, adding children from year to year to my fatherless brood, not working, because what would be the point? A job would just be one more terrible enslaving insult"(pp.122-23). Earlier, N. says "I wonder about all the poor women, the whole world full of poor women—men, too, of course—who have to do jobs they don't want to do"(p.121). N. (and "Johnson" behind her) are one here in a powerful identification of an educated, middle-class White woman with the poor and the dispossessed of society, the masses of people who know that their only choice in life is between a job with little dignity, advancement, and money, and welfare, with its heavy stigma. Realizing the ignominy and savage unfairness of this fate, N. herself plumps for welfare, if necessary, in a rebellious and sympathetic identification with the dispossessed of society, and in particular with Black women.

IV

There are a number of Black characters in *Shadow*, men like Clyde, Ev's estranged husband, AJ, her lover, Big Raider, Osella's boyfriend and nightclub promoter. They all have relatively minor roles in the story. However, the two Black housemaids or domestics in the Hexam household, Osella and Ev, are major characters. Osella, originally from the South, goes mad and accuses N. of hexing her (an accusation, as N. admits, with some validity in social and racial terms). She is also preternaturally sensitive to N's love affair, denouncing her as a whore both to Gavin and later, obsessively, over the phone directly. In a terrifying scene, just before Osella abruptly leaves the Hexam home, N. encounters her maid coming down the stairs "raving mad. I had never seen anyone raving mad before. There is no mistaking it when you look close. What did you do? And *then* I saw that in her hand beneath her apron she was carrying the bread knife"(p.84). She now wonders in a panic whether Osella has already slaughtered her young children upstairs, but, hearing the children, N. is able to maneuver them out of the house around the dazed, sweating maid who has already burned N. in effigy upstairs, a knife savagely pushed through the belly, the legs of the symbolic doll burnt into stumps.

Walking fast down the street with her children, escaping from the potentially homicidal Osella, N. is self-possessed enough to make a comment typical of the sensitive, meditating, female intelligence at the center of the work: "It is strange to be fleeing for your life along your own block with no one noticing much"(p.86).

At this point, Osella leaves, and the second major Black character, Ev, arrives. But it would be misleading to suggest that Johnson presents Osella only negatively. Osella actually serves as a gauge of N's own development, of her "éducation sentimentale." One day N. takes Osella out to a graveyard where her husband John Henry is buried. Osella visits the grave while N. waits for her in her car. After a while, N., because of her own family responsibilities, decides to tell Osella that they have to get back home. Expecting to find Osella mourning in sedate self-control, she is astounded and frightened at what she beholds: "she [Osella] was upended on the ground, her garters showing, and the bulges of bare skin above her stockings, her fat body shaking all over, her cheek laid against the earth, her hands pounding the earth with rage and despair, rage and despair the expressions of her contorted face"(pp.55-56). Soon after, when Osella returns, re-composed, to the car, N's solicitous behavior is met with a snarl and some reverberating words: " 'What do you know, in your jeans, wearing them jeans? You don't think it makes no difference if a poor nigger's dead. You gonna find out, you gonna find out' "(p.56).

Indeed, N. does find out what passion and a lost lover or beloved can drive one to. But N. also comes to realize Osella's humanity by being able to see that the massive Osella's grief in love is just as human and heart-breaking as her own. If once, N., with some haughtiness and distance, could ask herself about Osella, "where beneath those huge breasts did she feel her heart beat," in lines that perhaps parody Blake's "The Tyger" and mock Osella as well, her own experience of grief and terror and loss makes her, as we shall see later, more accepting of Osella, and makes her realize, too, that Osella's madness, like Ev's hopelessness and doom, has much to do with her position in White society. Osella can be regarded as a kind of "dark" double to N.—both will lose their beloved, both are distracted by sex, both relate maternally to N's children, though partly as rivals. Osella is in a way N's id, a titanic, primitive force out of the South, and, in her anti-witch strategems against N., out of a more primitive past as well.

A specter of White guilt, Osella swells near the end of *Shadow* into an extraordinary image of primitive, vulgarized, super-female sexuality, encompassing and belittling in *Shadow* all White sexuality which, ironically and masochistically, pays her to entrance and belittle it. It is not accidental that Osella continually speaks of N. as a "little bitty woman," implying something minute too about N's sexuality, and that she serves as a maternal caricature of Gavin's acute childishness.

With Ev, N's second domestic, a far different relationship obtains. Ev is not obsessive or insane. She is battle-scarred from marriage and love, and so pushed in and self-contemptuous from being repulsed by White society that she can fall asleep on a bus with lighted cigarettes in her hand, burning herself. When she and N. first meet, both are desperate for each other, Ev needing the job badly, and N. needing someone to help with the house and the children (so that N. could continue to pursue her Graduate studies). N., furthermore, needs a stabilizing human presence in the house like Ev now that Gavin has left her. Theirs too is a doubles relationship: "We were like two halves of a mirror. . . . Ev was the more desperate. Like me, her husband had left her"(p.104).

N., on one occasion of racial violence towards Ev, comes to see that her identification with Ev is closer than she had realized. Visiting a retirement home one day with Ev, Ev tries to use the swimming pool, only to be physically threatened by a huge man brandishing an iron pipe (pp.207-08). When N. rushes with righteous indignation to her defense, the man also turns on her. Ignoring all of N's social and racial credentials of respectability, he is ready to bash her head in, too. She notices earlier that when she has Osella in her car, she is harrassed by police in a way she never is when driving alone.

Ev is more a part of the Hexam family (minus Gavin) in its public-housing days than Osella ever was, and thus the signs of impending violence and terror pull the two women, White and Black, mistress and servant, close together. Both of them have plenty of reasons for thinking that men both known and unknown are after each of them, husbands, lovers, or just local rapist-maniacs who have been quietly watching them for weeks, months. Finally, Ev is attacked while taking some laundry at night into the darkened laundry room where someone strikes her heavily on the back and runs off. Ev dies a few days later. Though a police inspector regards her death as a result of Ev's alcoholism, this interpretation doesn't really explain the terrorization, which resumes before long. The police account is that Ev died from over-drinking ("acute pancreatitis"—p.218), which the attack might have aggravated, but did not basically cause. N. comes to think that Osella attacked Ev, and there are grounds for thinking so. Osella resented Ev taking "her" place in the Hexam home and denying her access to the Hexam children. N., further, discovers in the laundry room a heavy glass ashtray (probably used by the assailant) from the Club Zanzibar where Osella performs.

But even if Osella were the attacker, and it is never made clear that she is, there is a deeper horror. It is one comprised of the racism in American society itself that would drive Ev to drink, to feel deep self-contempt, to waste herself and allow her men to abuse her because she felt worthless. As N. acutely says of Ev, "if she'd been White living up on the hill, she would have fewer reasons for drinking her insides away so she would die at a blow"(p.219). This perspective lends a certain irony to the Police Inspector's claim that Ev died of "unknown causes." Whether Ev was murdered by an assailant or by her contemptuous dispossession by White society, she, N. is convinced, was still murdered.

Thus, if some of the tension of *Shadow* derives from its not being clear whether someone is after Ev or N., or both, the suspense is deepened by the sense that, through identification with Ev (and N's liberalist guilt), the terror applies to them both. N. feels committed to discovering the murderer, or at least the attacker, of Ev, partly because she interprets the attack as meant against herself as well. Through this identification she symbolically suffers for White racism, but she also thereby acknowledges her acceptance of her own "shadow" side.

V

For N. too harbors something of a murderer in herself. Her Bess "self" feels guilty about being a rebel of love and defiantly uncooperative (and even childish) with Gavin when he attempts, rather pretentiously, to patch up their marriage following his confronting N. about her adultery. But she also admits to herself that she would like Gavin dead, and is tempted on one occasion to kill him. N. and her husband are on a camping trip in Colorado, and at one moment when he is fishing on a height overlooking a fast stream at the bottom of a gorge, she thinks of pushing him into the water. Her next thought is that it would not be *deep enough*. Then she has a strong guilt response. This leads to one of the overt passages in *Shadow* depicting the self and its permutations and mysteries:

> . . . remembering the pounding power of my first impulse, I have never been sure why I did not push Gavvy. What is the real reason? I wish the real reason would be that I am an ordinary, sane, non-homicidal person, even the sanest of whom must sometimes be aware of homicidal thoughts, and these were mine. But there was some extra urgency in my first calculating judgement that will always make me wonder or darkly know that I only hesitated because I thought it wouldn't work.(p.132)

N. shortly after observes that Andrew has desired his wife Cookie's death, too. The fact that he imagines her death in the form of a car or plane crash, with all the horrible disfigurement likely to attend such a death, suggests a certain savagery (and desperation) on the part of the "decent," law-abiding, respectable Andrew. But the quotation above also makes us wonder about N. herself. She asks what is the *real* reason for her not pushing Gavin into the gorge, and one is meant to wonder which is the real or basic self here, the civilized N. horrified at her savage urge, or the one she wonders about herself, the murderer who wouldn't push her husband into the stream mainly because it might not have *worked*. Are both of these selves in N. real? If there is a murderer in N., does that extreme characteristic distance one from her, or, as N. possesses the persuasive authority of the point of view in *Shadow*, is it implied that the reader had best look into his own shadow selves?

Another aspect of N. as a murderer (or "murderer") is suggested by the ambiguity surrounding her possible pregnancy by Andrew and her miscarriage in the Sears Auto Annex late in the novel. Early in *Shadow*, after receiving a "death letter" from Andrew in which he informs N. of his wish to end their relationship, she thinks of aborting. She gets her doctor to insert an IUD, then has a reaction of traumatic guilt on going home when she encounters her front door not only "hacked and slashed," but covered with what looks like blood, vomit, and crankcase oil: " . . . when I came home and saw that door, it seemed to me that it was smeared with the murdered new life; fetal membrane and blood from inside me, that was my first thought. But of course I don't really know whether I was ever pregnant at all, or maybe I still am, so I hope I am not to be pursued by this ugly guilty thought forever"(p.7).

Front home doors readily symbolize the persona of the house dweller or owner. Thus an "attack" on such a door is a vicarious assault on the person(s) within the door. If, to make matters more complicated, the house-dweller sees the blood of her aborted fetus on the savaged door, she is identifying with the murderer but also implying that she deserves to be his victim. Being attacked from the outside, by someone else, N., by killing her fetus, also (in her own mind) murders her potential child and thus in a sense could feel that she is murdering part of herself in using an IUD—she becomes her own murderer. The miscarriage N. finally has in the Sears Annex serves to climax her sense of complicity in the violence surrounding her and rampant in the world. Feeling both like a murderer as well as a victim because of her wish to prevent any offspring from her rejecting lover embodies a guilt, vulnerability, and generalized fear of reprisal in N. not to be ignored.

It is important here, and for the whole novel, to realize what all this self-as-murderer material means in terms of N. as a reliable narrator. A would-be murderer usually would not bear sizable narrator authority, yet the whole tenor and weight of N's role, of her character and characterization, belies this interpretation. For a crucial aspect of N's character and self (or selves) is that she is almost brutally honest with and about herself; unlike the "analyzed" Bess, N. confronts the gorgons inside her.[5] At one point she even admits that she believes in murder, and also asks (not states) insightfully and revealingly that "if someone is trying to kill you, do you maybe deserve it?"(p.16). Johnson's using "you" here cunningly implicates the reader in this metaphysics of murder.

A passage from D. H. Lawrence's *Women in Love* provides us with a possible gloss of the enigmatic question above. Early in Lawrence's novel, Rupert Birkin says to the doomed Gerald Crich, " 'It takes two people to make a murder, a murderer and a murderee. And a murderee is a man who is murderable, . . . a man who in a profound if hidden lust desires to be murdered.' "[6] Is N. murderable? Does one of her selves desire to be murdered, out of guilt for her adultery, or for hostility towards her children, out of guilt for her murderous feelings towards her silly, careerist husband? Is she murderable because she also believes in *murdering*, for the sake of freedom in love? For the price of her rebellion in love is that she must fight for her rebel self, not only against her "social" self, but also against the massed (if partly random and impersonal) hatred, jealousy, and violence of the time.

When N. is still living with her husband, Gavin reveals some shocking regressiveness, which underlines the deeper horror and violence in *Shadow*. Outside her husband's study window one day, she catches a sight of Gavin sitting on Osella's lap like an infant. On another occasion, she wakes up at night in bed and realizes that Gavin in not in bed. Going through the house, N. discovers that he is lying in one of the children's cribs.

Possibly Johnson is laying it on rather heavily to discredit Gavin so strongly. The complaint has in fact been levelled against her that all men come off badly in *Shadow*.[7] Andrew, at first presented as an attractive, mature male, is finally revealed as a conformist coward, and though the Black men, AJ, Big Raider, and Clyde, come across as authentic minority males sizably disfigured or corrupted by White society, their depiction is not flattering to them. But it seems to me that the crucial consideration is not whether males come off well in a woman's novel, but whether they seem or feel authentic. There is no question about the authenticity of the males in *Shadow*. If, finally, all of them are unattractive (in different ways), that is an understandable outlook in a novel filled with terror, evil, and perversity. Certainly, plenty of celebrated novels written by men have not been generous towards women, and with less justification than Johnson might have. In addition, most of the *female* characters in *Shadow* are not very winning types, either.

But the real horror and ugliness in *Shadow* is domestic and relational—the (Bess) Harvills who have no love for each other but go through the motions of married life, the sterile marriage between Andrew and Cookie Mason, or between Gavin and N.; these relationships constitute the true location of the quiet terror and insidious madness in modern married life that N. both feels, is affected by, and is trying to escape. The vomit on N's car window, the slashed doors and tires, the hanged pet cat, the harassing and vicious phone calls are all "Gothic" excrescences of the warfare and agony of the hearth and home (in the case of Ev and Clyde, and even, once, of N. and Gavin, the violence is literal). And N's own hysteria of paranoia, of "detective" suspicion, of an acute sense of victimization structures the social and marital life surrounding her—it may be the structure of a nightmare, but like most dreams, murkily contains some crucial truths or illuminating evils if one probes or "detects" them with sufficient insistence. Thus it is appropriate now to probe the role of the "Famous Inspector" and male power in *Shadow*.

VI

The Famous Inspector is one of the dominant shadows in *The Shadow Knows*. He seems to be on N's mind almost as much as Andrew or the "Murderer," and in one striking alignment, is regarded, along with the "Rapist-Murderer," Gavin, and even Andrew, as possibly being the Culprit. The Famous Inspector is a mythic male image, society's official guardian, prober of the mind of the guilty (especially rebellious or adulterous women). But he is significantly more. He is the symbol of male rationality, the male genius of literal-minded cause-and-effect thinking, the Superego's lieutenant against immoral, irresponsible, and, especially, independent-minded women. He is Freud, the psychiatrist, the adult male hierarchy, even something of the Judeo-Christian God, and though he is not literally in the firm of Briggs, Harvill, and Mason, he is, as relentless and anti-subjective lawman, on their "team" in spirit.

That Andrew is also in that firm suggests an ominously tilted sense in *Shadow* of irresistible patriarchal power (which in part could account for a certain hysteria in N's rejection of Gavin's attempt to accommodate her love affair with Andrew). One could feel, again, that Johnson is loading the dice against men in *Shadow* only if he is blind to the fact that the alignments of power between the sexes even in the "real" world are as melodramatically polarized as the Briggs law firm and Detective Superego are against husbandless and powerless women like N. and Ev. If male readers complain that Johnson is rough on her male characters, they should remember or realize that men still run most of the basic social, economic, and political institutions and organizations in most countries in the world, certainly including the United States. Johnson's oblique bitterness and outrage at excessive male power has deep justice behind it.

The Famous Inspector, who both worries and fascinates N., is, again, also God as Patriarch, the male-created God who censures and resents women, and keeps them in line by the numinous threat of legal, moral, or even transcendent authority. He is also part of N. herself in her fine capacity for ratiocination and as the "Superego" of her guilt. However, her love of justice, finer, deeper than his, is her own. Whether or not N. wants to kill Gavin (unlike others in *Shadow*, she faces such thoughts in herself), she does want to know who attacked Ev, not only to insure her own safety, but to satisfy racial justice and ethical principle.

Yet it is typical of the subtle, reflexive mentality behind *Shadow* and of N's tough honesty that no sooner does N. think, rightfully, of justice for Ev than she asks herself whether she would like it applied to herself as an adulteress. That doesn't seem so attractive to her(p.207), so she opts for mercy, only to ask if people like Osella and others deserve mercy. When the real Inspector enters the "case," and, after analyzing it, decides that Ev is a victim of "unknown causes," N. cannot accept that: "'Please, someone has killed poor Ev!'"(p.204). This follows an exchange between the two that helps to give a large frame to the novel by confronting, respectively, the female and male opposition between justice to the individual (especially a Black, lower-class female individual) and social concord:

> '. . . you can't evade the fact of murder by calling it something else,' I protested.
>
> 'But you can diminish the degree of social destruction it causes. If it seems to people that the world is a place full of violence and crime, and that murder is not followed by discovery and retribution, then they are encouraged to indulge their desperation by violence and murder. Perhaps they feel they should, to perpetuate a certain view of life . . . '
>
> 'I am familiar with those arguments,' I said, ' but I am not a believer in capital punishment.'
>
> He smiled. 'If, on the other hand, the world presents its smoothest cheek, then people will not strike at it. They will hesitate to interrupt peace and order. Therefore, sometimes we don't call murder murder.'
>
> . . . .
>
> 'We call it unknown causes.'(pp.203-04)

It is easier to dispose of the murder of a lower-class Black by calling it death by unknown causes, because murder suggests to the White community of middle- and upper-class people that violence and crime are running rampant (that is, penetrating White neighborhoods), whereas covering up murder gives a sense, though spurious, of order and security. Such a cover-up becomes a case of mercy to the White society at the expense of justice (not to mention mercy) to Blacks. From the Inspector's outlook, whether society or a murderer killed Ev shrinks in importance when the peace of mind of society, particularly White society, is at stake. Ev becomes a kind of sacrificial victim to the need for maintaining the illusion that society is harmonious and that people are not venting hatred and violence on others. But Ev's death indicates that they really are venting hatred and violence, and the hiding of this social disharmony is in effect what Inspector Dyce is perpetuating. Dyce is implying that Ev is not important enough socially or racially to deserve the minimal attention that a homicide deserves at the very least, or even that she is a homicide and thus a possible victim of criminality and injustice. In trying to resist the suppression of the fact or possibility that Ev was murdered, N. externalizes her convictions as a social rebel and libertarian, in addition to being a rebel of love. That she extends her nonconformity from love into social or racial issues indicates the extent of N's human loyalty and compassion, qualities which are mirrored in her doubles relationship with the love-scarred, self-destructive Ev, and, later, even with another of her shadows, Osella. It also shows that N. can transcend her obsessive awareness of the Inspector (both Famous and real-life), and thus mature.

The real horror behind all of this material about sexual justice is that society, rather than a lurking, mysterious murderer, might be more likely to "do" N. "in," as in a way it "did in" Ev. First, through divorce proceedings mainly controlled by men, it attempts to doom N. to petty, sub-professional, low-paid work. It has her maid's death investigated by a police official who wants to reduce everything in the case to its most literal and unimaginative and thus unjust level. Finally, most terrifyingly, it has even persuaded some women to its viewpoint. That is to say, the narrative points to Bess, N's "close" friend, not only as an individual representing and arguing for an adaptive, conformist life for all women, including N, but also as a vindictive and dangerous shadow enacting her own justice on her vulnerable friend.

VII

N. on one occasion intuits that Bess is a friend to her and to other disadvantaged people, because Bess enjoys other people's misfortunes(p.220). She does so, because after trying unsuccessfully for years to have a child, she finally has one that is retarded. N. also recognizes that Bess is alienated from her worst or most challenging emotions, unlike N. who has them all too close to her consciousness. If one of the shocks in *Shadow* is seeing Gavin in Osella's lap, the image of White male power in the very hands—or lap—of one of the races that it has repressed, the emergence of the "dark" Bess is an even worse shock.   Yet Johnson has given hints earlier in *Shadow* that Bess might harbor a shadow side.   I have already indicated that Bess resents N's attempts to have a free sexual life and a professional career, while Bess, according to N., lives a "safe" life(p.236). Also, Bess would resent N's four normal children.   Never- theless, the extent of Bess's resentment, a frighteningly menac- ing rage, provides one of the climaxes of the novel.   It occurs after N. has been taken home from the Sears parking lot where she has her miscarriage (thus losing her last physical vestige of Andrew's love).   Bess has offered, like a good friend, to spend the night with her, while N. recovers from her miscarriage.   She also finds out, through a telephone call that she asks Bess to make, that Andrew, who, after an unexpected and short letter rejecting their relationship, and then affirming his love to N. again, has once more gone back to his wife.   N. in other words is overwhelmed with misfortunes, having lost her lover, her baby, and her "good" dark side in Ev, which sometimes seems to be the time in life when even more troubles or threats arise.

At this point, she is suddenly confronted by a menacing shock: Bess makes it plain that she hates N. Johnson's handling of this revelation is perfectly in keeping with the horror-mystery genre that she is utilizing for sophisticated purposes. N. wakes up in her bed, prompted by the same almost subconscious or ele- mentary force that drives her to break out of a conventional deadening marriage and to detect madness around her in Gavin, Osella, and others, to discover Bess standing by her bed unusu- ally close.   Startled, N. sees Bess hiding an expression, but "reads" it anyway: "It was hate. I wasn't exactly surprised just then. You get used to this"(p.238).

Bess identifies part of her deep resentment:

'You can learn to do without love. Everybody does,' she said.

'No, I never will do that, I hope,' I said.(p.238)

" 'You are a taker,' " Bess hisses, shortly after.   " 'You wouldn't work, you expect to have your own way' "(p.239). Bess is so be- side herself, or, in another part of herself, with rage, that she appears ready to attack N., who gets out of bed quickly and goes into the living room "as if looking for something"(p.240). What she *finds* among other exposed objects in Bess's open purse is a "heavy long strong knife, . . . one that you might slash tires with, or doors."(p.240)..

Bess's knife becomes one of the culminating and pivotal symbols in the whole work, unifying the two strands of detective thriller and somber meditation on contemporary domestic and social life. The knife cuts from fantasy into reality, from N's self-protecting yet self-diminishing paranoia to the core of her real danger. She says earlier in *Shadow* that she is always walking on the edge of a knife. Now the knife has been found in someone's purse who might grasp it and use it against her. The horror of this grave physical danger, though, is perhaps less than the horror of this Other Bess, the Dark self now emerging, with appropriate terror, at night when her foe is weakened.

A more accurate way of stating the Gothic and realistic-psychological horrors here—and it would apply to *Shadow* generally—is that they are one. The knives in Bess's mind and the knife in her purse are in effect the same knife, and they are the same knife, the same symbolic weapon of homicidal, luna-tical rage, that is filling the newspapers with stories of rape and murder and vandalism that N. reads about so obsessively. In Bess the external and internal worlds of violence concentrate, and they now converge on N.

N. has to spend the whole night with her former friend, pretending to sleep in her room while Bess paces like a lunatic back and forth in Ev's bedroom, muttering malice about love and about Andrew being a philanderer to N. through the wall, like the Unconscious speaking "home" truths to the Ego. The result of all the day's shocks, her miscarriage, the idea that Bess might be her vicious harrasser and Ev's attacker, thrusts N. towards a new plateau of realization:

> . . . Ev is dead, and it is really Bess in there walking around and my hand is on her long knife concealed under my pillow. Yet I could not believe it. I have a slow mind for distinguishing the actual from the unbelievable: is that really Gavvy on Osella's lap? Has he struck me? What do I feel? Is the future to stretch on forever without the real voice of Andrew or the urgent tenderness of his embraces; is that madness in Osella's eyes or is she only pretending?'
> (p.243)

This passage sums up N's crises: her loss of Ev, her loss of, and obsession with, Andrew, her shocking discovery that her best friend is perhaps her worst enemy and mad as well, the traumatic discovery of her husband's perverse regressiveness. A major concern is madness—the world around her seems to be losing its sanity, or, put another way, revealing its latent insanity which makes N's lament and longing for Andrew's love all the more tormenting. But all this nightmare is the necessary darkness before the dawn; it is, moreover, an illuminated or illuminating darkness. N. now sees what she must do in order to act purposefully. She may not know yet, nor may ever know, who the real assailant of Ev and pursuer (if any) of herself are—but Bess vividly embodies possibilities of pernicious evil. The important thing is that N. has now begun to go on the offensive. She began it by responding instinctively to Bess early in the evening, and following her instincts by finding Bess's knife, then, later, keeping it in her possession, thus disarming Bess and arming herself. She stays clear of Bess all night, and next morning realizes that though Bess will act like her hatred was simply a therapeutic catharsis in regard to an old friend, N. will *know* that it was real hatred and that Bess had a real knife in her possession (it is relevant in this regard to point out that Bess is a sizably larger woman than N.). N. may ask herself, "'Do you actually know what you think you know?'"(p.249), but she knows she will cut relations with Bess.

She also decides that she will resolve the case, the "murder" of Ev, especially as the Famous Inspector, cut down to mortal size as the sceptical and literal-minded Inspector Dyce, has disposed of the case as one of death due to "natural causes." N. won't accept this judgement, and has the resolve stemming from her night surviving mad Bess, which included a new vision of and identification with the sex-demented Osella: "It is as if Andrew, not I, were dead, and I alive battering at him in a frenzy of desire and panic, just trying to get the tiniest flicker of a smile to cross his face. Oh, now I can understand Osella battering the ground above John Henry's coffin"(p.237). Andrew *is* dead in spirit, in the spirit of his new sexual being created in his relationship with N., but N's new understanding and acceptance of Osella indicates a turning for her. Her accepting her shadow in this small group of Black and White women mourning for or suffering from their lost or violent men is both humanizing for N., and empowering. She can now pursue the "case" to the end. And she can also think of doing something else, that would terminate the Gavin-Andrew-Osella-Ev phase of her life: "I'm going to move out of those units"(p.260).

VIII

But first N. must confront the Club Zanzibar; she must make the Dark Descent into a racial and psychological underworld in order to resolve the assault on Ev, and thus her relationship and human obligation to Ev. N. takes on a bit of the character of her "animus" or male self, the Famous Inspector, prepared in her quest even to use detective cunning and male ratiocination as well as "female" intuitive and instinctive quickness and certainty. In so doing, she is for the first time in the novel also prefiguring a new potential wholeness of character. However, she still has two major experiences to undergo and assimilate.

Outside the Club Zanzibar N. looks at a poster of the naked Osella, and asks, "What is the connection between sex and murder? . . . . The naked Osella makes everything clear"(p.282). There is a hint in this passage that Osella might have wanted to attack both Ev and N. for Big Raider's philandering interest in them. But much of *Shadow* concerns the connection between sex (and love) and murder or violence, the subtle interrelations of these ostensibly polarized emotional realities. This is another way of describing the governing metaphor in this novel of darkness as fear, hatred, perversity—madness and ignorance raging everywhere, the very opposite of the converging order of the detective story, in other words, of commercialized fantasy and synthetic, superficial mystery.

What does happen at the Club? It is not that N. realizes anything new about Osella as a prime suspect. Especially after finding the Zanzibar ashtray in the laundry room, she already suspects Osella (a heavy smoker). But she also suspects Big Raider and now, after the long night following her miscarriage, Bess too. The fact, according to the Inspector, that the ashtray blow could not possibly have killed Ev ignores the subtler consideration that someone still might have *wanted* to kill Ev. But it is more consonant with the complex artistic seriousness of *Shadow* to keep this mystery unsolved. All of the suspects had motives, or, to move to the plane of universal and impersonal violence and insanity, it might have been anyone.

The Zanzibar sequence might or might not clear up the "murder mystery," but it does provide a climax to some of the main sexual themes in the novel. The central event of the Club is the appearance of the all but naked Osella, oiled, garishly made-up, "calling to mind one of those frightening and horrifying fertility goddesses with swollen bodies and timeless eyes and the same engulfing infinitely absorbing quality Osella radiated now"(p.267). Perhaps the key phrase here is "infinitely absorbing quality." Looking around the room, N. notices Gavin in a front seat, and though accompanied by a young woman, he gazes at Osella "with the fixed and rapt hypnotized stare of a slave, he was transfixed." Osella's commercialized sexuality is such an excess, such a belittling of all norms of sexuality and sexual love, that it not only mocks "White" sexuality, but inverts all standards, so that the bizarre, the gigantic, the monstrous embodies new norms that sanction the "normally" unlawful or immoral. As N. says to herself outside the Zanzibar, "Reproved is mostly what I felt [in looking at Osella's poster]. The question of murder momentarily receded before my immediate sense of shame and inadequacy. Murder and other enormous acts seemed right in scale"(p.263).

Osella may appear to be the arch-mistress of some Black, female perversion of White values. She may see herself as a Sex Goddess breaking through White racism. But, as her act is so successful, and as Big Raider is her promoter, it is clear that Osella has mainly changed from a racially-victimized domestic to a sexually-exploited pawn of a Black man.

Gavin's presence and behavior at the Zanzibar also merits consideration. His presence there, a successful, still young, White lawyer mesmerized by Osella's form of "Black Power," suggests a curious intimacy of perverse emotions between Blacks and Whites. Keeping Gavin's earlier acts of domestic regressiveness in mind, one can say that American White-male institutional dominance, as strong as ever in the 1970s, is represented by Johnson as being corrupt at its root—its sexual emotions or culture is depraved, "infantile," perniciously unbalanced. The Master today, like Osella's Southern college-President employer (who used to go off into the woods with little girls, and expose his genitals to Osella), is also the slave of abnormal impulses.

Osella in turn consummates all the misspent and anarchic energy in the entire novel. As a Felliniesque, primitivist sex goddess, she embodies the raw, surging monstrousness of sex in modern society, its failure to move into the currents of love and marriage and ordered, happy life. She represents sex out of proportion and control, grossly enlarged, commercialized, and endlessly unsatisfied. And that she packs people into the Zanzibar every night (indeed, with a camera present and the cords, a transformer, and microphones, it all begins to resemble a contemporary media Event) suggests an intimate complicity of the White world in the perversion not only of sexual emotions and values, but also of their relations with Blacks. On the level of N's sexual rebellion, this condition provides oblique justification for her nonconformity in love; she has opted out of the corrupted White upper-middle-class world represented by the Gavin Hexams, the Bess Harvills, and lastly by the Andrew and Cookie Masons. N. talks to Big Raider with something of the confidence of the Famous Inspector assimilated into her psyche, informing Raider (though mistakenly) that Osella murdered Ev, and that if he does not stop Osella's phone harrassments, she will make sure the police get incriminating evidence about Osella, especially if anything should happen to her, N. She thus pressures the formidable Big Raider into freeing her life of Osella, and of her White, middle-class guilt about Osella. One event remains for N., before she will be truly ready to move from the "units" and possibly begin a new life.

Driving home from the Zanzibar, N. thinks of the Masons together and of herself apart, alone. She has some savage fantasies about wreaking revenge on Cookie, though they are qualified by being phrased conditionally ("Maybe I will years from now strangle their cat, . . . hit, stab Cookie" (p.237). Further, she perceives this conduct as being warped. This fantasy also, once again, identifies N. with the murderers, the attackers, the violent and the vindictively demented, and suggests on one important plane that Lawrence's murderer and murderee are in N. one person. If a person has a *hidden* lust to be destroyed, exposing that lust, making it conscious and facing it, might be purgative and healing. An important difference between Bess and N. is that the former, through psychoanalysis, placates her inner devils by assuming that they are an essential part of human nature, and thus have to be tolerated rather than challenged, a pessimistic, even cynical, outlook hardly restricted to Bess. N., on the other hand, confronts her feelings by trying to lead a life that takes them seriously; she doesn't live exclusively from the passions, but they clearly play a big role in the major decisions and acts of her love and family life. This is to say that N. is basically more honest and courageous than Bess, although, as she is aware, she is open to charges of egotism and self-centeredness—such of course is the risk of any individualist or nonconformist ethic. Her consciousness of this danger, which is also a consciousness in touch with her unconscious in ways that detect danger and compel a finer love, is the force that will keep N. alive, developing, open to growth. She reflects as she heads home to her husbandless housing unit that love would heal her hatred, but that no one will be making genuine love tonight, not the Harvills, not the Masons, not Osella. And not N. Instead, she will be raped.

Getting out of her car in a whirl of strong emotions and reflections, N. is for once unaware of her surroundings, a dangerous state for most people in certain situations. Suddenly assaulted, she cannot identify the rapist. It could be anyone, Black or White, husband or lover, neighborhood maniac—or, as Johnson archly observes in the McCaffrey interview, "I also felt that you might suspect that the Famous Inspector was the rapist"(p.213), which is tantamount to saying that the rapist could be almost any man, that all men harbor evil, and that, ultimately, what feminists call the patriarchy is responsible for sexual violence towards women.

But Johnson extends evil generally to both sexes: "the shadow represents simply the evil that lurks within all men—again, not meaning men as males, but mankind" (p.213) —in other words, both sexes. And when N., shortly after, during the rape, asks herself "Are men all the same in the dark?"(p.275), she not only amplifies the basic theme of potential universal complicity in evil, but also administers a strong and justified female retort to the old male-chauvinist saw that all *women* are the same in the dark.[8]

The rapist, who is strong, is able to force N. into her own car again. For a short time she is frightened that he might also try to kill her. She struggles, and continues to struggle during the rape. But a curious ambiguity or ambivalence develops during the rape. N. says she struggled when first attacked, but as the event progresses, she makes statements like "I mean I think I was struggling," and, a little later, says this: "So wrapped up was I in my thoughts and my dread I may have, for all I know, moved rhythmically according to long habit with the deep purposeful thrusting inside me of the organ of this unknown man or maybe I lay there unresentfully"(p.275). After it is all over, N. says "I was shaking with terror and amazement and also with a strange elation. . . . I don't know. I felt happy"(p.276).

According to Johnson, the rape scene has evoked a lot of criticism,[9] and one can see why. Superficially, it seems as if N. is enjoying the rape. The traditional sneaking suspicion of some men about women's experience of rape is that often women either encourage and/or enjoy the rape. And N's admission that she may have moved rhythmically during the rape adds fuel to the fire—though she is not sure she did and it was partly because her mind was overwhelmed with the final questions and thoughts of a possibly dying person. Yet it is probable that women undergoing rape might move rhythmically not because they want or enjoy sex with a rapist but the sooner to terminate the experience, and, also, by "cooperating," perhaps significantly lessen a rapist's murderous post-sex guilt or self-disgust. Some men (and women) will readily berate this strategy, but some women have possibly escaped horrible disfigurement and even death by practising it, and it could be strongly contested that the raped woman should be the final arbiter in the matter. Also, in N's case, there are no longer any husbands or lovers to feel guilty about.

But there is no certainty that N. is really following such a strategy. Johnson says, probably more out of generosity than conviction, that criticism of the scene is "probably justified," yet provides her own retort to it. After stating that she did not at all intend to imply that N. had enjoyed the rape, she says this: "I meant that she was simply in on all this, too . . ."(p.212). Earlier, she observes that "the rape scene was meant to be a final symbol of ambiguity and everyone's complicity in evil"(p.212).

First, how is N. "in on all this?" What is her complicity in evil? This consideration was partly broached earlier in the chapter in discussing N's own murderous tendencies, one aspect of the connection in *Shadow* between love and death, sex and murder. Johnson, I feel, is implying above that N., with her somewhat excessive sense of evil and danger in the world and around her, contributes to the general and extreme violence and terror of the contemporary world. By being a "murderee" in Lawrence's sense, by projecting and transforming her guilt into terror, she adds to this aura of violence and malice. Further, by engaging in serious erotic rebellion and living closely to her instinctual life, she runs the risk of becoming a murderer in spirit if not in fact (how close, after all, *was* N. to pushing her

husband to his possible death?).   The Famous Inspector might
not care about or understand that kind of "distance," but a
serious novelist does.   N. is potentially both a murderee and a
murderer; yet she is also a decent, kindly, sensitive and intelligent human being.

So, what *is* N., essentially?   And if this character, with
whom, because of the first-person narration, we feel so at ease
that even for male readers there can be substantial identification
and sympathy, is full of dark as well as "light" selves, what, the
narrative implies, do we make of *ourselves*?   In this context, the
opening sentence of *Shadow*, "You never know, that's all.
There's no way of knowing," reverberates with an endless ironic
booming that carries us back to the great pessimists and sceptics
like La Rochefoucauld, Pascal, and Hume.   But there is also
affirmation in the fact that N., with all her complicity in the
emotional sickness and violence of the time, is also trying to
purge herself of these forces—such is her quest.

N., then, by my lights, is a substantially good person with
a demonic aspect of which she is seriously conscious.   If this
evaluation is tenable, it makes her characterization stronger, for,
without rendering her a basically unreliable narrator, N., with
this Forsterian blend of good-and-evil, becomes a more complex
character and *Shadow* a psychologically and philosophically
more compelling fiction.   One never knows whether people are
planning to kill N. or were trying to kill Ev.   It seems possible,
even probable, that some of the harrassment N. receives is connected with her nonconformist life and code, but one cannot be
certain.   Thus the ambiguity of the rape scene is fitting, for it
purposely does not clear up more than one matter, but that
matter is crucial to N. and to *Shadow*.

What N. realizes after the rape is that she has now encountered extremity, and yet "here I still am"(p.276).   Short of
being killed (but thinking briefly during the rape that she might
be killed), she has finally experienced the shadow she has
dreaded all along, and has survived it.   This survival becomes
the major breakthrough in the novel for N.   She has faced her
conception of the worst, survived what she has both dreaded,
and, for exorcistic reasons, desired.   From now on, perhaps,
things will be better or different.   Ironically, it sounds like the
rape has both terminated her Old Life and violently inaugurated
the possibilities of a New one.   As N. says, "I feel better. You can
change; a person can change. . . . Your eyes get used to the dark"
(p.277).

N's response to the event is clearly affirmative. As I have already argued, this response is not due to her enjoying the rape, which would be prurient and perverse, and thus would reduce *Shadow's* fineness of sensibility. Merging the Jungian shadow with the detective-mystery shadow is hard to resist in reading this novel. Jung's concept may itself be somewhat sensationalistic and melodramatic, yet for this final climactic and transformative scene it might be illuminative. I will suggest that N. in the rape sequence finally meets her "shadow," and finds that encounter emotionally consummative, satisfactory, and liberating. This shadow is all men, and thus represents a composite male archetype the acceptance of which means that N. accepts death and therefore life—as well as men. Her "night journey" into the Zanzibar opens N. psychologically to the acceptance, as distinct from the enjoyment, of the rape which in turn engenders a possible rebirth for her. If this interpretation seems either too "literary" or Jungian, I would indicate that Johnson herself intimates the pre-conditions for it by implying that on one level in N's mind, all men are potential assailants, and in a very real sense, she is half-murdered by Andrew's betrayal and Gavin's unmanliness. Bereft, abandoned, N. has nothing left, and yet everything, and it is the rape that "helps" her to begin to see in the dark, to live, that is, from deeper recesses of self.

Trying to figure out, among all the men she knows, who the rapist might be, N. concludes that "Perhaps it doesn't matter at all"(p.276). The specific man doesn't matter because psychically the trauma of the rape exorcised her guilt and fear, and made her feel like she had paid the cost of the free life she has elected. N. of course doesn't *deserve* to be raped (some males would think she does), but it is a possible consequence of the conditions of life and love that she has chosen, and she, understandably, has not been able to face or accept that consequence.

Protected by neither husband nor lover, she survives rape, and feels renewed by it, not because she "enjoys" it, but because she enjoys surviving it and transcending all her terrors. She has undergone what Terrence Des Pres describes as the "demonic sublime,"[10] and by associating herself with the agent of terror, transcends both. In Jungian terms, N. has absorbed her shadow *and* her animus (the male rapist combines both psychic components), and thus has gotten a new lift of life force. Instead of re-creating Des Pres's entire and complex chain of thought in relating terror to the sublime, I will merely repeat his summary of Schopenhauer's view of what Des Pres calls "the sublime's essential dialectic": "Terror and dissolution of human individuality on the one side, and on the other 'a power beyond all comparison superior' because the beholder, who is now also the *participant*, has completely identified with terror—so completely, indeed, that it seems his own idea."[11]

There is certainly an inexorable sense in which terror seems N's own idea (even if she is not dissolved by it), for reasons some of which I have tried to detect.   N. embraces terror, "accepts" the rapist, again, not out of sexual desire, but because it is only by merging with and thus incorporating the terror that she can transcend it.   That N. experiences her transcendence in terms of violent, coerced sex rather than love resolves *Shadow* with appropriate irony.   For rather than the ideal resolution of romantic love with an institutionally compromised Andrew, the horror of rape is the consummatory gesture which, proclaiming that modern sexuality is violence or a sham, thrusts N. beyond sex-and-terror into the possibilities of a new life, a different sexual consciousness, and thus a new self. It is a tough-minded vision indeed that allows a rape to serve as the basis of an isolated, principled woman's regeneration, after rejecting her husband and her social and false friend, Bess, and losing her lover and her maid and close friend Ev.

Having to go through N's ordeal to work towards a new life or self might not seem to be worth it, but the narrative logic of *Shadow* indicates that there is no other choice for an N. to achieve authentic existence. The first words of *Shadow* are "You never know," but when that "you" includes the shadow, then one does have the chance or the power to know what one's basic life choices are. If one doesn't make the right choice and try to live it, then his or her life will not only be terrible—like the life of Gavin, of Bess, and especially of the fainthearted Andrew, it will be the quiet desperation of the living dead.

An idea in Kenneth Rexroth's long poem *The Heart's Garden, The Garden's Heart* can serve in resolving some of the mystery of *Shadow*. Says Rexroth, "The solution of the problem of knowing/And being is ethical./Epistemology is moral."[12] The old epistemological concern that humans cannot know themselves, that we are all a mystery, to ourselves and to others, can breed a moral and creative passivity, possibly even cynicism and nihilism. Rexroth's lines imply that we have a responsibility to know ourselves, that moral or ethical conduct leads to or even embodies valuable self-knowledge, and that feeling and behaving morally would dissolve the "mystery" or inscrutability of the self. Responsibility, virtue, magnanimity, honesty, courage and other primary values of character embody self-knowledge, or, if they do not, they can precipitate or consummate it. The problem is thus what philosophers call a "pseudo-problem." In this perspective, N's behavior and values are illuminating. She may be herself puzzled, even horrified, with the mystery of being as terrorization, of ignorance as a life risk, but what she is trying to make of her life amounts to a kind of moral epistemology. There resides in N. an invaluable "knowledge" of herself and of existence in regard to love, decency, the universality and perversity of violence, the value of friendship, of racial equality and community, of intellectual courage. Whatever one cannot know, one can know and activate these values and states of being. Assimilating and realizing these values may not be everything, but they are plenty for a lifetime, and their implementation into personal life and society would go some ways towards reducing the dark domain of the shadow, of menace, hypocrisy, racism, greed, jealousy—ultimately, of murderousness.

VIII

Such is the hard-earned authority of selfhood in *The Shadow Knows*. *Shadow* continues the exploration, elaboration and humiliation of the self observable in all the writers in this study from Dostoyevsky, James, Hardy, Conrad, and Céline, to more recent writers like Ellison and Bellow, as well as in the experience of extremity described in my treatment of incarceration and torture (see chapter ten). Despite all the degradation, misery, and unrelenting analysis that these writers impose on the fictional selves in their novels, what also emerges is—with the exception of Dostoyevsky's Underground Man and perhaps of Céline's Bardamu—a dignity of endurance and coherence in the image and concept of the self. It leads us in fact to wonder whether a still operable definition of the modern self could be the dedicated striving of a human being to make his or her existence coherent and meaningful.

A creature of radically conflicting purposes, the self posits a dimension of individual being that is unique, inimitable, original. In this facet of life all possibility for the particular, specific, uniquely realizable existence resides. The self, like its ancient ancestor and contemporary, the soul, may be a myth or an illusion, as certain systems of philosophy and the social sciences, and whole political regimes, contend, but it defines as true and irreducible something we know in our center of being. That these writers try in different ways to get to that center by relating or contrasting it with the Other, whether as community or collectivity, beloved or enemy, or as Hardy's "fervorless" universe, is an enduring part of their achievement.

Notes

[1]Le Clair, Tom, and Larry McCaffrey, eds. *Anything Can Happen: Interviews with Contemporary American Novelists* (Urbana, Illinois: University of Illinois Press, 1984), 211. All further references in this chapter to this work are to this text.

[2]According to Sandra Gilbert, *The Shadow Knows* "is first of all a sort of bitter parody of a genre invented by 19th century men, the detective story." ("Abandoned Women, in all Senses," *The Nation*, 220, June 14, 1975, 730).

[3]Johnson, however, has claimed to have "solved the mystery in the novel for the reader," McCaffrey, Op. cit., 211.

[4]Diane Johnson, *The Shadow Knows* (New York: Knopf, 1974), 302. All further references in this chapter to this work are to this text.

[5]One could have mentioned witches here, rather than gorgons, for "witch" is a recurring word in *Shadow*, used by both Osella and N. to refer to N. hostilely or disparagingly. As Sandra Gilbert has pointed out, " . . . N.—her married name is *Hexam*—does, in some part of herself, believe she is a witch, an abandoned woman in the bad sense, whose unconsciously cast spells have doomed her to abandonment in the sad sense"(p.730). Osella does genuinely feel hexed by N., and N. is wise enough to translate her maid's superstition into the racial and economic terms of White power over Blacks. But I also hesitate to use "witches" for "gorgons" in the text, because, despite Johnson's claim that she might not have thought out the witch material sufficiently (McCaffrey, Op. cit., 214), the term is used complexly enough to suggest that it might bear strong positive associations as well as negative ones. If N., as Gilbert states, may sense the bad witch in herself, it is in part a reaction of conscience coming

from the same sphere of values that Bess, the Famous and real Inspectors, and the Briggs, Harvill, and Mason law firm occupy and endorse. Also, at one point when N. vehemently rejects Gavin's dishonest (and only) attempt to suggest that they reconstruct their marriage, she states that a witch part of herself had acted up (p.92). This "inner witch" is, to my mind, relatable to at least two striking womanly traditions. One of them is the Mujer Brava, the Bold or Angry Woman in Hispanic culture who decides to resist conventions and openly live her own life on her own terms, almost always a dangerous intention for most women in either Latinic or North American society. The Mujer Brava symbolizes rebellious womanhood defying traditions, powers, or sanctions (Tilly Olson's *Silences* (New York: Dell/Laurel Book, 1983) is a compendium of such male sanctions: for example, women are wives and mothers, not artists). N. has something of the Mujer Brava in her; this "witch" element is part of the cutting edge of her exploration and growth, though it also results in much pain and terror for her. Another witch tradition is that described by the 19th century French historian Jules Michelet, who, in his book, *Satanism and Witchcraft*, urges the thesis that witches or "witchery" was an inevitable human response to and release from the grinding socio-economic misery and political oppression, that the witches of the late Middle Ages and later eras were symbolic rebels fighting a merciless, male-dominated social order. That such an interpretation may contain a pre-Marxist or revolutionary character does not sizably diminish its symbolic and perhaps even its literal value. Mary Daly's interpretation of "witchery" in *Gyn/Ecology: the Metaethics of Radical Feminism* (Boston: Beacon Press, c1978) places more stress on the psychological-religious hysteria and wrath induced in institutional author-ities (mainly male, "patriarchal") by women who either actually opted for a "Mujer-Brava" life, or, probably a far larger category, of women falsely accused by religious, sexual, or opportunistic paranoids of being in sexual league (as in the Black Mass) with the Devil. Put generally and soberly, women who want as much sexual and general freedom as men are "diabolical," because they threaten male institutional power and control, and, if Daly's figures on the traditional Western treatment of witches are accurate, have been put to death by the millions: "It is computed from historical records, "Daly states, "that nine millions of persons were put to death for witchcraft after 1484, or during a period of 300 years. The greatest number of this incredible multitude were women"(p. 183[n]). Another authority Daly cites (Rossell Hope Robbins, *The Encyclopedia of Witchcraft and Demonology*) "gives a typical conservative estimate of 200,000." Whether or not there is such a thing as an archetypal memory or Collective Unconscious, N. has better reasons than she might think for feeling at times deep dread because of her general individualism and rebelliousness.

[6]D. H. Lawrence, *Women in Love* (New York: Viking Press, 1960), 27.

[7]Johnson has admitted that in *Shadow*, "all the men come off badly but that she is not misanthropic towards men, and in *Lying Low* presents them as amiable" (McCaffrey, Op. cit., 201-02). She doesn't in *Lying Low* present *all* men as amiable, though, for the novel is encircled with a malignant and ominous aura of personal homicidal violence (the Zodiac Killer) and institutional (prison) violence, both male.

[8]Benjamin Franklin, in a "Letter to a Young Man," heavily implied the same vicious idea in advice to the effect that if the Young Man had delicate

feelings about seeing the face of a middle-aged woman that he was having sexual intercourse with, he should put a bag over her head. (This document can possibly be found in the Rare Books Room of the University of California, Berkeley; it was read there by me around 1955).

[9]*Anything Can Happen*, Op. cit., 212.

[10]Terrence Des Pres, "Terror and the Subline," *Human Rights Quarterly*, v.5, no.2, May 1983, 145.

[11]Ibid., p.143.

[12]Kenneth   Rexroth,   *The   Heart's   Garden,   The   Garden's   Heart* (Cambridge, Mass.: Pym-Randall Press, 1968).

II.

SELVES IN MODERN NON-FICTION PROSE

D. H. Lawrence's "Pornography and Obscenity"—
Sex, Society, And The Self

I

D. H. Lawrence's well-known essay "Pornography and Obscenity" was written in 1929, a year of fine essays by Lawrence, including the audacious "Introduction to these Paintings," "A Propos of *Lady Chatterley's Lover*," "Nottingham and the Mining Country," and, dipping back into December 1928, the short but magnificent "spirit-of-place" piece called simply "New Mexico." Having gotten *Chatterley* in its third and final version completed in January 1928, and *The Man Who Died* by mid-1928[1], Lawrence must have felt in a retrospective mood. He would go on in 1929 to write two impressively meditative works, *Apocalypse*, his iconoclastic commentary on the *Book of Revelation*, and *Last Poems*, completed during the last 3 or 4 months of his life. Despite their retrospective cast, these two works possess considerable speculative and imaginative vitality.

Thus it is not surprising that a man both literally and imaginatively as close to death as Lawrence was in 1929 should still feel sufficiently alive to write not one but two major essays on the topic of sex during the last six-seven months of his life. His writing "A Propos" at this time is understandable. *Chatterley* was triggering a rage of attention, critical and legal, and some kind of apologia for it seemed in order. But during the months in which this essay was developing, another one also was written which possibly has as much of a right as "A Propos" to be considered one of Lawrence's greatest essays.[2]

According to Frank Kermode, "Pornography and Obscenity" is the work by Lawrence "that has kept best as a contribution to the continuing debate" on sex.[3] One can focus on Lawrence's contribution even more closely by saying that the distinction of this essay resides in its conferring a crucial onto-logical dimension upon the topic—for Lawrence (and this holds for much of his best work), sex is a touchstone of being. In this

chapter I want to show that Lawrence's extended definitions of
the words pornography and obscenity probe the deepest recesses
of human nature. I hope to extend this reading of his famous
essay by relating its ideas to some aspects of our contemporary
erotic culture, as well as by suggesting some shortcomings in
Lawrence's elaborations of his definitions. I will also attempt to
relate Lawrence's conceptions of pornography to his view of its
impact on the self, a powerful aspect of his thought on this
subject. The organization of "Pornography" moves from rejected definitions of pornography and obscenity to an elaboration
of Lawrence's own understanding of the terms; this outlines the
path of my own discussion as well.

II

     When people define what pornography and obscenity
mean, Lawrence refuses to take their definitions of these key
words seriously because people respond to them, not from their
individual, authentic self, but from what Lawrence, both acutely
and snobbishly, calls their "mob" self. He sees two categories of
meaning (including understanding) arising from these two
selves, "mob" meaning and "individual" meaning. People responding from their "mob" side, the side nurtured and controlled by modern mass culture, are "incapable of imaginative
individual responses."[4]
     Adding to this problem of genuine response to
"pornography" and "obscenity" is the relativity of the two terms.
People vary markedly among themselves about the meaning of
pornography and obscenity, as they have in different eras.
Lawrence mentions how Aristophanic comedy shocked the people of his time, but evidently did not faze the ancient Greeks
themselves. When we instance Attic theatrical humor in
"comic" routines (used as interludes to the longer tragedies) like
Cyclops catching and buggering some of Ulysses's crew,
Lawrence's point becomes clear. Lawrence puts this issue of
sexual relativism in a maxim that men are likely to enjoy more
than women, "If a woman hasn't got a tiny streak of a harlot in
her, she's a dry stick as a rule"(p.64). Lawrence of course is not
saying that all women are pornographic (stemming from the old
definition that pornography pertains to the description of harlots

and their trade), but he is implying that cut-and-dried definitions are useless for words as deeply controversial and relative as pornography and obscenity. If, as W. H. Auden once said, a poem reads the reader, perhaps a person's definition of pornography and obscenity also "reads" him.

Nevertheless, this equivalence of female sexual desire, lust, or even sexual activism of aggressiveness with harlotry is one of a number of areas of Lawrence's sexual thinking that feminists would sharply criticize, and rightly so. For implicit in Lawrence's harlot maxim is a stigmatization of female sexual energy and desire. One could even claim that some sexually active or expressive women are "dry sticks," as their sexual extroversion is, as with some men, more an expression of a power drive than of a need for erotic fulfillment. Men may, like William Blake, want the "whore"-like "lineaments of gratified desire" in a wife or girl friend, yet if they find it, men will partly censure the woman for a "wicked" area of her sexuality which they actually crave and even encourage. This is a dangerous contradiction in the male psycho-sexual make-up that Lawrence doesn't address in "Pornography."

Beyond the relativity and the inauthenticity of response to the two terms lies the thorny issue of intention. According to Lawrence, some people feel that any conscious effort by a writer or artist to arouse sexual desire is pornographic. Lawrence's rejoinder is acutely suggestive:

> It is the old vexed question of intention, become so dull today, when we know how strong and influential our unconscious intentions are. And why a man should be held guilty of his conscious intentions, and innocent of his unconscious intentions, I don't know, since every man is more made up of unconscious intentions than of conscious ones. I am what I am, not merely what I think I am (p.67).

One is sexually what one is, not what, or only what, he thinks he is. The idea that we should be held responsible for our unconscious as well as for our conscious nature is associated with depth psychology, but applied to sexuality in terms of intention not only to arouse someone sexually, but also to be sexually aroused, it has important ramifications. One is that sexual or erotic manifestations of behavior are interwoven with our deepest recesses of being, which, comprised of a reservoir of other assimilated and genetically endowed "material," give our sexual character the critical role of reflecting our deeper self.

Lawrence of course dramatized this ontological function of sex memorably in his greatest novels and short fiction; it became part of his novelistic vision of 20th century character and fate. But if we briefly apply this touchstone to modern sexual culture, with its emphasis, among other things, on lax standards of sexual morality, the commercialization of eroticism, and sexual sensationalism in mass media, the results are revealing. Not only is an imagery of sexuality visible that adumbrates the inner quality of modern being; one source of modern deracination and alienation stands exposed as well.

Considering further the charge that sexual arousing in art is pornographic, Lawrence moves into one of the memorable passages of the essay: "Half the great poems, pictures, music, stories of the whole world are great by virtue of the beauty of their sex appeal. Titian or Renoir, the Song of Solomon or *Jane Eyre*, Mozart or Annie Laurie, the loveliness is all interwoven with sex appeal, sex stimulus, call it what you will"(p.68). Lawrence in a short late essay called "Sex Versus Loveliness" puts it figuratively: "sex and beauty are one thing, like flame and fire. If you hate sex, you hate beauty. If you love *living* beauty, you have a reverence for sex"(p.50). And an intimation of his metaphysic appears on the same page in a plant metaphor that relates sexuality to both the inner and outer self: "Sex is the root of which intuition is the foliage and beauty the flower."

Sex and beauty, warmth, flower—Lawrence's equation is full of basic life and nature elements, standing in opposition not only to the "grey-Puritan" censorship of sex but, particularly in our own day, to the even darker, highly contrived imagery of explicit film pornography. "The right sort of sex stimulus," Lawrence concludes this section of his argument by asserting, "is invaluable to daily human life. Without it the world grows grey"(p.69).

At this point in "Pornography," Lawrence turns to his own definition of pornography. He is emphatic about what he thinks it is and what he would do about it:

> Even I would censor genuine pornography, rigorously. It would not be very difficult. In the first place, genuine pornography is almost always underworld, it doesn't come into the open. In the second, you can recognize it by the insult it offers, invariably, to sex, and to the human spirit.[1]

> Pornography is the attempt to insult sex, to do dirt on it. This is
> unpardonable. Take the very lowest instance, the picture-post-card
> sold underhand, by the underworld, in most cities. What I have
> seen of them have been of an ugliness to make you cry. The insult to
> the human body, the insult to a vital human relationship! Ugly
> and cheap they make the human nudity, ugly and degraded they
> make the sexual act, trivial and cheap and nasty(p.69).

Lawrence's point that secrecy is essential to pornography
is no longer true, in view of the growth of the film, book, and
magazine erotic sub-culture, from *Hustler Magazine* to the
"breakthrough" film *Deep Throat*, culminating in the "snuff"
films in which pornography terminates in actual sadistic
murder. A newspaper statistic once indicated that at least ten
million Americans attended "adult" films in 1978 (this
supposedly was large-screen cinema, not including the countless
25¢ porn-film arcades throughout the land. Gloria Steinem, in
her 1984 book, *Outrageous Acts and Everyday Rebellions*, states
that magazine and film pornography sales comes to 8 *billion*
dollars a year. Pornography is hardly secretive or covert anymore: to adapt H. Rap Brown's maxim about American
violence from the late Sixties, "porn" has become as American
as cherry pie. Yet it is also world-wide. The increasing commercial dissemination of x-rated cassettes for use in the privacy of
the home—and for parties—and of "R" and "X" rated TV
channels embody an ironic return to Lawrence's point about
pornography and secrecy—for these new methods of purveying
pornography both insure secrecy and make it unnecessary—a
paradise for the sensually self-brutalized.

Nevertheless, Lawrence's point about secrecy has relevance because it relates to a guilt and shame felt by men (and
women) about sex, as well as to a hostility towards women, and,
according to Gershon Legman, towards their genitals,[5] significant signs of misogyny which Lawrence does not consider. It
relates as well to his contention that pornography tries to "insult
sex, to do dirt on it." If we take "dirt" to mean—as it clearly
seems to mean—excrement, then pornography, Lawrence is
saying, shits on sex, something he regards as very common
("how strong is the will in ordinary, vulgar people, to do dirt on
sex") (p.70). The supposedly polarized attitudes towards sex of
the Puritan and the average man is regarded by Lawrence as a
kind of unified and thus prevalent outlook. Lawrence's average
man views the achievement of sexual intercourse as a victory, as

a way thus of degrading the female sexual partner, which he attributes to the nearness in such a person's mind of the pro-creative and the excremental functions of the human body. Although Lawrence claims these two functions to be utterly different ("Sex is a creative flow, the excrementory flow is towards dissolution, decreation . . . ") (p.70), he claims that the "two flows become identical" in degraded people, people who are porno-graphically conditioned or influenced: "Then sex is dirt and dirt is sex, and sexual excitement becomes a playing with dirt, and any sign of sex in a woman becomes a show of her dirt"(p.70). One recalls however that he allows his hero, Mellors, in *Chatterley* to sodomize the heroine of that late novel on one occasion, and we know from the close critical readings of *The Rainbow* and *Women in Love* that both "good" as well as "bad" characters fail to keep these two adjunct "flows" distinct.

Without going into Lawrence's doctrinal justifications for this identification,[6] I would say that Lawrence in "Pornography" is simplifying the complex "polymorphous-perverse" sexuality subtly present in his major novels. Lawrence must have wanted this essay to have a polemical impact for a broad audience, and in such an arena one tries to keep his ideas simple, lucid, direct. Perhaps an implicit elitism can be detected here as well as in other important last-period works like *Etruscan Places* and *Apocalypse* if Lawrence is implying that a more profound, but dangerous, sexuality is available to the Masters of Reality, but that for most of us, something a little more clear-cut is safer, and sufficient.

But Lawrence broaches a central idea when he claims that pornography occurs when "there is sex excitement with a desire to spite the sexual feeling, to humiliate and degrade it . . . "(p.71). One way to spite sex is to treat the other body (or one's own) as an object, a thing, a medium for self-gratification. Objectification of another person destroys the reciprocity integral to a vital rela-tionship. If sexual love is a form of Martin Buber's I-Thou dialogue in an interaction of aroused flesh and tenderness, porn-ography, to which lust is the fuel, leads to an "It-It" experience. At its worst, it becomes a sadistic-masochistic relationship, in which both "master" and "victim" are victims of their own de-humanization (even if one of the partners is more overtly degraded).

Thus, pornography, one can infer from Lawrence's definition, is a double involvement with sexuality. It is a series of actions, but it is also a certain attitude towards the actions embodied in an act that is both sexual and a contemptuous travesty of sex. One sexual partner inserting a whip handle into the body of another is both symbolizing and viciously mocking phallic-vaginal copulation in the general sense; he (or she) is simultaneously having intercourse with, while deriding and "mastering," the person and being of the other.

Lawrence may not have lived into our liberated Seventies and Eighties to see what pornography coming out of the closet (or the men's smoker) would look like: the perverse, slick, flamboyant insolences of *Penthouse* and *Hustler*, the sex-fleshy cinematic stage of John Holmes and Seka, the post *Naked-Lunch* frontiers of black-leathered S-M bondage and anal fist-fucking. Yet he must have had a premonition of such extremes simply from those picture post-cards, sold "in the underworld" ("of an ugliness to make you cry," he grieves, and it is a real grief: "The insult to the human body, the insult to a vital human relationship") (p.69).

Norman O. Brown has described Lawrence as "that paradoxically conservative philosopher of sexuality,"[7] and in some ways his label is correct. In Lawrence's other famous essay on sex and love, "A Propos of *Lady Chatterley's Lover*," he makes a majestic case for the integrity and utter necessity, individualistically and politically, of fidelity and the family. In the context of the sweeping political and commercial totalitarianism of the 20th century, however, such an affirmation is incorrectly viewed as merely conservative. Lawrence views the state as capable of taking over all aspects of private and personal life. He also thought that the function of the family (created and sanctioned, he asserts, by the Church, and made into a sacrament) is to keep a man—he doesn't include women—free to a degree, giving him "his little kingdom of his own within the big kingdom of the State."[8] "The marriage tie . . . ," Lawrence says earlier in the essay, "is the fundamental connecting link in Christian society"(p.97).

This sounds conservative, certainly, even a bit like T. S. Eliot waxing eloquent on the Idea of a Christian Society. Father Tiverton, in his book *D. H. Lawrence and Human Existence*, thought that Lawrence was close to Catholicism in his last years, and that a good long talk with someone like Baron von Hügel would have set him right. Perhaps it would have, but what

Lawrence it talking about here can be understood in terms short of conversion. He is attempting to relate the utter necessity of sex and love to ritual of some kind, whether as the nature analogies of growth and decay of the great pre-Christian Mediterranean cultures, or as the elaborate procession of holy days central to the structure of the Christian year. Lawrence is longing for a symbolic structure with which to gird his definition and sense of sex, love, life, and death, something which modern industrial societies, with all their complexity, lack. He had a preternaturally deep sense of the relation of human life to the life and rhythms of nature, an attunement that helped to keep some of his work clear of doctrine, whether conservative or radical. Lawrence also realized in the 1920s that societies were only going to get worse. As his sexual pedagogue, Mellors, says to Connie in *Chatterley* in a letter near the end of the novel, " 'there's a bad time coming. If things go on as they are, there's nothing lies in the future but death and destruction for these industrial masses.' "9

Loving copulation would not keep this bad time from arriving, nor, unlike Yeats, did Lawrence have a basic ambivalence about the "second coming." Yet it is surely radical in the deepest sense to suggest that a microcosm of erotic integrity was as valid a gesture against collective pornography and symbolic objectification as any. And if it seems contradictory for a man to preach sexual integrity in an essay based on a novel itself based on infidelity, that risk of contradiction is a measure of how far (again, how radical) Lawrence would go to repudiate a respectable but dead marriage by contrasting it with a vitally living relationship. Marriage being made in bed is an adage easily attacked, but it dramatizes for Lawrence the place and mode of being for a regeneration of the self and the other. In that ultimate sense *Chatterley* is a radically ontological novel in which sex is a synecdoche of our entire being. The ostensible conservatism in "A Propos" is thus rendered less conservative than it at first appears.

Lawrence, especially in his last writings, the work of the mid-Twenties on, was primarily a pastoral writer, one who interpreted either the present or the past against a vivid cast of Golden-Age models. From 1925 to 1930, he saw a gorgeous, simpler, nobler past embodied in the Etruscans, the ancient Greeks, the old Mediterranean world, the long, silent ages of Italian monastic life. He wrote in the late Twenties like a man still seeing a Golden Age as the Iron Age was descending like a gray wall between viewer and the resplendent image. This is the better side of his conservatism (it had its uglier aspect), and its implicit Mediterranean pastoralism is in part the proper context for both *Chatterley* and the two big essays as well as for his perspective on early 20th century sexual culture.[10]

III

I asserted earlier that Lawrence was mistaken to see secrecy as an indissoluble element of pornography. His attitude was undoubtedly influenced by the repressiveness and hypocrisy of Victorian mores casting their shadow upon the Edwardian era, the years of Lawrence's young manhood. What his reaction would have been to the dynamical, successful commercialization of sex of our day is interesting to comtemplate. Certainly he would have been revulsed by the "philosophers" of sexuality like Hugh Heffner, Bob Guccione, and Larry Flynt, who neatly combine "free thinking" with big money-making. He would have made short shrift of these huckster-epistemologists who pose women in highly artificial erotic positions and insist that any sexual response to them resides in, and is induced by, the mind of the beholder. To this incredible effrontery, or to the subtler eroticism that he thought resided in a work like *Jane Eyre* or *Tristan Und Isolde*, he would counter with Boccaccio, whose sexual stories are nothing if not sexually open-handed. In the story from *The Decameron* of the "deaf-mute" gardener in a nunnery (full of young, sex-starved nuns), there certainly is nothing secretive about the sexuality, whereas the smothered, oblique, obsessive forms it assumes in Richardson's *Pamela* or Charlotte Brönte or Wagner struck Lawrence as being far closer to pornography than *The Decameron*. That the very obliquity, the concentrated self-consciousness, of sexuality in these works also embodied serious esthetic concerns would not have impressed Lawrence, and one can understand Lawrence's point about a certain involutedly erotic character to such works without feeling that they are artistically unworthy. Though Lawrence applauds Titian and Renoir, we today tend to find Renoir too overt, "gemütlich," "bourgeois"; and the direct, opulent sensuosity of both artists either embarrasses or bores us, because of our Modernist and post-Modernist acerbity of taste.

No, Lawrence's chief insight about pornography is its insulting of sex. His stress on the secretiveness of sex is partly valid as far as people experiencing pornography goes, but its availability is no longer really covert, or covert enough as to appeal only to a small minority. Today respectable middle-class people not only speak of longing to see a porn film or of going to a triple-x motel, but see the film and go to the motel. Things have changed since the Twenties.

Or have they? The next step in Lawrence's argument in "Pornography" concerns the effect of pornography on the individual. This is a major phase of the essay, and the second half of it. Lawrence's contention is that pornography leads to masturbation. He proceeds to discern the subtler effects of masturbation in a figurative sense, as a metaphor of our modern malaise, a mode of 20th century death-in-life.

Pornography, asserts Lawrence, provokes masturbation. He calls it, as others have, a vice, and a form of self-abuse (and from a philosophical standpoint, the "self" in that familiar phrase harbors ontological facets that I will probe later in this chapter). Lawrence's stand on masturbation again reflects his significant libertarian aspect: "When the grey ones wail that the young man and the young woman went and had sexual intercourse, they are bewailing the fact that the young man and the young woman didn't go separately and masturbate. Sex must go somewhere, especially in young people. So, in our glorious civilization, it goes in masturbation."(p.72)[11]

For decades advanced opinion about masturbation held that masturbation is better for a person's psychological health than repressive self-denial. Sometimes this permissiveness evinces a rather colorless, hygienic character, as if masturbation were as neuter-value or "contentless" as urinating on need or brushing one's teeth. Before commenting on this, I would first like to extend briefly Lawrence's contention that "the mass of our popular literature, the bulk of our popular amusements, just exists to provoke masturbation"(p.72). Not enough attention is given to the subtle, insidious interconnections in American society between soft-core eroticism and pornography. The first is far more pervasive in the mass media through television, films, magazines and ads in innumerable forms. Silk stocking, high heel, brassiere, and lipstick ads, ads with seductive women draped around cars or in tight jeans, movies R-rated not only for violence or profanity but for erotic material and emphasis, articles on more, better, or subtler copulation and how and with whom (besides spouses) to achieve it, TV "sit-coms" full of deliciously sexy young people and situations—our society is super-saturated with soft-core eroticism, not primarily to promote masturbation, as Lawrence holds, but to promote viewing and buying and to provide short-term consumption goals and gratifications with a roseate glow of easy, vicarious sex.

That masturbation, or what Lawrence infers is a masturbatory sensibility, results from mass-media eroticism is, as he claims, probably true.   That this soft-core eroticism also makes hard-core eroticism (or pornography) more desirable, and, ultimately, licit, should be self-evident.   If some people can, or know where to, draw the line between acceptable and unacceptable eroticism, others, judging by x-rated film box-office receipts, can't or don't.   America, Anaïs Nin noted in 1967 in her seventh *Diary*, seems full of "so much puritan disapproval, so much of the spectator and the voyeur."[12]   Commercialized voyeurism, easier to encounter than sexual contact, adds to the pervasive alienation already giving mass societies their atomized character. As soft-core eroticism in our media is primarily designed to attract viewing or to sell commodities by lending them sexual or "sexy" allure, one can ask whether even soft-core eroticism is decent or even permissible.   The connection between shapely L-eggs—stockinged legs ad and a porn-queen writhing in professional ecstasy is perhaps not so distant as might be thought, at least not in the mind of the human male, prone as he is to quick, high-charged sexual excitation by voluptuous objectification of the female figure.

Whether or not such a contention is true, Lawrence discusses the result in terms which if applicable to our time suggest a serious condition in the body social. He argues first that masturbation may be inevitable but is not therefore natural. He cites the shame, futility, and guilt it causes, and, more serious, its habit-forming character, climaxing his censure in strong terms: "Instead of being a comparatively pure and harmless vice, masturbation is certainly the most dangerous sexual vice that a society can be afflicted with, in the long run"(p.73). Is Brown's conservative philosopher of sex beginning to show his hand?

Lawrence contends that masturbation involves only loss, that, unlike sexual intercourse, it provides no give and take, no "reciprocity": "The body remains, in a sense, a corpse, after the act of self-abuse. There is . . . only deadening. There is what we call dead loss"(p.73). There are a lot of figures of death here; they point to Lawrence's conviction that masturbation, because it is only an expenditure, a one-way flow of energy, kills something in us. "In sexual intercourse, there is give and take. A new stimulus departs. Something quite new is added as the old surcharge is removed. And this is so in all sexual intercourse where two creatures are concerned, even in the homosexual intercourse"(p.73).[13] The allusion to "the homosexual intercourse," somewhat disingenuous on Lawrence's part, nevertheless dramatizes how dangerous he thought masturbation ("onanism," he also calls it, with a certain Old Testament severity). Sexual intercourse in itself is not necessarily being idolized by contrast: "Two people may destroy one another in sex," a statement of some weight, coming from the author of *The Rainbow* and *Women in Love*.

What Lawrence appears to be suggesting is that masturbation is a form of sexual solipsism, an intricate involvement in the self cut off from any renewal or inspiriting from the outside. Sexually encountering another human being can be a kind of dialogue, a physical drama of words and flesh, a ballet of accommodating wills and emotions. In masturbation, a person engenders or encounters the figments of his or her overheated erotic imagination. Often enough, these figments are the stars of television, movies, and "girlie" magazines, or they can also be the girl or wife, the boy or husband, next door; only in that sense does the outside world invade the inside one. Otherwise, it is all an erotic drama in the brain, a sex theatre-in-the-round of a single mind with one three-dimensional protagonist and one or more "flat" characters. This closet drama becomes an abuse of the self if we understand the self to acquire much of its integrity and distinctness through the character of its interaction with, and achievement in, the real or external world. Actually having intercourse with (for men, let us say) Morgan Fairchild or (for women) Robert Redford is one thing, a real event of some (if variable) magnitude; but winning her or his heart and body in a masturbatory fantasy is a cheap cheat, the self consciously and vulgarly deluding itself. It is a belittling of our deepest being.

This I suspect is Lawrence's position on masturbation and might account for why he regards it as such a deadly vice. It degrades the "soul," our sense of our essential or best self, and makes self-development harder or even impossible. In this way,

Lawrence implies, masturbation is an ontological evil, a vice of, even beneath, character. Those who are not so deeply affected by their masturbation are, from this perspective, not (as Joseph Conrad would have it) worthy of the Test, of high aims in character or achievement. This ethical position is harsh, certainly, even, as I shall try to show, partly unsound or untrue, but in view of the broad permissiveness of the last few decades, it might not be totally uncommendable. No one has ever gained anything worth gaining by not struggling for it, and some of this struggle has entailed certain kinds of self-denial.

IV

A major passage in "Pornography" emerges from Lawrence's discussion of masturbation:

> The only positive effect of masturbation is that it seems to release a certain mental energy, in some people. But it is mental energy which manifests itself always in the same way, in a vicious circle of analysis and impotent criticism, or else a vicious circle of false and easy sympathy, sentimentalities. The sentimentalism and the niggling analysis, often self-analysis, of most of our modern literature, is a sign of self-abuse. It is the manifestation of masturbation, the sort of conscious activity stimulated by masturbation, whether male or female. The outstanding feature of such consciousness is that there is no real object, there is only subject. This is just the same whether it be a novel or a work of science. The author never escapes from himself, he pads along within the vicious circle of himself(p.74).

Lawrence is describing a symbolic masturbatory type among professionally creative people, writers, artists, scientists. This intellectual hyperconsciousness, typical, Lawrence claims, of modern artistic creativity and literary criticism, represents, again, a form of sexual solipsism; it is unreciprocative and narcissistic, because it revolves solely on the pivot of the self. Lawrence's assertion that there is no real object, only a subject, has nothing to do with the significant monistic areas in his writings in which he transvaluatively surmounts the traditional subject-object polarization of perception and phenomena to effect or approximate a union between perceiver and perceived. Rather, he is intimating in the quotation above that the writer or thinker makes himself (or his self) the subject of his scrutiny in a manner or form that produces a closed-circuit microcosm of self-exhausting consciousness. Self-consciousness and self-exploration become equivalences and ends in themselves, and thus a psychic centripetality and kind of figurative masturbation. The Other, the World, the Object is either ignored or beyond realization by the author. Lawrence would have included Proust within this category, and one does not have to accept that verdict to acknowledge that the great French author's thorough-going analyses of events, emotions, and ideas have at times seemed excessive to others besides Lawrence.

What Lawrence is describing here as an ontological effect of masturbation goes beyond masturbation, however. More than a few heterosexual and homosexual relationships are intensely, even brutally, unreciprocative and narcissistic, and thus are not genuine relationships. Lawrence himself accused women (as instanced in the character Bertha in *Chatterley*) of using men masturbationally and thus exploitatively to gratify themselves sexually. Although this does occur, it is an odd thing to emphasize in view of the greater tendency of men to use a woman's vagina (or rectum) for exclusive self-gratification, and to feel justified in both doing so as well as in being indifferent to orgasmic satisfaction for a female partner.

As an iconoclastic and apocalyptic mind, Lawrence is sometimes given to sybilline pronouncements as stunning as they might be hard to prove by objective argumentation and evidence. To be sure, Lawrence was no historian or sociologist (though he wrote and published a history textbook); he was, however, something rarer—a sage, sometimes. When he says in his fascinating essay on Cezanne, "Introduction To These Paintings," that the impact of syphillis on the English mind partly accounts for the absence of a significant English tradition of the painted nude, Lawrence makes a case by mentioning the ravages of syphillis among 16th and 17th century British royal families, and the heavy sense of the "pox" in Shakespeare's plays. But when he goes on to say that "The terror-horror element [induced by syphillis] which had entered the imagination with regard to the sexual and procreative act was at least partly responsible for the rise of Puritanism, the beheading of the king-father Charles, and the establishment of the New

England Colonies,"[14] one gapes. Yet even as audacious and un-
provable as these propositions seem on one level, on another
they feel *partly* true.   When, again, Lawrence says in
"Pornography" that "the real masturbation of Englishmen began
only in the 19th century"(p.74), one wonders how this claim
could be verified. Lawrence might be thinking of the deep deracination and disorientation that set into English culture with the
development of industrialization, and the consequent dislocation of economic stability and thus of the intimate self. Along
with this might have gone increased interest in fantasy and
romance fiction of little literary merit, conceivably a symbolic
form of masturbatory involvement in the unreal, the fantastic,
and the sublimated erotic. Or he might be inferring cause from
effect, seeing the modern age as devitalized.
     Whatever the history or cause, the sense of devitalization
in 20th century society Lawrence feels with acute perception:

> It [masturbation] has continued with an increasing emptying of the
> real vitality and the real *being* of men, till now people are little
> more than shells of people. Most of the responses are dead, most of
> the awareness is dead, nearly all the constructive activity is dead,
> and all that remains is a sort of shell, a half-empty creature fatal-
> ly self-pre-occupied and incapable of either giving or taking. Incap-
> able either of giving or taking, in the vital self. And this is mastur-
> bation [sic] result. Enclosed within the vicious circle of the self,
> with no vital contacts outside, the self becomes emptier and emp-
> tier, till it is almost a nullus, a nothingness(p.74).

     The   point   is   hammered   home   through   incremental
repetition.   Both literal and figurative masturbation destroy
vitality, impair or stymie one's deepest energies. Accordingly,
there is no Buberian "Thou" here because the "I" has become all-
absorbing or absorbed through a sexual sensibility that turns one
in on one's self, cutting the individual off from rejuvenating
exchange with the Other or the "Thou," and trapping him in the
"vicious circle of the self." One reason Lawrence is a great 20th
century author is because he demonstrated in his fiction and
verse that a human being could die in many ways before he
finally died biologically. He realized that people in our time died
in or because of their psycho-sexuality, died, as the expression
has it, by inches, or through a traumatic change or a crucial
collapse of will.   The self, psychologically or sexually self-
absorbed, deprived of enlivening contact, shrinks and hardens
within itself.   It doesn't appreciably lessen the value of

Lawrence's stricture here to observe that this psychological or sexual solipsism has often occurred in married women, concubines, and mistresses, and, also, though to a far lesser extent, in married men (who have traditionally had the challenges and satisfactions of the outer world to compensate for domestic or bedroom frustrations).

This psycho-sexual diminution Lawrence relates to a self-consciousness resulting from a masturbatory perspective: "The vicious circle of self-consciousness that is never *fully* self-conscious, never fully and openly conscious, but always harping on the dirty little secret"(p.75). This "vicious" circle of masturbation in part results from a sexual gamut with the pure lyric and lily at one end and the smoking-room story at the other. One pole makes the other, Lawrence insists: "They are counterparts, and the one is as pornographic as the other"(p.75). One evokes or calls into being the other, necessitates it. This gamut is also a circle, and the metaphor of the circle of psycho-sexual entrapment of the masturbatory self is in turn a metaphor as well for a condition of self-consciousness that to Lawrence was the special plight of the 20th century individual. For to be self-conscious means to be so focussed on and jailed in the self that one dissipates one's possibility of a true or deeper or "natural" self. Lawrence's own jargon for this lost naturalness was "blood-consciousness." Dislike that Fascistic-sounding phrase as one may, it nevertheless embodies a compelling metaphor of ideal being in an era of synthetic or self-indulgent solutions.

Thus when Lawrence talks about self-consciousness, he is also talking about the results of giving in to the "dirty little secret," of surrendering to the masturbatory mode of sexuality and consciousness. We saw earlier what the problem was with his solution to this Secret—bringing the Secret out of the closet doesn't necessarily get rid of the "dirtiness." Pornography now, instead of evaporating, is still there, more overt and lewd than ever. Lawrence thought you might kill sexual vitality itself in killing the "dirty little secret," and indeed part of the vitality of sex for perhaps many people resides in the thrill, the dark numinosity, of its "dirtiness," in its purple glow of illicitness, of giamour, of being forbidden as adultery or being innately immoral. Perhaps these dimensions of sexuality—rendered ever more intense by modern frustrations, tensions, dissatisfactions, depersonalization, and greater leisure time, abetted by a partly fraudulent sexual revolution—make the "dirty little secret" and rampant eroticism far more deeply rooted in both our private being and our societal structure than ever before. In a world that, generally speaking, lacks humane direction or leadership, in which love and fidelity lack meaningful institutional sanction, sex becomes an all-permeating eroticized libido, its sharp excitements substituting for more civilized values, activities, commitments. Like watching television, the modern engrossment with sex becomes a way of killing time in an interior life that has become a mode of doing time.

Late in the essay Lawrence rises to a climax of poignant desperation and self-transcendence:

> If my life is merely to go on in a vicious circle of self-enclosure, masturbating self-consciousness, it is worth nothing to me. If my individual life is to be enclosed within the huge corrupt lie of society today, purity and the dirty little secret, then it is worth not much to me. Freedom is a very great reality. But it means, above all things, freedom from lies. It is first, freedom from myself, from the lie of myself, from the lie of my all-importance, even to myself; it is freedom from the self-conscious masturbating thing I am, self-enclosed. And second, freedom from the vast lie of the social world, the lie of purity and the dirty little secret. All the other lies lurk under the cloak of this one primary lie(p.79).

Freedom "from myself, from the lie of myself, from the lie of my all-importance, even to myself"—Lawrence is not saying that one, one's self, is unimportant. He is claiming that self-consciousness and obsession with the self are "masturbatory," that the pith of one's self is intimately related to the individual's pattern of psycho-sexuality. Thus, this pattern is important, even crucial, because it helps to shape and determine our innermost being. The "lie of myself," then, is one's solipsistic sense of his sovereign and socially inaccessible being, and the cracked sexual sensibility caused by being stretched between the poles of "purity" and the "dirty little secret." Sex must go somewhere, says Lawrence. One of the places he thinks it goes is right into our "soul," making our central sense of what we like to think is best or permanent or most desired in ourselves either envenomed with corruption or wholesome, even whole. "Sex is the root . . . "—if that is so, then it penetrates indeed into our soul, into our un- or underconscious, even into the carbon and electricity and fluids of our sub-human being. If sex is so deeply rooted, no wonder it is on people's minds today. No wonder as well that an exploitative society can make its members so obsessed with it, keep it on and under our minds so much that it runs us more than we run it. And by keeping our minds on sex too much, we keep it that much off other vital, even crucial concerns: from art to environmental pollution, from the state of one's soul to surviving the "Nuclear-Bomb-Age."

IV

As already mentioned, Lawrence's sexual views have been considered by some writers to be conservative, even reactionary. I have suggested that Lawrence's sexual ideas also contain a libertarian dimension, especially when he is addressing official repressive censorship. But Lawrence's views on masturbation have their own repressive and narrow-minded side. First of all, masturbation doesn't provide only "mental" relief, as Lawrence contends; it also offers physical relief. And it does so often enough for people who usually have no other—or better—means of sexual release: prisoners, enlisted men and women, widows and widowers, young and older children, bed-ridden people, and so on. One indeed could argue that if such categories of people (and there are others) did *not* masturbate occasionally, they would have an advanced case of that modern malady that Lawrence calls Sex-in-the-Head. This consideration does not necessarily invalidate Lawrence's argument that masturbation leaves or can leave one null; it complicates it by suggesting that many human beings have no other sexual recourse, and are understandably prone to risk possible nullity for the sake of relief from sometimes even excruciating longings.

Lawrence also speaks of the guilt and other destructive effects induced by masturbation. Although one cannot doubt that these effects occur, or at least have occurred in the past, we have come since Lawrence's time to feel that such guilt is a culturally implanted attitude, linked with all the old Puritanic prohibitions about "self-abuse." One feels guilty and shamed about masturbating because we are told as children that masturbation is wrong, immoral, "wicked." If that is the charge, the punishment for masturbation (a terrible word) is that we will either go crazy or become infertile. Our recent sexual emancipation has of course asserted precisely the opposite notion, that lack of sexual expression (including masturbation) would make us neurotic or even psychotic, and perhaps sterile too. The point is less that the Golden Mean might apply here as well than that sexuality (like pornography and obscenity) is extremely relative and thus partly at the mercy of any culture's theoretical and practical definitions of it. Not only is one what one is sexually, as Lawrence rightly urged earlier; one is in part also what one's society tries to bend one into being.

In addition, Lawrence's censure of masturbation verges on being inhumane when silhouetted against the efforts of modern women to liberate themselves sexually. Some women view and protest the sexual role of women traditionally as being masturbatory cavities for men; they want instead to explore and develop their own intrinsic female sexuality and sensuality. Touching their bodies becomes a form of self-exploration, and clitoral masturbation a mode of self-discovery denied them, they claim, by patriarchal conventions. Females have experienced forms of sexual inhibition different from, and probably deeper than, those encountered by males during sexually repressive eras; their sexual emancipation is thus all the more justified and urgent. Masturbation in this light becomes a valid dimension of sexual definition and development of a woman's self. This consideration suggests some inadequacy in Lawrence's understanding and criticisms of masturbation.

Yet as long as sexual or sensual self-investigation leads to erotic self-obsession, it can be a pernicious threat to an individual's character structure or development. Lawrence in this vital regard is right; he is right, too, in denoting the dangers of the habit-forming aspect of masturbation, a serious vulnerability in an individual living in a society as permeated by the commercialization of eros as ours is. Whether from too much or too little sexual expression (including masturbation), depletion or diffusion of being is often the result: "the self becomes . . . almost . . . a nothingness."

V

Undoubtedly Lawrence speaks with some authority and intensity about pornography and obscenity because most of his important novels—*The Rainbow, Women in Love, Lady Chatterley's Lover*—had been described as one or the other.

Chatterley, accused of being pornographic *and* obscene, was banned for three decades in Great Britain and the United States. Certainly by Lawrence's definitions it was nothing of the sort. Whether or not the eroticism of *Chatterley* exhibits the openness or frankness that Lawrence applauded in Boccaccio or Rabelais could be another matter. Of course the sexuality in *Chatterley* is ideological, transvaluatively moral. In its way, it is as far from the saltier tales in *The Decameron* or *The Canterbury Tales* as one could get. Lawrence's purpose in *Chatterley* is doctrinal, noble, and also irritatingly heuristic; detractors have called it puritanical or reactionary.[15]   Moralist that he was, and great iconococlast in the tradition of Blake and Nietzsche, Lawrence does not give us a sexuality as direct and country-natural as that in a fabliau, as hilariously gross and bare-cheeked as the Miller Tales, whether Chaucer's or Henry's in the *Tropic* books, where desire and coupling are as plain and palpable as a smell, a stone, a blow. Rather, Lawrence would make sexual love tender, mystical, apocalyptical through an oblique craft of nature metaphors. He thus got only part of sex too, but certainly a part deserving exclamation, exposition and praise (despite the male provincialism and class snobbery in *Chatterley*). Whatever the faults of this last novel of Lawrence's, the following *Chatterley* passage exhibits a powerful eroticism that is anything but pornographic:

> He took her in his arms again and drew her to him, and suddenly she became small in his arms . . . the resistance was gone. . . . And as she melted small and wonderful in his arms, she became infinitely desirable to him, all his blood-vessels seemed to scald with intense yet tender desire, for her, . . . for the penetrating beauty of her in his arms, passing into his blood . . . softly he stroked the silky slope of her loins, down, down between her soft warm buttocks, coming nearer to the very quick of her. And she felt him like a flame of desire, yet tender, and she felt herself melting in the flame. She let herself go. She felt his penis risen against her with silent amazing force and assertion, and she let herself go to him. She yielded with a quiver that was like death, she went all open to him.[16]

The best test of one's precept is one's practise of it. In this scene in which Constance Chatterley has a "blood-consciousness" experience of sexual love, Lawrence shows what he could uniquely do at his best. It is fashionable among some to laugh at areas like this in Lawrence's work today; they are beyond all this supposedly sentimental sensual tenderness. Also, they would view Connie's "smallness" here as a sign of Lawrence's chauvinistic diminishing of women's independence, a stricture more valid for other areas of Lawrence's works than for this ambiguous passage in which smallness suggests the shrinking of ego rather than of being.   Certainly, *Chatterley* is not the world of William Burroughs' drug-glazed pederastic sexscapes or of Henry Miller's sexual "realism," of "Miller," Fillmore, and the rest of his farcical buddies moving through the comic nightmares of ignoble lusts not necessarily untypical of the rest of us. *Chatterley* exhibits the other extreme, romanticized copulation, idyllic fucking, sex versus the Machine. So it is. *Chatterley* has its place in the pantheon of sex or erotic writing as much as the work of Chaucer, Casanova, and Miller.   After all is said and done, sex, in its capacity to galvanize, shape, and exalt or ruin people's lives, is a serious matter indeed, something that deserves our keenest attention and care.   Ancient cultures and many religions have tried to control sex by making it a sacrament, which is somewhat analogous to the Greeks calling the Furies the Kindly Ones.   This is wise, for sex, like death and birth, is one of the great numinous phenomena of existence and being.   Lawrence realized this, and probed its sinuous manifestations profoundly.

Near the end of "Pornography," Lawrence makes the basic distinction between fraudulent and genuine sexuality with which the entire essay is concerned:

> And perhaps one day even the general public will desire to look the thing in the face, and see for itself the difference between the sneaking masturbation pornography of the press, the film, and present-day popular literature, and then the creative portrayals of the sexual impulse that we have in Boccaccio or the Greek vase-paintings or some Pompeiian art, and which are necessary for the fulfillment of our consciousness(p.81).

"Necessary for the fulfillment of our consciousness" —Lawrence again sounds like a libertarian here, rather than like a reactionary instinctivist.   If his work sometimes seemed to stress the instinctive or subjective too much for some, he made it significantly clear elsewhere that he believed in an organic integrity: the root in the dark soil nourishing the flower of consciousness. "Pornography and Obscenity" is one of his great essays because it elaborates this metaphor expositively and memorably.   And though we seem to live in a period that is divorcing consciousness from the unconscious again, as in the American

Puritan or the English Victorian era, Lawrence's "Pornography and Obscenity," and his work generally, attests to a presence that fought this radical alienating and corrupting of our intimate being throughout much of his career.

Notes

[1] This data on the writing and publication dates of Lawrence's last essays is taken from Keith Sagar's book *The Art of D. H. Lawrence* (London: Cambridge University Press, 1966), 202, 203, 229.

[2] Harry T. Moore regards "A Propos" as the "finest of all his [Lawrence's] pronouncements on the subject of sex, literature, and censorship" (*The Intelligent Heart: The Life of D. H. Lawrence* (New York: Grove Press, 1962), 511). Some might regard *Study of Thomas Hardy* to be Lawrence's greatest essay, but it is long enough to qualify as a short book. Essay or book, *Study* ranks with his best literary criticism.

[3] *D. H. Lawrence* (New York: Viking Press, 1973), 146.

[4] *Sex, Literature, and Censorship*, edited by Harry T. Moore (New York: Viking Press, 1959), 66. All further references to this text will be documented by page numbers in parentheses in the paper.

[5] *The Rationale of the Dirty Joke: An Analysis of Sexual Humor* (First Series) (New York: Grove Press, 1968), ch. 6.

[6] Some fascinating, at times, brilliant, work on this crux in several major Lawrence novels can be found among critics like Colin Clark, Frank Kermode, Mark Spilka, Kingsley Widmer, and others. See Mark Spilka's "On Lawrence's Hostility to Willful Women: The Chatterley Solution," in *Lawrence and Women*, edited by Anne Smith (London: Vision Press, 1978); Kingsley Widmer, "The Pertinence of Modern Pastoral: the Three Versions of *Lady Chatterley's Lover*," *Studies in the Novel*, 5 (Fall 1973). H. M. Daleski, *The Forked Flame: A Study of D. H. Lawrence* (Evanston: Northwestern University Press, 1965), 304-11; "Critical Exchange: On "Lawrence Uptight: Four Tail-Pieces," *Novel*, V (1971), 54-70; Frank Kermode, *Shakespeare, Spenser, Donne: Renaissance Essays* (New York: Viking Press, 1971), 28-31; Mark Spilka, "Lawrence Up-Tight; or the Anal Phase Once Over," *Novel*, IV (1971), 252-67; William Empsom (*Essays in Criticism*, 13, 1) (January, 1963), 103. See also my " 'The Impossible Notation': The Sodomy Scene in *Lady Chatterley's Lover*", *The Sphinx: A Magazine of Literature and Society*, #14, IV, 2, 109-25, or in my *The Maze in the Mind and the World: the Labyrinth in Modern Literature*. (Troy, New York: Whitston Publishing Co., 1985).

[7] *Life Against Death: The Psychoanalytical Meaning of History* (New York: Random House, 1959), 181.

[8] This monarchy metaphor is revealing and perhaps not a metaphor at all, in view of Lawrence's strong advocacy of male domination in a marriage,

the sexual counterpart of the male-leadership ideas in much of his work of the 1920s. A king of course is a king by having subjects: in this case, wife and children.

[9]*Lady Chatterley's Lover* (New York: Bantam Books, 1968), 327.

[10]The importance of Italy in Lawrence's work, and not only in the 1920s, is amply and attractively set forth in Leo Hamalian's book *D. H. Lawrence in Italy* (New York: Taplinger, 1982).

[11]Earlier in "Pornography," after quoting the late British Home Secretary, Sir William Joyson-Hicks, mentioning improper books, and then stating that "these two young people, who had been perfectly pure up till that time, after reading this book went and had sexual intercourse together!!!," Lawrence, evincing a spirited libertarianism, says, "*One up on them*! is all we can answer. But the grey Guardian of British Morals seemed to think that if they had murdered one another, or worn each other to rags of nervous prostration, it would have been much better"(68-69).

[12]*The Diary of Anais Nin, vol. Seven, 1966-1974*, ed. by Gunther Stuhlmann (New York: Harcourt, Brace, Jovanovich, 1980), 46.

[13]Lawrence in a powerful passage from "A Propos" puts sexual interaction in grand mystical metaphors of marriage:

> Two rivers of blood are man and wife, two distinct eternal streams, that have the power of touching and communing and so renewing making new one another, without any breaking of the subtle confines, any confusing or commingling. And the phallus is the connecting link between the two rivers, that establishes the two streams in a oneness, and gives out of their duality a single circuit, forever. And this, this oneness gradually accomplished throughout a lifetime in twoness, is the highest achievement of time or eternity.
> From it all things human spring, children and beauty and well-made things; all the true creations of humanity" (Moore, *Sex, Literature, and Censorship*, 101-02).

[14]*Selected Essays* (Harmondsworth, England: Penguin Books, 1950), 312.

[15]According to Susan Sontag, "A country in which the vindication of so sexually reactionary a book as *Lady Chatterley's Lover* is a serious matter is plainly at a very elementary stage of sexual maturity." ("Psychoanalysis and Norman O. Brown's *Life Against Death*," in *Against Interpretation and Other Essays* (New York: Dell Publishing co., 1961), 257. But Sontag, whose views on the sexual politics in *Chatterley* hardly constitutes the last word on the subject, goes on to assert that Lawrence must still be defended "because many who reject him have retreated to an even more reactionary position than his."(p.257).

[16]*Chatterley*, Op. cit., 186.

"Only the insane notion that 'everything is possible' has expressed our deepest knowledge that far more is possible than we had ever thought."

Hannah Arendt, *The Origins of Totalitarianism*

" 'I even make statues talk.' " Oriana Fallaci, *A Man*

"Yet it is possible to practice the art of living even in a concentration camp, although suffering is omnipresent."

Viktor E. Frankl, *Man's Search for Meaning*

Incarceration and Torture:
The Self in Extremity

I

In a number of the fictional works examined so far in this book, the protagonists encounter extremities of experience in one form or another. Dostoyevsky's Undergroundling is utterly alienated, Tess and N. Hexam undergo a terrifying number of misfortunes, Celine and Ellison's narrators alternate between living at the center of societal violence and at the margins of society, and James's Marcher suffers an extremity of self-delusion, while Bellow's Hattie Waggoner approaches death alone in the desert of America and her old age. If we consider the place or plight of a number of protagonists in Modernist literature—Stephen Dedalus, Paul Morel-Birkin-Mellors, Lord Jim-Nostromo-Axel Heyst, *Under the Volcano's* Consul and Thomas Mann's Leverkühn, Orwell's Winston Smith, Beckett's cripples—it is apparent they occupy by their very psychological, esthetic, or ideological constitution an isolated position in relation to society that confers on their lives a tension, even a desperation, implying an extremity of experience.

But to lend our pursuit of the self a dimension of more overt extremity, I would like to scrutinize the implications for self of three twentieth-century accounts of imprisoned or tortured human beings, two of the works non-fiction and one famously fictional. I do not mean to imply in stressing non-fiction works in this chapter that they provide a better example of the self in extremity than fiction does: a variety of short and long fictions, from Yukio Mishima's short story about ritual disembowelment, "Patriotism," to Arthur Koestler's novel *Darkness at Noon* (and George Orwell's *1984*, the fiction I will examine briefly in this chapter) disproves such a contention. Yet in Viktor E. Frankl's book *Man's Search for Meaning: an Introduction to Logotherapy* and Jacobo Timerman's *Prisoner Without a Name, Cell Without a Number*, one beholds two extraordinary documents of the self in the extremity of incarceration and/or torture that richly deserve scrutiny as non-fiction prose literature of the self. This comparison will be amplified by shorter references to incarceration-and-torture material in such writers on the topic as Bruno Bettelheim, Terrence Des Pres, Aleksandr Solzhenitsyn, and Jean-Paul Sartre. One definition of the self that I would like to induct for this chapter is that of the self as a multifold sense of psycho-physical reflexivity that tries to cohere, persist, and survive in the face of degradation, pain, death, and the threat of these extreme conditions. Psychic reflexivity or consciousness would seem to be a crucial and determinative aspect of selfhood, an endless if intermittent inner scrutiny. It is also consciousness that makes the experience of physical and psychic suffering so extreme in the accounts I present, as it was a high ethical consciousness that drove prison and torture victims, whether of the concentration camps or of other collectivistic horrors, to survive in order, as Des Pres has described it in his stunning book, *The Survivor: An Anatomy of Life in the Death Camps*,[1] to bear witness. Bearing witness is as good a way as any, especially in the bleak underworld of authoritarian terror, of validating the idea of the self, and will as such represent an implied primary definition of self underpinning this chapter.

Incarceration and torture are obviously two (sometimes united) forms of extreme experience. Other kinds of experience, such as deep grief, sexual desire or lust, greed, love, and anger test the self in its vulnerabilities and steadfastnesses. Yet being deprived of physical freedom, especially for an indefinite period, and being exposed to malicious physical violation or even mutilation of one's person, constitute distinctively terminal events. Probably few individuals are prepared to endure captivity or torture. Thus, in experiencing them, most people have only their inner reserves or physical resources to help them to endure extreme humiliation and psychological or physical disintegation, and to protect them from madness or suicide. It would require a very stout soul to take calmly what happened to Jacobo Timerman one early morning in April, 1977, when twenty men broke into his Buenos-Aires apartment:

> They uprooted our telephone lines, took possession of our automobile keys, handcuffed me from behind. They covered my head with a blanket, rode down with me to the basement, removed the blanket, and asked me to point out my automobile. They threw me to the floor in the back of the car, covered me with a blanket, stuck their feet on top of me, and jammed into me what felt like the butt of a gun.

No one spoke.[2]

Later in the day, somewhere else, lying blindfolded on the ground where he had been flung, Timerman feels something like a gun-barrel against his head and the lethal words " 'I'm going to count to ten' " spoken to him. It will be significant later in this chapter that as the Counter counts, Timerman, thinking he will be shot in the head when the number ten is reached, writes: "Was it [his threatened murder] what I desired? Yes, it was what I desired," and "Wife, children, I love you. Adiós, adiós, adiós"(p.10).

The intricate horror of these experiences would probably daunt, even terrify, most people. If it didn't terrify Timerman (he doesn't say that it did), this might be explained by his having partly expected such a visit. As publisher and editor of an eminent Argentine newspaper called La Opinión, Timerman had openly criticized the government's repressions of civil rights and citizens, a dangerous enterprise in a militarist society. Timerman knew that not only enemies or critics but even middle of the roaders were all considered real or potential foes of the regime, and therefore were likely to disappear from their homes, their jobs, or other places suddenly and swiftly. As an outspoken critic of the despotic Argentine military junta, Timerman, in a situation similar to that of Pedro Joaquin Chamorro (the Editor of the Nicaraguan newspaper La Prensa assassinated by Somoza), undoubtedly knew that his life or freedom was imperilled during his editorship from 1971 on.[3] So a police "visit" probably did not surprize him. This knowledge, if it lessened the shock of his situation, probably did not lessen its terror.

The mode of apprehension (it was not an arrest) that Timerman describes is clearly intended to strike terror into the captive; terrorization is part of a strategy of softening the victim up so that he or she will do or say what the captors want. In the process, the victim's self is or can be destroyed; whether it is so temporarily or permanently depends on the character or nature of the victim. It is significant that Timerman, when asked if he wants to say his prayers because he supposedly is about to be shot, says nothing. This behavior points ahead to one of the major survival resources of the self—and of Timerman's self—in *Prisoner*. Before dealing with these resources at length, however, it is more convenient at this point to introduce Frankl's *Man's Search for Meaning*, for it describes a form of captivity and pressure, as well as a style of self-preservation, that will differ significantly from Timerman's, and thus silhouettes *Prisoner* more effectively by preceding it.

II

Frankl's *Search* is one of the numerous books dealing with an inmate's personal experience of the Nazi concentration camps. What makes it a distinctive work within this genre is hinted at in its title: Frankl suggests that concentration camps are endurable and even provide an opportunity to create value by forging meaning out of extremity, particularly the extremity of the pain, privation, degradation, hopelessness, and misery of concentration-camp life. Although held in the vicious grip of brutal circumstances, a human being still has one great residual power, "the last of the human freedoms—to choose one's attitude in any given set of circumstances, to choose one's own way."4 He elaborates this major theme shortly afterwards: "the sort of person the prisoner becomes was the result of an inner decision, and not the result of camp influences alone. Fundamentally, therefore, any man can, even under such circumstances, decide what shall become of him—mentally and spiritually. He may retain his human dignity even in a concentration camp"(p.105).

This sounds noble, but Frankl sets these inspiriting words over against some harshly sobering facts. Early in his account, he admits that "only those prisoners could keep alive who, after years of trekking from camp to camp, had lost all scruples in their fight for existence"(p.7). If there is any doubt about the meaning of the foregoing sentiments, Frankl sweeps it away decisively by the end of the paragraph: "the best of us did not return," a position I will probe later in the chapter. Further in the book, Frankl states that "most men in a concentration camp believed that the real opportunities of life had passed. Yet, in reality, there was an opportunity and a challenge. One could make a victory of these experiences, turning life into an inner triumph, or one could ignore the challenge and simply vegetate, as did a majority of the prisoners"(p.115).

The prisoner who gives up has lost his faith in the future, and is therefore doomed: "With his loss of belief in the future, he also lost his spiritual hold; he let himself decline and became subject to mental and physical decay. Usually this happened quite suddenly, in the form of a crisis . . . the prisoner refusing one morning to get dressed. . . . No entreaties, no blows, no threats had any effect. He just lay there . . . lying in his own excreta, and nothing bothered him any more"(p.118).

By saying that the majority of the prisoners ignored the challenge of the camp, Frankl effectively places the loftly ideals in the book within a context of grim facts about how people did fare in the camps. His is not a facile idealism. Yet Frankl's account is permeated by a glow of tragic affirmation. Indeed, some of Frankl's attitudes resemble the traditional (if austere) tragic humanism of growth through suffering, and of the creating of meaning and value in life by accepting and assimilating one's suffering.

Such an achievement depended, paradoxically enough, on accepting the reality of concentration-camp life. Because of the brunt and misery of that life, the temptation was strong to act as if it were unreal, and this, insists Frankl, was dangerous. Instead of making the best of camp life, of developing possibilities for something positive, some prisoners saw camp life as unreal, a reaction which led to their losing their grip on life(p.114).

Making the best of camp life and taking it seriously at first seem unlikely, yet one has to remember human flexibility, the positive side of human malleability. Frankl strikingly relates this flexibility to the relativity of pain and suffering in a key point: " . . . suffering completely fills the human soul and conscious mind, no matter whether the suffering is great or little. Therefore the 'size' of human suffering is absolutely rela-

tive"(p.70). That "absolutely relative" might justly disturb a fastidious mind, but the basic idea is implied grandly just before it
in Frankl's contention that " . . . it is possible to practise the art of
living even in a concentration camp, although suffering is omnipresent"(p.69).

No matter how horrifyingly different concentration-camp
(or any other) experience is from one's "normal routine civilian
life, it has a whole gamut of satisfactions, joys, challenges, failures, and achievements latent within it "world." A good example can be found in Timerman's book at the very beginning of
the work. In a dramatic opening, Timerman says that the cell he
is kept in is so narrow that at its center he cannot extend his
arms. But it is long enough for him, lying down, to stretch out
his whole body: "A stroke of luck," he claims. Obviously, it
would not be a stroke of luck to a free man used to so much
physical space that the thought of extending his limbs or even
walking or running in any direction as far as he wants to is a
freedom he doesn't prize sufficiently.   Timerman mentions,
however, that in his previous cell he "was forced to huddle up
when seated and keep my knees bent lying down"(p.3).

On the other hand, Timerman misses his first cell because
it had a hole into which he could urinate and defecate. In his
"present" cell, he has to ask the guards to conduct him to the
lavatory, a complex routine. They don't always heed his calls,
and so he sometimes excreted on himself. Again, in "normal"
life, people take the relieving of these needs for granted.[5]
William Faulkner once said that making love and defecating
were the two acts for which humans need privacy. Yet one of
the big shocks to an individual is how many "liberties," upon
which rest varying degrees of self-composure, self-acceptance,
and even self-recognition, he takes for granted, and, when they
are taken away, how staggering the impact on the psyche and its
stability can be. As an educated, civilized, and prosperous professional man,[6] Timerman in his regular life must have lived with
all or most of the amenities of 20th century material culture. He
must have been accustomed to privacy and comfort as he per-
formed his private functions day to day in his Buenos Aires
apartment.   Suddenly his life undergoes a violent wrenching,
and he finds himself grateful to be in a very narrow cell (not a
room) where he can get rid of his body wastes (if inelegantly).
After all, if the alternative is to have one's wastes remain on (or
even in) one's body, the differences between a cell with a hole

for voiding excrement and a cell without one becomes perhaps as large as the cell with a hole and an expensive apartment for one's luxuriantly free use.

One begins to feel the living veracity of Frankl's term "absolutely relative." Indeed, part of the power of Timerman's narrative is his openness about details of his 30-months' incarceration. His "I do it on myself" has a Zolaesque candor lacking in Frankl's book, which is rather scant on naturalistic or ugly details, as well as about descriptions of torture or beatings. The following passage is typical of Frankl's understandable brevity and generality about physical abuse and sadism in his camp: "after a time we again heard the lashings of the strap, and the screams of tortured men. This time it lasted for quite a while"(pp.23-24).

I am not thirsting for bloody details. Yet Frankl's tough-minded and beautiful idealism would carry more authority if weighed against a fuller description of the terrible and continual pains and horrors that he and his camp mates had to endure. "Doing it on himself," as Timerman must, certainly a significant and vivid detail of his experience of imprisonment, also means that he had to get permission to get his clothes clean. Thus he had to wait naked in his cell—sometimes for days—or until his clothes dried, undergoing the dreadful vulnerability of being naked for what must have seemed like an eternity. Timerman talks about experiencing an overwhelming isolation, but the reader also is left to think about the degradation a human being forced to befoul himself must feel, especially around "clean" guards who might make the most of the opportunity to scorn and insult one for a smell anyone would give off if coerced into the same condition.

It would appear from *Prisoner* that Timerman had great fortitude, and was able to stand such degradation, as he was able to survive terrorization and pain and (worst of all, he claims) memories of better times and places. Frankl too speaks of naked-ness, at one point in an affirmative light. After taking the first camp shower, part of a ritual that severed the inmates from their previous lives, the men suddenly laugh: "we knew that we had nothing to lose except our so ridiculously naked lives"(p.24). This is wisdom indeed, and probably has nothing to do with one's previous education, work, or class. A grimmer and figur-ative nakedness appears later in Frankl's book when he describes the stripping of one's past sense of his own worth: "We all had once been or had fancied ourselves to be "somebody." Now we were treated like complete nonentities . . . the average prisoner felt himself utterly degraded"(p.99).   Whether physically or metaphysically, a concentration-camp prisoner (Frankl) and a political and ethnic prisoner (Timerman) experienced an ontological nakedness, yet both men apparently were able to summon inner reserves to withstand their degradation, and to ward off the various forms of disintegration that could and did result for many others, from depersonalization to insanity and suicide.

III

One is threatened in these two situations of brutal confinement with being reduced to an object, a thing, an "animal." Loss of self respect, of a sense of one's moral or physical integrity, of one's innate worth or right to minimal decency and respect threaten to warp or crush the self until one capitulates (where capitulation is desired by captors) or commits a suicide of the will.   One becomes clay in the hands of one's political captors or ideological torturers. As Hannah Arendt says in universal terms surely true for much of the 20th century:

> What totalitarian ideologies therefore aim at is not the transfor-
> mation of the outside world or the revolutionizing transmutation of
> society, but the transformation of human nature itself. The concen-
> tration camps are the laboratories where changes in human nature
> are tested, and their shamefulness therefore is not just the business
> of their inmates and those who run them according to strictly
> "scientific" standards; it is the concern of all men. Suffering, of
> which there has been always too much on earth, is not the issue,
> nor is the number of victims. Human nature as such is at stake . . . [7]

Human nature being at stake is another way of saying that the durability of the self and of the validity of the concept of the self is also at stake.   George Orwell's O'Brien in *1984* is a character famous (or infamous) for his anti-self stance that human nature is transformable; a person can be dehumanized by so betraying what he holds most dear that he has no unity, no moral center, no mental or emotional coherence.   The "horrifying" motto of the effects of O'Brienism in *1984* is Winston Smith's tortured cry and betrayal of his beloved,

"Do it to her!"

Both Timerman and Frankl admit that some people can be changed or "bent." One of Timerman's major charges is that political liberals and Argentinian Jews allowed themselves to be intimidated into silence at government acts of antisemitism in the country. And Frankl too observes more than once that maintaining belief in one's self, in the value of one's being, under the stripping, debasing pressures of concentration camp life, was very difficult, and that many prisoners succumbed, understandably, to a reduction, perversion, or "transformation" of their selves—they became objectified.

Yet both authors significantly suggest that a healthy, even life-saving, aspect resides in possible responses to being treated as an object. Early in *Search* Frankl suggests that getting the proper perspective on a concentration-camp experience is difficult. A prisoner obviously cannot have the proper objectivity of detachment. Yet detachment too is not entirely desirable, for, as Frankl says: "Only the man inside knows"(p.8). Part of the problem Frankl and Timerman face is trying to communicate the utter pith, the resonances of the actuality, of their experiences, something they both feel to be impossible. Words convey only so much, and if a person has not experienced electrification of his or her genitals, or lay next door to another room filled with the screams of a person being tortured, an impenetrable curtain separates word from meaning as deed. In order, Frankl implies, to capture the essence of a camp experience, one must not only be an inmate, but also be an object.

Hannah Arendt quotes Bruno Bettleheim suggesting something else protective about object status or reality for camp inmates: "It seemed as if I had become convinced that these horrible and degrading experiences somehow did not happen to 'me' as subject but to 'me' as an object. This experience was corroborated by the statements of other prisoners. . . . It was as if I watched things happening in which I only vaguely participated. . . . This cannot be true, such things just do not happen."[8] In a very real sense, people do experience these degradations as objects. The degradations make objects out of them, but if this process can be assimilated so that one's inner esteem, one's "real me," is not seriously bruised or pierced, then this "objectification" becomes a process of serving and saving the self. What occurs appears to be a kind of "beneficial" schizophrenia whereby the portions of one's being that stands most in need of remaining intact or uninjured are protected. One "vaguely participates" in enforced abasement because only part of the psyche is forced into involvement; some other part of one's being remains in the darkness of the self, refusing participation in order to survive. This object "ideal" is presented in its more negative aspect as well:

> Under the influence of a world which no longer recognized the value of human life and human dignity, which had robbed man of his will and had made him an object to be exterminated (having planned, however, to make full use of him first . . .)—under this influence the personal ego finally suffered a loss of values. If the men in the concentration camp did not struggle against this in a last effort to save his self-respect, he lost the feeling of being an individual, a being with a mind, with inner freedom and personal value (pp.78-79).

Yet, again, some kind of acceptance of one's self as an object could, according to Frankl, be life-saving:

> Apathy, the blunting of the emotions and the feeling that one could not care any more, were the symptoms arising during the second stage of the prisoner's psychological reactions, and which eventually make him insensitive to daily and hourly beatings. By means of this insensibility the prisoner soon surrounded himself with a very necessary protective shell(p.35).

The crucial question then arises how one saves his self-esteem while allowing himself to be self-protectively desensitized. Is there some kind of psychic economy here that cancels out contempt and abuse? And does a point get reached where the emotional or psychic capital finally becomes exhausted, and the strategy of de-sensitization becomes self-devouring? Or, to use another order of metaphors, do human beings possess varying numbers of selves that—rather like D. H. Lawrence's "dark gods" in his witty and provocative Benjamin Franklin essay—come and go, and that while one self is sacrificed or hurt by brutal treatment, another self keeps the "soul" firm, free from madness or violence? Using a Freudian and Jungian metaphoric schema, one could perhaps say that for prisoners (and others, in different areas of life) who survive harsh treatment, the ego has absorbed it in defense of the self. This, one grants, is a rather mechanistic way of putting what must be an organic or fluid relationship between the (still hypothetical) constructs of the ego and the self, for a blow to the ego would also affect the self. Yet is it possible that the relation between ego and self would vary for different people and would absorb external punishment differently (as well as *internal* punishment, if we consider how the Superego can respond to the spectacle of one's degradation)? Perhaps one can approach this question obliquely by considering what two concentration-camp writers, Bettelheim and Des Pres, have described as a key, if not basic, camp-inmate behavior.

Frankl's contention that "the best did not survive" in the camps has been seriously challenged by Des Pres in *The Survivor*, in which he contests at length that some of the best *did* survive, and did so through what was best in them. But Des Pres's real disagreement is not with Frankl but with Bettelheim. Bettelheim says that the prisoners' feelings could have been summed up as follows: "What I do here or what is happening to me doesn't count at all; here, everything is permissible as long and insofar as it contributes to helping me survive in the camp."[9]   Bettelheim supports this survival code further when he claims that "One had to comply with debasing and amoral commands if one wished to survive; but one had to remain cognizant that one's reason for complying was 'to remain alive and unchanged as a person' "(p.157).   Bettelheim qualifies this position and even more so the one preceding it significantly in his contention that "to survive as a man not a walking corpse, as a debased and degraded but still human being, one had first and foremost to remain informed and aware of what made up one's personal point of no return, the point beyond which one would never . . . give in to the oppressor . . . "(pp.156-157).

Bettelheim's last point here seems close to Des Pres's idea that "The distinction is between those who live at any price, and those who suffer whatever they must in order to live humanly"(p.19). (However, the people who tried to "live humanly" would sometimes be the ones who got killed—beaten to death, for example, if they even watched as the SS beat another inmate up or dead) (pp.125,139). But Bettelheim appears to be contradicting himself; on the one hand, he says "everything is permissible" as long as it helps one to survive the camps; yet, on the other hand, he insists that everyone possessed an ethic of what he would not tolerate even at the cost of his life—in other words, not *everything* is permissible.

According to Des Pres, the real dynamic to camp-survival is quite different from Bettelheim's somewhat contradictory thesis in *The Informed Heart* on how inmates survived. Bettelheim, Des Pres claims, says that the inmates behaved like "incompetent children," "identified with the SS," became a shapeless mass, and lacked autonomy(p.185). Des Pres, on the contrary, claims that the inmates were organized, and used their organization both to run a Black Market (thus helping to acquire amenities that made their lives more bearable) and to help one another (and even groups of children) covertly: "Prisoners survived through concrete acts of mutual aid, and over time these many small deeds . . . grew into a general fabric of debt and care"(p.157). Earlier, Des Pres quotes Eugen Kogon as stating that "In every concentration camp where the political prisoners attained any degree of ascendancy, they turned the prisoner hospital, scene of fearful SS horrors that it was, into a rescue station for countless prisoners' "(p.139). "In extremity," Des Pres observes a little later, "life depends on solidarity"(p.141), and he assembles a variety of impressive camp-life witness-participant accounts to support his interpretation.

In terms of self theory, Bettelheim claims most inmates behaved childishly, whereas Des Pres claims that their behavior was superlatively adult in a number of ways, including their ability to maintain their sense of self, of purpose and worth by integrating the Other as part of themselves. Knowing, according to Des Pres's material, that there was not only one person but a whole community of crucially concerned members on the same "team" would conceivably have amplified or heartened the self deeply: one in many, many in one, a reciprocal formula of brotherhood whereby the objectifying world of the SS was offset by the humanizing one of mutual aid, gift-giving, and acts of sometimes perilous generosity.

It is less to my purpose to choose between Bettelheim and Des Pres's interpretations of concentration-camp types and behavior (though I would certainly want to believe that Des Pres is right) than to observe that if Des Pres *is* right, what we find in the Nazi camps is one of the greatest instances of human cooperation, "heart," and perseverance on record. Like building a home out of bare rocks with hardly more than one's hands, the prisoners, by Des Pres's account, shaped a humane culture of the self and the Other in the most barren, degrading, and torturous of circumstances.

IV

Timerman's treatment of objectification in captivity and extremity is markedly different from Frankl's strategy for self survival, and one of the most distinctive and amazing sections of *Prisoner*, particularly in its embodiment of "feminine" passivity as a strength. He too felt that it was a good strategy to make an object of oneself, but during torture what Timerman recommends and claims he practised is passivity: "Some fought against being carried to the torture tables; others begged not to be tortured; others insulted their torturers. I represented sheer passivity. . . . This passivity, I believe, preserved a great deal of energy and left me with all my strength to withstand the torture"(p.34). This strength is crucially needed, Timerman observes, because in experiencing torture, "A man is shunted so quickly from one world to another that he is unable to tap a reserve of energy so as to confront the unbridled violence":

> That is the first phase of torture: to take a man by surprise, without allowing him any reflex defense, even psychological. A man's hands are shackled behind him, his eyes blindfolded. No one says a word. Blows are showered upon a man. He's placed on the ground and someone counts to ten, but he's not killed. A man is then led to what may be a canvas bed, or a table, stripped, doused with water, tied to the ends of the bed or table, hands and legs outstretched. And the application of electric shocks begins. The amount of electricity transmitted by the electrodes . . . is regulated so that it . . . hurts, or burns, or destroys. It's impossible to shout—you howl. (p.33)

One withstands these sudden and remorseless waves of pain and fear by *not* acting or feeling as if one were a ". . . normal human being. The vegetable attitude can save a life"(p.35). This appears to be a strategy of acceptance, but it is so in the traditional craft of rolling with the punches. That this strategy requires a latent will of rock should be suggested by the fact that most intentional and malicious impositions of unpreventable pain are frightening, often terrifying, to most people, and that the impulse even of a tactically passive torture victim would be to enter into cooperative or resistant interaction with the torturers. As Timerman puts it:

> . . . I always managed to reconstruct the mechanism of withdrawal, and thus was able to avoid lapsing into that other mechanism of

tortured solitary prisoners which leads them to establish a bond
with their jailer or torturer. Both parties seem to feel some need of
the other: for the torturer, it is a sense of omnipotence, without
which he'd find it hard perhaps to exercise his profession—the torturer needs to be needed by the tortured; whereas the man who's tortured finds in his torturer a human voice, a dialogue for his situation, some partial exercise of his human condition—he asks for
pity, to go to the bathroom, for another plate of soup, he asks for
the result of a football game(pp.37-38).

"I was able to avoid all that," he concludes. His ability to
avoid all "that," though, was the result of a larger strategy which
he calls the "mechanism of withdrawal." What this mechanism
involved was the obliteration of memory, of all the persons and
values and associations of normal life that, contrasted with his
prison life, would make the latter unbearable.

It is here perhaps more than anywhere else in the two
books that Timerman and Frankl differ. For Frankl, it is clearly
and triumphantly those very associations of family and wife and
home that help so much to keep him from going under in the
concentration camp, from becoming an object in the pejorative
sense. As he says near the beginning of his narrative, when the
prisoners are being received in transport junctions where being
directed to the left meant a judgement of imminent death, and
to the right work-camp and a lease on life, "Every man was
controlled by one thought only; to keep himself for the family
waiting for him at home, and to save his friends"(p.6). Later, in
one of the most moving passages in the book, Frankl reveals
what's on his mind during one of his long treks to slave-work,
bullied and gun-butted by guards in the brutal cold early
morning darkness: " . . . as we stumbled on for miles, slipping
on icy spots . . . we both knew each of us was thinking of his
wife"(p.58). What would be a truism becomes, under these ar-
duous, miserable circumstances, stirring words: "Then I grasped
the meaning of the greatest secret that human poetry and human thought and belief have to impart. *The salvation of man is
through love and in love.* I understood how a man who has
nothing left in this world still may know bliss, be it only for a
brief moment, in the contemplation of his beloved"(p.59).

This apotheosis is lent poignancy when Frankl soon
informs us that his wife even then had already died in another
concentration camp; yet, even if he had known that she was
dead, he would still have contemplated her image. "This intensi-
fication," Frankl concludes, "of inner life helped the prisoner

find a refuge from the emptiness, desolation, and spiritual poverty of his existence, by letting him escape into the past." The key word here for taking his last sentence properly is "escape." Frankl, as mentioned earlier, makes it emphatically clear that one was not to lose his grip on the present, even if that present were the living nightmare of concentration-camp life. He doesn't advocate escapism, but does propose meditation on experiences, people, and values in one's past that would strengthen one for the present, and even bestow hope in one's future.

That this strategy has its weaknesses Frankl himself concedes. The new prisoner especially felt a longing for home and family so intense that it almost consumed him(p.31). According to Bettelheim, " . . . old prisoners did not like to be reminded of their families and former friends. When they spoke about them, it was in a very detached way . . . they had come to hate all those living outside the camp, who 'enjoyed life as if it were not rotting away' "(p.165). Bettelheim elaborates these points later in *The Informed Heart*: "To avoid so much guilt, frustration and pain [through being removed from family life] one withdrew emotionally from one's family and those aspects of the outer world one was still strongly attached to. But while these emotional ties made life in the camp more painful, the alternative of denying, repressing, and loosening them all robbed the prisoner of what might have been his greatest source of strength"(p.192). In his last sentence, Bettelheim in effect takes a position between Timerman and Frankl. Des Pres, using the evidence of a survivor of a Soviet slave camp, supports Timerman's position (as does Solzhenitsyn in *The Gulag Archipelago*): " 'The experienced Russian camp inmates kept advising us to forget—for our own sakes—our past lives. Otherwise, they maintained, homesickness would soon undermine our resistance' "[10] Des Pres goes on to make a point that concurs with Bettelheim, Frankl, and Timerman's views and experiences: "Those who begin to 'live in the past,' as we say, inevitably lose their hold on the present. They become less attentive, less disciplined, and in the end they die"(p.218). Whether a middle ground between oblivion and remembrance of family and home was a viable ideal or strategy, it was one that many prisoners and inmates fell into, but as Bettelheim, Des Pres, and Frankl all indicate, remembering the past always posed the risk of forgetting the present, making one particularly vulnerable to all the brutal dangers and menaces of camp life that could impinge on one anytime.

The theme of longing for home provides us with a bridge back to Timerman's "mechanism" and position on confronting captivity and torture, for he too is deeply concerned with the problem of memories of the past, of home and family and wife. Timerman's tactic was not to think: "To think meant becoming conscious of what was happening to me, imagining what might be happening to my wife and children; to think meant trying to work out how to relieve this situation, how to wedge an opening in my relationship with the jailers. In that solitary universe of the tortured, any attempt to relate to reality was an immense painful effort leading to nothing"(p.35).

Frankl's approach is the more obviously "humane" one. It is winning in its combination of self-interest and magnanimous memory of others, dear ones, friends, helpless or weak victims. Timerman's position by contrast *seems* a bit heartless, not to mention being very difficult in its asceticism. His effort instead is directed away from the past, from what was going on around him, and from his own present: "I tried to maintain some professional activity, disconnected from the events around me"(p.37). He would think about a book he was working on (presumably before capture), or how to organize a bookstore(p.36). It all seems rather bloodless and cold.[11]

Timerman appears to be even reprehensible in a passage in which he mentions getting a letter and some scented candy from his wife, to whom he has been married for twenty-seven years. His reaction at first seems excessive: "the image of my wife's face is unbearable in this place. How I cursed my wife that day! How many times I told myself I wouldn't read her letter, I wouldn't eat the candies"(p.84). The world of his wife reminds him of the *un*naturalness of his present prison cosmos, " . . . this world I've already accepted and that is real, that corresponds to the inscriptions on the wall, the odor of the latrine matching that emitted by my skin and clothes, and these drab colors, the sounds of metal and violence, the harsh, shrill, hysterical voices. And now this world, so heavily armored, so solid and irreplaceable, without cracks, has been penetrated by a letter and two candies. . . . She says that she'd kiss me a thousand times if she could. But that is what she fails to understand: she cannot. In a rage, I throw the letter into the latrine . . . "(p.85). The "chief enemy," concludes Timerman, "is not the electrical shocks, but penetration from the outside world, with all its memories"(p.85).

Solzhenitsyn, a man even more familiar with the inside of prisons or places of incarceration than Timerman, Frankl, and Bettelheim, concurs with Timerman about the need to wipe out one's past: "From the moment you go to prison you must put your cozy past firmly behind you. At the very threshold, you must say to yourself: 'My life is over. . . . I shall never return to freedom. I am condemned to die. . . . For me those I love have died, and for them I have died' "[12] Solzhenitsyn offers these precepts as a way of resisting being crushed in body and spirit (and one always remembers the genitals of Russian inmates being crushed, according to *Gulag Archipelago*, under Stalinist boots as a touchstone to every precept for prison survival), of standing the pain, when we are shackled to our outrageously ironic human vulnerability to pain, and when people one loves remain alive.   Like Timerman's, Solzhenitsyn's strategy would seem to require Herculean fortitude.   Yet human beings, when put up against the wall of extremity, sometimes reveal extraordinary resiliency or resourcefulness.   Some of these latent selves emerge, which ordinary civilian or civilized existence would not have evoked, and show a capacity for renunciation, defiance, and endurance worthy of Plutarch's "Great Lives."   Class, sex, and age would seem not to have been significant in terms of classifying people who enobled or degraded their selves under outrageous pressure.   Yet it is perhaps the most brutal arithmetic conceivable in human experience to see what is left of the self after, as Solzhenitsyn tells us, one has undergone two or three beatings on one's sciatic nerve with a rubber truncheon (held down, of course, by henchmen) as the pain explodes in one's head and one breaks one's fingernails scratching the floor in agony, or, as Oriana Fallaci recounts in both *Interviews with History* and her novel *A Man*, her former husband, Alexis Panagoulis, tortured by the agents of Greek Premier George Papadoupolis, on one occasion has inserted into his penis a metal knitting needle which is then heated by a cigarette lighter, and, on another, has a very badly cut finger sewn up without anesthetic.[13]

For some, the pain from the shocks, the beatings, the "knitting needles" would be the worst; for others, the anguish of lost love and domestic associations and authority is most unbearable.   Who would have the authority to say which type of pain is worst, which type of pain it is more noble to endure or more ignoble to break under?   If it can be said that pain creates the reality of infinity for the tortured, that it is a shockingly dark or violently bright universe that can seem—or be—temporally or spatially endless, any strategy that brings the "finite" universe of the bearable or the painless back (Freud's definition of pleasure as the absence of pain becomes poignantly relevant) would seem resoundingly justified.   Ursula Le Guin in *The Dispossessed* presents the phrase the "autism of terror," the capacity of terror (including pain and the threat of pain) to restructure reality "fantastically" around the most vulnerable or defensible contours of the self, something most of us might experience only fleetingly during painful or exceptional moments of our otherwise "normal" daily existence.   But terrorizing pain radically and violently questions or reshapes many of the assumptions we carry daily about ourselves, our environment, others, life itself.   What it makes of us is instant "essentialist" philosophers, for we suddenly assess the relation of our strengths and weaknesses to a potentially pointless testing as sharp as a scalpel or as dynamic as an electric wire—indeed, the questioning and the sharp edge or hot wire are all too often one, and our "answers" and our later reflections about our answers, often tell us, as Kingsley Widmer has observed,[14] what terror has subtracted from our essential being, or what our essential being is under extremity. This is perhaps an excessively harsh definition of selfhood, a consideration I will discuss later in the chapter, but it has the effect of wringing from us self-knowledge that we may never have otherwise come upon, and of devising strategies of transcendence of self and the alienated Other (the torturer) that project news bases of being and thinking.

Of the two approaches to enduring captivity, confinement, and/or torture, Frankl's, again, seems the more human and attractive.   But if Timerman's "Program" is regarded as a method of survival, a strategy for retaining some kind of sanity and integrity and independence, then it too, if not entirely attractive, is impressive, even awesome.   One would be hard-pressed to achieve Timerman's "feminine" passive resistance, his subtly resistant non-resistance.   What an overwhelming temptation it must have been, and must be, to cry out for mercy or in outraged fury as a torturer applies—or threatens to apply—an electrode to one's moistened genitals, when, as Timerman says, the pain is either so overwhelming or so "shockingly" sudden that one can't shout or scream, but only moan. (The horror here is compounded at the thought of a gag and its sadistic use: stuffed into the mouth of the victim to silence or choke his/her cries of reaction to the bodily torment within him, this action concentrates or condenses his agony by not even allowing the body and mind the minimal "relief" of venting one's pain and/or terror through screaming, yelling, swearing, or moaning.   One thus faces the possibility of becoming, not Timerman's tactical, life-saving "vegetable," but a squirming, agonized hunk of dehumanized flesh, a denatured object whose condition also (if only symbolically) denatures the tormentors).

Like Timerman, the victim can be "left enclosed in a small cell for forty-eight hours, his eyes blindfolded, his hands tied behind him, hearing no voices, seeing no sign of life, having to perform his bodily functions upon himself"(p.34).

Timerman's situation here brings to mind the sentiments of Alexis Panagoulis in *his* cell: "Tomorrow is not another day when existence has nothing human about it,"[15] and evokes as well a despairing passage from Bettelheim's *The Informed Heart*:   "Nobody had a watch.   It is difficult to imagine what additional hardship it was not to be able to gauge how soon the horror of forced labor would end.   If, driven by foremen or guards, one spent one's limited energy too soon, one might begin to slow down, be 'noticed,' and soon 'finished off' "(p.140). Time for all three men here becomes eternity, either of a claustrophobic nightmare of enclosed space and no variations of day and night, or of the strain of brutal work virtually without end and with the likelihood that if one were to be convinced of the endlessness of the labor, and give up, it would mean a sudden and violent end to both work and life.   It is a cliché of doing time that time is one of the worst menaces, an endlessly wily enemy continually to be coped with, defeat by which could lead to capitulation to captors, madness, or suicide.   It is no wonder that some incarcerated men, like Panagoulis, "made friends" with mice, cockroaches, and spiders.

Under such physical and mental duress, madness suggests itself, as well as suicide.   Indeed, Timerman admits to having considered suicide often.   At times it even seems to him like a delicious fruit(p.88).   Hands tied, eyes blindfolded, Timerman found suicide to be a temptation.   But even this time-filling, contemplative delight, which is one way of soothing the self's continual abasement by one's captors, is abandoned (at least, by

Timerman), "for it becomes too obvious a subterfuge . . . you realize that you're not going to commit suicide and once again comes the feeling of defeat"(p.91). Thus the victory of holding out against the torturers, of telling nothing, of putting up with the prison microcosm of cockroaches, dried vomit on clothing, and the stench of shit and rotting inedible meat, is punctured, according to Timerman, by the humiliation one feels in knowing he won't—or can't—commit suicide.

Bettelheim describes the objective or external conditions present in a concentration camp that could lead to suicide: " . . . it was the senseless tasks, the lack of almost any time to oneself, the inability to plan ahead because of sudden changes in camp policies, that was so deeply destructive. By destroying man's ability to act on his own or to predict the outcome of his actions, they destroyed the feeling that his actions had any purpose, so many prisoners stopped acting. But when they stopped acting they soon stopped living"(p.148). Thus, the camps encouraged suicidal feelings by deliberately making life shapeless or meaningless. Yet, to make matters worse, the SS wanted to control suicide: "The stated principle was: the more prisoners to commit suicide, the better. But even there, the decision must not be by the prisoners"(p.150), thus depriving the prisoner of his or her last gesture of self-determination.

Camp prisoners might also have wanted to kill themselves (or allow themselves to go insane), because, Des Pres informs us in an overwhelming chapter from *The Survivor* called "The Excremental Assault," they were in continual danger of "virtually drowning in their own waste"(p.64): "Everybody in the block had typhus . . . it came to Belson Bergen in its most violent, most painful, deadliest form. The diarrhea caused by it became uncontrollable. It flooded the bottom of the cages, dripping through the cracks into the faces of the women lying in the cages below, and mixed with blood, pus and urine, formed a slimy, fetid mud on the floor of the barracks(Perl,171)"(p.58). The point of all this "excremental assault" was to " 'destroy our human dignity,' "(p.69), which in turn would make inmates either more tractable or more prone to suicide.

In such cloacal circumstances, human beings come to realize how close the body is to the self or the soul: " . . . when conditions of filth are enforced, befoulment of the body is experienced as befoulment of the soul"(p.71). With befoulment of the soul comes the greatest menace to a human being's integri-

ty and self-acceptance.   Yet, despite being covered with shit,
prevented by guards from relieving themselves, forced to ignore
the wanton and brutal beating, humiliation, or even killing of
other prisoners for minor "offenses," some prisoners managed
to keep an inner core of themselves alive and intact.   Whether
this urge to survive was due to altruism, to a deep sense of
autonomy, or to a goal to live for is less easy to confirm than that
this bone-deep will not only to live but to live right betokens the
glowing, inner existence of a self.

Translated to Frankl's world of values, Timerman's
achievements would perhaps have seemed or felt more
substantial to him, for they would make his immense suffering
more meaningful.   Frankl presents an "existentialist" context for
much suffering:

> When a man finds that it is his destiny to suffer, he will have to
> accept his suffering as his task; his single and unique task.   He will
> have to acknowledge the fact that even in suffering he is unique
> and alone in the universe.   No one can relieve him of his suffering or
> suffer in his place.   His unique opportunity lies in the way in which
> he bears his burden.
>
> For us, as prisoners, these thoughts were not speculations far re-
> moved from reality.   They were the only thoughts that could be of
> help to us.   They kept us from despair.(pp.123-24)

Perhaps this outlook would have given Timerman
comfort and solace.   It appears not to have done so, though it
apparently lightened Frankl's burden and misery.   But Frankl's
tragic humanism here might not have appealed to Timerman
for a major reason that I will soon explore.   It is easy enough to
say that in accepting one's suffering one defines his individual
meaning or worth, but when captors are kicking one in the back
(or in the genitals, a camp-introduction ritual, according to
Bettelheim), cutting one's body (as one is tied down) with a
sharp implement, half-drowning one in a stream or a bathtub,
such lofty philosophic notions are not readily remembered, and
it is only Frankl's own credentials as a concentration-camp
victim that justify his uttering them.

V

But the thought, the image, lingers of the sheer ravaging

dehumanization of the self in the extremity of confinement or torture (and in a profound sense, confinement and torture are one and the same). In addition, what happens to the self in the psychic extremity of the vagueness of Timerman's captivity? Like Kafka's Joseph K., Timerman was never told why he was arrested; no official accusation was made against him. Neither was he apprehended for being a journalist—or a Jew(pp.71-72).

The Jewish or anti-semitism theme in *Prisoner* is the main reason why this book seems to have a darker cast over its narrative than *Search* does. Frankl does not minimize post-captivity let-down, or the problem of new freedom for men brutally pent up for years. When they do get free, they are numb to its meaning: "its reality did not penetrate into our conscious-ness . . . "(p.139). Returning home sometimes proved to be disap-pointing or disillusioning. One is not greeted warmly, some have (like Frankl) lost members of their family, and bitterness results: "A man who for years had thought he had reached the absolute limit of all possible suffering now found that suffering has no limits, and that he could suffer still more   . . . "(p.146).

This is one of those balancing negativities in Frankl's carefully weighted narrative strategy of affirmations and nega-tions that endows his book with powerful psychological realism and moral wisdom.   Yet even this strong anti-climactic disillusion is subsumed under the curiously forceful realization about one's life's possibility as a humanly creative challenge. Men in the camp who showed a suicidal bent, who felt that life had no more to offer them, were talked back into accepting life on a simple yet profound shift of "terms": " . . . it was a question of getting them to realize that life was still expecting something from them"(p.126).   One man was reminded that he had an adored child waiting for him in another country; another, that he had a series of books to finish that only he could finish.

Timerman does not seem to offer these richly positive life-supporting propositions.   The main affirmation in *Prisoner* is embodied in his own personal heroism in his endurance of torture and terror by agents of the harshly repressive Argentine junta, as well as in the heroic practising of civil rights as an intrepid libertarian journalist and editor (which activity drew sinister attention to him in the first place). But there is a despair and anger and shock within *Prisoner* that is attributable to sev-eral important factors.   One of them is the recrudescence of a virulent anti-semitism in the last quarter or so of the 20th century, *after* the Nazi German experience of the Second World War. The other is the complicity in silence that Timerman accuses the Argentine Jewish community of. He conveys some of the complacent historical presuppositions and sinister implications of this alleged silence in a major passage of the book:

> What is frightening is to realize how content we feel because we suppose there are deeds that cannot be repeated. It is true that six million European Jews cannot be murdered; tortured and murdered. But if, only thirty-five years after this did happen, the Jew can be considered the enemy, tortured and killed for being that enemy, then he has kept his place in history, his historic condition persists. And his helplessness to change his relationship with history persists, as does the world's inability to help him or understand him.
>
> We were not all Jews in those hidden prisons. Many of us were. We Jews continued to be Jews, and being Jewish was a category of guilt... (p.135).

If being Jewish is a category of guilt, then one's Jewishness can be automatically objectified whether one likes it or not. As a result, even a strong (perhaps also arrogant) soul like Timerman's could, like Jews under the Nazi regime, feel self-hatred at times, "convinced by the Nazis that they were objects of hatred because they were intrinsically hateful objects"(p.126). This tendency would amount to viewing or even feeling oneself to be the most odious, horrible image conceivable and projected by another human being. Like Ralph Ellison's Invisible Man, the Jew in this context of self-odium is not an individual with nuances of being and personality and character all his or her own. Rather, he is a despised object, Kafka's odious humanoid-insect bereft of his precious individual humanity by a horrible league of conspiratorial hatred and self-hatred. The individual self is lost—and destroyed—in the projected and debasing stereotype.

The anti-semitism motif first bursts on the scene with violence during one of the many torture episodes that Timerman underwent:

> . . . they sit me down, clothed, and tie my arms behind me. The application of electric shocks begins, penetrating my clothing to the skin. It's extremely painful, but not as bad as when I'm laid down, naked, and doused with water. The sensation of the shocks on my head makes me jump in my seat and moan.

> No questions are asked. Merely a barrage of insults, which increase in intensity as the minutes pass. Suddenly, a hysterical voice begins shouting a single word: 'Jew . . . Jew . . . Jew!' The others join in and form a chorus while clapping their hands . . . (pp.60-61).

Timerman is bouncing in the air from the inevitable bodily reaction to the electric shocks, which are combined in amused laughter with his torturers calling him a "clipped prick" in the vicious anti-Semitic synecdoche. In one of the most heartbreaking passages of his book, Timerman says, so simply and so devastatingly, this: "in the solitude of prison, it is so sad to be beaten for being Jewish. There is such despair when they torture you for being Jewish. It seems so humiliating to have been born"(p.135). Coming from this brave and strong man, this is a lament to stir all but the heartless or totally ideologized into deep empathy with Timerman the Jew.

Part of the trouble of course is exactly that—the heartlessness of power-seeking, paranoiac ideologues. According to *Prisoner*, powerful military extremists in Argentina think that they are already fighting World War Three, that they represent a vanguard against what they regard as the Communist and Jewish World Conspiracy. If the disparity of power between the Jews and world Communism strikes one forcibly as an argument *against* the existence of a Jewish power center threatening to, say, right-wing Latin American regimes, Hannah Arendt provides an illuminating point: " . . . it must be possible to face and understand the outrageous fact that so small (and, in world politics, so unimportant) a phenomenon as the Jewish Question and antisemitism could become the catalytic agent for, first, the Nazi movement, then a world war, and finally the establishment of death camps."[16]

A sinister implication of both the Arendt and Timerman passages on anti-Semitism is that if anti-Semitism could still whip a regime, during the 1970's, *after* the Holocaust, into a frenzy of paranoid accusations and viciousness, this frenzy signals something so lethal and unrelenting in man's need to find "objects" for his hatred as to suggest both that his hatred, however irrational and unjustified, is virtually bottomless, and that it may indeed perpetuate itself until the human universe is destroyed. And when the hatred of the Jew is both linked to the deadly paranoia of an assumed World War Three, it makes the existence of the hatred in one passage in *Prisoner* seem tantamount to a will to press the Nuclear button:

> . . . hatred of the Jew was visceral, explosive, a supernatural bolt, a
> gut excitement, the sense of one's entire being abandoned to hatred.
> Such hatred was a deeper expression than the mere aversion
> aroused by an enemy, for it expressed, in addition, the need for
> a hated object and the simultaneous fear of that object—the almost
> magical inevitability of hatred. One could hate a political pris-
> oner for belonging to the opposite camp, but one could also try to
> convince him . . . make him understand his error, switch sides. . . .
> But how can a Jew be changed? That is hatred: eternal, intermin-
> able, perfect, inevitable.(p.66)

Essential questions thus arise: how can a human being be
changed or humanized who feels such hatred? How can a savage anti-semite or racist be made to see this "Object" of odium
(and fear) as a brother or sister, as the mystical Other? *Is* there,
for the persecuted Jew (or minority), an Other? In one of the
most moving stretches of *Prisoner*, Timerman examines the
idea of whether there is an Other for the contemporary Jew:

> In this world of tribunals and of the accused, I search fervently
> for the relief that should be forthcoming from the Other, if truly
> we belong to that vast little group of victims. But once again I find
> only consolation, not identity. I find the consolation of solidarity,
> but not that of inevitability, for though we share the same aspir-
> ations, his guilt is not inevitable, and he will always be lacking
> the guilt needed to reach me. And if he is unable to reach me, it
> means that I am united with him, but not he with me. Not in the
> fullness of my guilt, which I possess in its totality, but which he
> possesses only in part.
> There will always be a place where I'm alone, totally alone be-
> fore my judges, who are also his judges, and before whom I appear
> in his company, but suddenly abandoned by him in that singular,
> inevitable, incomparable, dark, and superb solitude that always
> begins with the same ritual: "Are you a Jew?"(p.112)

One of course can respond to this passage by saying that
there are other Jews. But Timerman's point is ontological, and
profound: that any indictment based on the charge (however
spurious and vicious) that one is *genetically* evil, *born* "wrong,"
is bound to be overwhelmingly isolative, harrowingly guilt-
making.[17] Any racism is an attempt to transform human nature
or the self from its innate and complex combination of process,
flexibility, and permanence to a hypostatization that makes one
eternally, unchangingly greedy, dirty, lustful, lazy, all the evil or

base qualities that racists thrust upon their dark opposites in order to make their own insufficiencies and evil more sufferable. Timerman's vision of "inevitable" guilt (for it is visionary in its intensity), if it evokes Kafka's metaphysics of mystical indictment, also evokes Arendt's thesis: that racism can be seen as part of a large mechanism of ideology and objectification whereby totalitarian *and* authoritarian regimes attempt to transmute human nature itself, and thus invalidate individualism. Such an enterprise represents a fundamental assault on the self, *and on every self.*

Authoritarian political terrorization can in effect make David Hume's hypothesis of the fictitiousness of the self "valid," by so shattering the mind or "soul" that it not only violates the fundamental logic of addition and betrays the most cherished value (the Other), but does so in full willingness. These extreme developments describe the last one-fifth of Orwell's *1984.* Thus it is worth examining this political Gothic novel, for, as probably the most violent onslaught in 20th-century political fiction on the integrity and even on the existence of the self, *1984* could possibly be used to test the values of endurance and suffering in *Prisoner* and *Search,* as it in turn can be tested by the values of Timerman's and Frankl's books.

VI

1984 is dystopic satire, and as such makes use of exaggeration in all propriety. Yet it also places such stress on naturalistic detail as to suggest that its treatment of reality in key areas of theme and character is to be taken literally. Among its primary material is the subject and test of torture, and its effects of pain, terror, resistance, and collapse. The final part of the novel, Section three, is in the main devoted to seeing whether the Party can "get inside" a victim or enemy. Winston Smith and his lover Julia claim earlier that it cannot. Section three shows with brutal emphasis and ostensible finality that it can. In the process of showing how utterly the Party can violate and degrade someone, a lot of violent narrative material is marshalled to make a convincing case for the capacity of pain and terror to transform human nature.

It begins with the major reversal in the novel, the capture

of Julia and Winston as lovers by O'Brien and his henchmen in the antique shop where the lovers have been meeting secretly against Party regulations. Both are forced to stand at attention, utterly vulnerable to brutes. Julia is viciously punched in the stomach. Later, in a dungeon, Winston knows that he is going to get savagely struck, but does not know when or where. Then he knows:

> The elbow! He had slumped to his knees, almost paralyzed, clasping the stricken elbow with his other hand. Everything had exploded into yellow light. Inconceivable that one blow could cause such pain! The light cleared and he could see the other two looking down at him. The guard was laughing at his contortions. One question at any rate was answered. Never, for any reason on earth, could you wish for an increase of pain. Of pain you could wish only one thing: that it should stop. Nothing in the world was so bad as physical pain. In the face of pain there are no heroes, no heroes, he thought over and over as he writhed on the floor, clutching uselessly at his disabled left arm.[18]

This first encounter with terrible pain is only a taste of what is to follow. And the realization, suffering such pain, that one could never want more pain in order, generously, to decrease someone else's pain, is an omen of the nihilistic climax in which the lovers are agonizingly wrenched into making admissions that totally destroy their love and their self-respect.

Taken into custody, Winston is mercilessly beaten in order to extract a confession of disloyalty to and betrayal of the Party:

> How many times he had been beaten, how long the beatings had continued, he could not remember. Always there were five or six in black uniforms at him simultaneously. Sometimes it was fists, sometimes it was truncheons, sometimes it was steel rods, sometimes it was boots. There were times when he rolled about the floor, as shameless as an animal, writhing his body this way and that in an endless, hopeless effort to dodge the kicks, and simply inviting more and yet more kicks, in his ribs, in his belly, on his elbows, on his shins, in his groin, in his testicles, on the bone at the base of his spine. There were times when it went on and on until the cruel, wicked, unforgivable thing seemed to him not that the guards continued to beat him but that he could not force himself into losing consciousness(p.198).

One suspects that most people would collapse under such treatment, would sign anything or sign anyone away just to stop the pain and horror of such unrelenting violence against the body and mind. Yet it should be asked whether exposure to absolute brutality is a fair test of the self or of its integrity. Orwell's point, it would at first appear, is that in a totalitarian society, the individual hasn't got a chance. The massive power of the State would annihilate any individual bravery or resistance, ultimately, every sense of self or self-worth.

Needless to say, this sort of treatment of people has occurred already, not only in totalitarian or authoritarian societies (Timerman's Argentina), but in the basements of police stations in "open" societies. What, however, could keep these physically-abused persons from total hopelessness, one conjectures, is the fact that outside of that police station there are free individuals whose freedom means the right to protest and fight such institutional dehumanization. And in our age the existence of relatively free societies along with authoritarian ones means the freedom and power of persons or groups in *some* areas of the world to put pressure on the repressive regimes to stop institutional cruelty and the gross abuse of civil rights. Orwell, however, posits a world in which freedom or libertarian authority no longer exists. Such is the gloom and doom of his futuristic polity, and such too is his interpretation of totalitarian reality. It is a reality in which total, unendurable pain can be imposed on one individual by another, in which an individual can be not only destroyed but liquidated, and even vaporized. As O'Brien tells Winston, in the process of trying to break his will, " 'You must stop imagining that posterity will vindicate you, Winston. Posterity will never hear of you. You will be lifted clean out from the stream of history. We shall turn you into gas and pour you into the stratosphere. Nothing will remain of you . . . "(p.210).

On one occasion, Winston, showing he still has some spunk in him, challenges O'Brien: " 'Somehow you will fail. Something will defeat you. Life will defeat you.' 'We control life, Winston,' " states O'Brien, " 'at all its levels. You are imagining that there is something called human nature which will be outraged by what we do and will turn against us. But we create human nature. Men are infinitely malleable' "(p.222).

O'Brien here speaks with the insolent omniscience of at least two modern traditions, Marxist political ideology and modern science, or, at least, a popular conception of scientific authority. O'Brien or Orwell did not know of recent ideas of

genetic engineering, but if he had, this extremely potent knowledge could well have been harnassed in *1984* for ends of
political and biological determination and control unparallelled
in civilization.   An infinitely malleable human nature would
mean the destruction of the self, the very stuff of individuality
and individuation.   Yet one can suggest that if, as O'Brien contests, human beings are infinitely malleable, they are also amaz-
ingly resourceful and flexible.   Indeed, as Frankl says near the
end of *Search*, "every human being has the freedom to change at
any instant.   Therefore, we can predict his future only within the
large frame of a statistical survey referring to a whole group; the
individual personality, however, remains essentially unpredictable.   The basis for any predictions would be represented by
biological, psychological, or sociological conditions.   Yet one of
the main features of human existence is the capacity to rise
above such conditions and transcend them"(p.207).[19]   O'Brien's
virtual answer to this exciting libertarian contention is that it
takes at least a spark of rebellion or an inch of autonomy to
generate such self-assertion and liberty, and that the Party (or a
totalitarian society) can destroy such stimuli.   This ultimately
assumes complete power and domination, global conquest, as
the hysterical enemies of Communism and Capitalism warn,
and that fate is neither here yet nor inevitable (though even
global conquest is preferable to a more likely fate that would end
incarceration and torture forever through global nuclear annihilation).

O'Brien uses the tortured Winston as a negative image of
the "spirit" of man that, Winston asserts, would fight a totalitarian state. O'Brien shows Winston what he looks like in a mirror, the miserable result of a process of breaking him down. But
this is obviously unfair, for the human spirit is not fully registered by human beings only at their worst, but also at their best
(although the best in some emerges precisely under the
definitive pressure of extremity).   And even O'Brien admits a
little later that Winston is a " 'difficult case. . . .   In the end we
shall shoot you' "(p.226).   But they won't shoot Winston until
they break him completely, until, that is, he betrays Julia utterly
by his willingness to substitute her for torture he finds
unbearable.

Parts of Jean-Paul Sartre's *Being and Nothingness* seem
almost like a gloss on Section Three of *1984* in Sartre's meditations on the interrelations of torturer (sadist) and tortured, for

freedom is at stake here too: " . . . the sadist does not seek to suppress the freedom of the one whom he tortures but to force this freedom freely to identify itself with the tortured flesh."[20]

O'Brien wants Winston to fully and "freely" accept the proposition that two and two are five if the Party says so. This state of mind Sartre calls abjuration: "In fact no matter what pressure is exerted on the victim, the abjuration remains *free*; it is a spontaneous production, a response to a situation; it manifests human reality. No matter what resistance the victim has offered, no matter how long he has waited before begging for mercy, he would have been able despite all to wait ten minutes, one minute, one second longer. He has *determined* the moment at which the pain became unbearable"(p.523).

As Sartre suggests, though the tortured person is obviously in bondage, he also retains the basic freedom of choosing how long to endure the pain (which of course is one reason why some torture victims long to pass out, and why perhaps their deepest anguish concerns how much pain they and their bodies can endure without losing consciousness or sanity). This is not the kind of freedom most people want to exercise or have tested, but, as Des Pres observes, "The first condition of extremity is that there is no escape, no place to go except the grave"(p.61). To make matters worse, "The sadist," claims Sartre, "posits himself as 'having all the time in the world ' [Like O'Brien]. He is calm, he does not hurry. He uses his [torture] instruments like a technician"(p.523). Here again we see time threatening to become eternity for the victim, which is the worst of all times for the thought to strike one, as it does the hero in Bernard Malamud's *The Fixer* that "whenever he had been through the worst, there was always worse"(p.12). Such a thought is perilous because it can lead to Sartre's "abjuration," the verbal act or sign of self-defeat that could signal the onset of self-dissolution. Sartre describes this abjuration in terms of the victim's freedom bending or breaking under the leisurely will of the "technician": "The spectacle which is offered to the sadist is that of a freedom which struggles against the expanding of the flesh and which finally freely chooses to be submerged in the flesh. . . . In the abjuration a freedom chooses to be wholly identified with this body; this distorted and heaving body is the very image of a broken and enslaved freedom"(p.524).

It is recognized that abjuration can lead to a point of no return, one in which the soul is so contracted or violated by intentional torment that life no longer feels worth living, one's life no longer feels natural or "right."   Against this nihilistic state, Sartre poses the idea that the very "world" of torture and sadism and implements of pain posit the absolute freedom of the Other, indeed that this freedom makes the existence of the world of torture possible(p.526). This may be so, yet it strikes me as a philosophic generalization of dubious merit at least to the victim being tortured. Sartre's concept of freedom here would not likely comfort Winston when O'Brien tells him, in a typical torturer's ploy, that the victim's deepest fear and phobia is known and is to be "implemented" against him (or her).

Winston's deepest fear is rats, and his final ordeal is to have his head affixed to a metal cage containing large, very hungry rats that, when a door is released, would plunge right into Winston's face, eating through it.   Winston, fighting off panic, controls himself enough to realize that there is one safe way out: "he had suddenly understood that in the whole world there was just one person to whom he could transfer his punishment—one body that he could thrust between himself and the rats"(p.236).

In an ugly scene near the end of the novel, Julia and Winston admit to each other that they had both wished the torture they could not bear on the other. Julia had earlier said that the Party can't get inside of you. But the recessed narrator of *1984*, some aspect of Orwell, insists that they *could* get inside of you: "There were things, your own acts, from which you could not recover. Something was killed in your breast . . . "(p.234).

VII

1984 ends with Winston loving Big Brother, his will utterly broken.[21] This abject condition represents "Orwell's" image of rebellious, libertarian humanity pulverized by the grinding, merciless power of the Party and the State. Yet that is not the final word on the matter. First, O'Brien himself admits that the panic one experiences on confronting his most feared torture does not involve courage or cowardice. He says that the reaction here to self-preservation is instinctual, comparable to lunging for a rope when falling from a height or to breathing for air after being immersed in water too long(p.234). Most human beings might have their price or limit of endurance (some don't), but one can question whether the power of absolute brutalization properly judges an individual's deepest being. Winston may scream, " 'Do it to her!' ", but it is likely that he would have submitted, as more than a few persons would, to a variety of *other* torments without betraying his Julia.

In completely destroying virtue, totalitarian force shows less the fragility or finally the non-existence of self or soul, than it does the triumph of absolute evil combined with absolute power, and in *that* extreme sense shows the only, cynical way in which O'Brienism's Might Makes Right has meaning. Further, if Lord Acton's apothegm about power is correct, then the more totalitarianism consolidates all the power, the more it corrupts itself to a point of possible or even crucial weakness that offers the conditions for an overt emergence of self in the form of potentially key rebellions or resistances. The pessimism of *1984*, which verges on nihilism, seems all the more relevant today as both large and small nation-states consolidate political, economic, and military power at the expense of their constituent peoples. Yet Winston's fight against Big Brother is itself meaningful, and Orwell's sense of reserves of power within the Proles, the lower classes, is not to be discounted entirely.[22] But there is something else, too, a lingering, almost subliminal, symbolic action in Section Two of *1984* that deserves high-lighting. A newsweek film early in the novel depicts a war scene at sea. A number of people are helplessly adrift in a lifeboat, an enemy helicopter hovering right over them. Horrible destruction is imminent, as the copter will soon drop a bomb on the small boat. A refugee woman, a mother, tries to protect her child from the oncoming massacre by covering her boy with her arms, ineffectual as her gesture will be(p.11). This poignant image of selfless love sticks in Winston's mind when, later, he contemplates the "outmoded" values of the narrative past, in the late Forties, even after a Second World War. Winston remembers about this "past" era, before Party values had officially repudiated personal feelings, impulses, and values, that "What mattered were individual relationships, and a completely helpless gesture, an embrace, a tear, a word spoken to a dying man, could have value in itself"(p.136).

This image of the poignantly protective mother and Winston's humane reflections do not, to be sure, constitute the primary meaning of *1984*, but they are important, because they represent implicit Orwellian values in harmony with certain values of Frankl and Timerman. All three writers indicate, if in different ways and in Orwell most faintly, that resistance to despotism is a valuable human activity. Frankl and Timerman equate endurance with survival and thus with life itself. Endurance becomes both a mode of and an argument for the viability of the self, though it is manifested differently in each man. Endurance for Frankl acquires meaning through the humanizing assimilation of suffering, and thus in a sense requires suffering. Endurance for Timerman does not "invite" suffering in Frankl's mode, but through a psychology of passivity works *with* the force and edge of the captors' violence so as to lessen its force and dull its edge and terror while conceding to the torturers nothing from within. Orwell appears to be indicating in *1984* that endurance cannot withstand *sufficient* suffering, that the brave or resistant self, if up against complete, technologically sophisticated, force, cannot persist. Further, *1984* appears to show conclusively that along with the unendurability of suffering goes the integrity and the validity of the self.

But this nihilistic transformation of endurance and suffering in *1984* overlooks the novel's status as satire, which by its generic nature allows for such disproportions of power and vulnerability. Indeed, what is amazing, and latently affirming, is that, as Lillian Feder has suggested, Winston survives as long as he does against such odds.[23] There is a profound sense in which Winston (with whom Orwell partly identifies) incarnates the heroicism of Frankl and Timerman in his resistant, libertarian individuality. Most probably, Frankl and Timerman too would have been broken in *1984*'s Room 101, but, as I have already contended, Room 101 is not a fair test of one's individuality. It is not a valid test of the endurance of the self. It is instead a raw, brutal, absolute manifestation of power by the state exercised by people with less real individuality and self than their victims. In *Prisoner* and *Search*, the author-protagonist and thus the self triumph; in *1984*, the self does not survive, but does fight so hard for realization and a culture of liberty that its struggles almost amount to a moral victory, the odds being so overwhelmingly what they are. *1984* is fiction, Juvenalian satire. The words of a historical person who endured an extended period of torture comparable to Winston Smith's, are inspiriting here: "The secret," says the unbreakable Panagoulis, "is not to resign yourself, never to feel yourself a victim, never to behave like a victim—not even when I was wasting away with hunger strikes."24   That is an ideal very hard to achieve, yet some individuals have achieved it, and even approximations of it can be excitingly life- and self-affirming.   One cheapens the idealism of endurance and survival, though, if one overlooks all those who became victimized, who were broken by unrestricted pain or pressure, all those among whom but for luck or circumstance one could include oneself.

VIII

What makes the self so strong, at least to Frankl, is not focusing on self or self-achievement. Frankl, in a powerful passage, rejects the popular psychologistic ideal of self-actualization:

> Human existence is essentially self-transcendence rather than self-actualization. Self-actualization is not a possible aim at all, for the simple reason that the more a man would strive for it, the more he would miss it. For only to the extent to which man commits himself to the fulfillment of his life's meaning, to this extent he also actualizes himself. In other words, self-actualization cannot be attained if it is made an end in itself, but only as a side effect of self-transcendence.
>
> The world must not be regarded as a mere expression of one's self.(p.175)

These ideas lead to Frankl's feeling that one owes *life* something, and thus suggest that self-fulfillment can primarily or desirably come through relating to others, an outlook reminiscent of Martin Buber's metaphysics of meeting and dialogue. One makes value through and with and for other human beings. This is of course not the same idea as the total suppression of one's self or being for a collectivistic ideal or group—a self-sacrifice for the Party.   But even the most seemingly self-involved activity, if it is genuinely creative, has a dimension of social value: it intimates life's richness or beauty or significance for at least one other human being, perhaps several, even many. Is this not a portion of the major paradox latent in so desperately hopeless a fictional projection of future25 society as *1984*, that we can benefit by Orwell's Juvenalian prophecy, make value by what we do in the present to prevent the closed worlds of "1984" from occurring?
But the problem today in our own 1980's is as grim as it is

in Orwell's 1984—and, militarily, even more pernicious.   Hannah Arendt's grave words, also written in the late 1940's, seem more applicable today than they did then:

> The total attempt to make men superfluous reflects the experience of modern masses of their superfluity on an overcrowded earth. The world of the dying, in which men are taught they are superfluous through a way of life in which punishment is meted out without connection with crime, in which exploitation is practised without profit, and where work is performed without produce, is a place where senselessness is daily produced anew.(p.431)

Arendt is writing about totalitarian countries, but with some adjustments, the senselessness, greed, and exploitation she describes can be applied to less repressed nations too, including the United States of the early 1980s. Against the appalling crises of the possible nuclear extinction of humanity and the earth, over-population and mass-starvation, destruction of resources, pollution, maldistribution of wealth in the contemporary world, world-wide racial, religious, and nationalist enmities, and a politically dangerous high technology, one still witnesses people like Frankl and Timerman, who can embody the reality, vitality, and integrity of the self. They vividly remind us of the humanizing potential for all individuals of the self's resiliency and endurance. This potential is found in a deep concern for others, for the self of others, and thus for the self and for one's self, and is evident in the arousing and poignant humanity in the ending of *Prisoner*:

> Have any of you ever looked into the eyes of another person, on the floor of a cell, who knows that he's about to die though no one has told him so? He . . . clings to his biological desire to live, as a single hope, since no one has told him that he's to be executed.
>
> I have many such gazes imprinted upon me. Each time I write or utter words of hope, words of confidence in the definitive triumph of man, I'm fearful of losing sight of one of those gazes. At night I recount them, recall them, re-see them, illumine them.
>
> Those gazes, which I encountered in the clandestine prisons of Argentina and which I've retained one by one, were the culminating point, the purest moment of my tragedy.
>
> They are here with me today. And although I might wish to do so, I could not and would not know how to share them with you.(p.164)

Notes

[1]Terrence Des Pres, *The Survivor. An Anatomy of Life in the Death Camp* (New York: Pocket Books, 1977). All further references to this text are to this edition.

[2]Jacobo Timerman, *Prisoner Without a Name, Cell Without a Number* (New York: Random House, C1981), 19. All further references to this text are to this edition.

[3]It should be pointed out that Timerman has been a controversial figure in recent years, particularly with the publication of *Prisoner*. The controversy can be subdivided into two aspects: 1- the Jewish question, and 2- the political question. The first issue I will only mention, as it is not central to my concern in this paper. Timerman's charges in *Prisoner* that the Argentine Jewish community has been silent about Argentine anti-semitism has met with some disapproval and disagreement, particularly among Argentine Jews. Part of the controversy centers on how serious anti-semitism in that country is and what it means: is it an omen of another Holocaust, or is it a transient event? The political question relates to the issue of Timerman's own integrity, and can conveniently be divided into liberal and conservative sides. The conservative position is implied in the following opinion from Mark Falcoff: "Jacobo Timerman was not kidnapped because he was a Jew, or probably even because he was protesting the conduct of Argentina's security force, but because his business partner was discovered to have intimate relations with one of the most important left-wing guerilla organizations in the country. Although innocent, Timerman . . . " ("The Timerman Case," *Commentary*, v. 72 (July, 1981), 22. Falcoff thus admits that Timerman was innocent of his partner's alleged complicity with left-wingers, and the semantic weight of "probably" in his diminution of Timerman's nobility should not be underestimated. In a later discussion of Timerman in the same journal, Benno Weiser Varon claims that "the doctoring of the [David] Graiver [Timerman's business partner] factor undermines Timerman's credibility. He who can omit facts may be tempted to add facts" (*Commentary*, v. 72, Dec., 1981), 15). Falcoff adds that "Timerman's newspaper *La Opinion* was Peronist, and it favored a military coup in 1976 (though this stand was not necessarily inspired by dishonorable motives—yet Timerman is *not* the American conception of a liberal—he *couldn't* have been, to make *La Opinión* a success in Argentina"(Op. cit., 18). The liberal outlook perceives a different Timerman. According to Robert Weisbrot, "the case against Graiver himself was based largely on the replies of a captured guerilla who was questioned under torture by security agents. These charges still await proof" ("Siege of the Argentine Jews," *New Republic* (June 27, 1981), 17. Aryeh Neier, in turn, states that "the Argentina Junta never brought any charges against Timerman involving Graiver . . . [thus] while it is possible to speculate as to the reasons Timerman was . . . kidnapped . . . , it seems likeliest that it was because his newspaper was critical of the Junta" ("Crimes of Silence Revisited," *The Nation*, v. 232 (Aug. 8-15, 1981), 116). Although hardly non-partisan on this issue, Falcoff makes a point that deserves to be mentioned in any assessment of the total meaning or motivation of Timerman's conduct either in captivity or when free: " . . . few political prisoners in Argentina or elsewhere have been so fortunate in the range and importance of the friends who have rushed to their defense, and few of those friends have been as suc-

cessful elsewhere" (Op. cit., 18). While a virtually unknown political prisoner is obviously in a more desperate situation than someone with Timerman's connections, the fact remains that Timerman endured thirty months of incarceration. Furthermore, the conservative writers seem to ignore the fact the Timerman attacks *left* as well as right-wing Argentine terrorism in *Prisoner*; they also blame the left for virtually everything that has gone wrong or reactionary in Argentina. In sum, the following generalizations about Timerman seems as fair or just as the present available evidence permits: Timerman was and is an influential and powerful man who *might* have one dubious business associate (or *had* one, as Graiver died mysteriously in a plane crash over Mexico a few years back), might not be a liberal of the American type, might or might not have assessed Argentine anti-semitism and Jewish response accurately, but definitely and openly did criticize political despotism and paid dearly for it.

[4]Viktor E. Frankl, *Man's Search for Meaning: An Introduction to Logotherapy* (New York: Pocket Books, [c]1959), 104. All further references to this text are to this edition.

[5]Not *all* people, of course. John Howard Griffin, in his book *Black Like Me*, the 1959 account of a White man passing for a Black in the deep South, describes a situation on a Greyhound-bus ride in Mississippi that should give pause about how readily one can take the satisfaction of bodily needs for granted in the United States:

> The driver turned back to me. 'Where do you think you're go-ing?' he asked, his heavy cheeks quivering with each word.

> 'I'd like to go to the rest room.' I smiled and moved to step down

> He tightened his grip on the door facings and shouldered in close to block me. 'Does your ticket say for you to get off here?', he asked.

> 'No sir, but the others'——

> 'Then you get your ass back in your seat and don't you move till we get to Hattiesburg,' he commanded.

> 'You mean I can't go to the'——

> 'I mean get your ass back there like I told you,' he said, his voice rising. (New York: NAL, 1962), 61.

[6]It seems fair to assume that the editor and co-owner of a major Latin-American newspaper is well off (if not wealthy).

[7]Hannah Arendt, *The Origins of Totalitarianism* (New York: Harcourt, Brace, [c]1951), 432-33.

[8]Bruno Bettleheim, "On Dachau and Buchenwald," quoted in Arendt's *The Origins of Totalitarianism*, 414-15[n].

[9]Bruno Bettelheim, *The Informed Heart: Autonomy in a Mass Age* (New York: Avon Books, [c]1960), 157. All further references to this text are to

this edition.

[10]Des Pres, Op. cit., 217-18.

[11]One should remember that Timerman's "last" thought before his fake execution on the day of his abduction is an expression of love to his family.

[12]Aleksandr I. Solzhenitsyn, *The Gulag Archipelago, 1918-1956: An Experiment in Literary Investigation, 1-11* (New York: Harper & Row, c1973), 217-18.

[13]Oriana Fallaci, *A Man* (New York: Pocket Books, 1980), 43.

[14]In a letter of March 12, 1984 to the author, Widmer's exact words were the following: "The knowledge of incarceration, and all the related arbitrary humiliation, becomes a touchstone of what freedom for the self really is, the fundamental nature of self definition against its loss. ..."

[15]Fallaci, *A Man*, Op, cit., 81.

[16]Arendt, Op. cit., viii.

[17]In one sense, any sympathetic or empathetic person is a Jew when antisemitism exists; yet few non-Jews are sufficiently empathetic to be "Jews" (or "Blacks," "Hispanics," "Native Americans," or "Orientals," for that matter). Timerman's point I feel, stands; to be a Jew is a special fate, an insignia creating an invincible solitude for the imprisoned and persecuted Jew.   People abominably treated "like" Jews—such as Panagoulis—perhaps come the closest to this forlorn estate, and yet even here not so, for Panagoulis's abiding, life-sustaining identification was that of an unyielding *Greek* rebel against tyranny.   An additional point suggested to me by Eric Patton, an English teacher and football coach, is that Timerman's loneliness as a Jew can be seen as particularly intense if contrasted with war prisoners who, whatever their misery, have the possibly consoling sense of a whole nation represented by their imprisonment, and thus a symbolically national sympathy and concern.

[18]George Orwell, *1984* (New York: New American Library, c1949), 197. All further references to this text are to this edition.

[19]Irving Howe, in a highly laudatory essay on *1984*, demurs with Orwell's implication in his novel that human beings are infinitely malleable: "even when consciousness has been blitzed, the 'animal drives' of man cannot be violated as thoroughly as Orwell suggests. In the long run, these drives may prove to be one of the most enduring forces of resistance to the totalitarian state."   ("*1984*:   History as Nightmare" in Orwell's *1984:   Text, Sources, Criticism* ed. Irving Howe (New York: Harcourt, Brace & World, c1963) 194).

[20]Jean-Paul Sartre, *Being and Nothingness* (New York: Washington Square Press, 1966), 523. All further references to this text are to this edition.

[21]Lilian Feder argues cogently that Winston's will is not *completely* broken in a discussion that stoutly defends the existence and persistence of the self in *1984*: "Half-drunk on Victory Gin, he [Winston] responds with 'violent emotion' to the news that Eurasia is gaining on Oceania. Some instinct remains that makes him hope for the destruction of the Party" ("Selfhood, Language, and Reality: George Orwell's *1984*, "*Georgia Review*, v. 37, no. 2 (Summer 1983), 405).

[22]Some commentators *would* discount the Proles entirely as a source of renewal or rebellion in a totalitarian society.   According to Philip Rahv, "an authoritarian state built on the foundations of a mass-society could scarcely afford the luxury of allowing any class or group to evade its demand for complete control" ("The Unfuture of Utopia," in *Orwell's 1984:   Text, Sources,*

Critism, Op, cit., 184-85). Orwell's valuation of the (British) working class is that it is closer to its instinctual life than other classes, and thus less vulnerable to victimization by State ideology or other forms of institutional deceit.

[23]Feder, Op. cit., 394. Feder makes a powerful case for the self by arguing for its importance especially in a totalitarian society: "The seven years that O'Brien . . . spends in surveillance of Smith and the time and effort he invests in interrogating and torturing him until his ultimate surrender of selfhood indicate quite the opposite: the self is the greatest challenge to a totalitarian regime's authorized versions of reality . . . "

[24]Fallaci, *Interviews with History,* Op, cit., 367-68.

[25]*1984* can of course be viewed as also depicting the present, as Richard J. Voorhees has done: "Far from being a picture of the totalitarianism of the future, *1984* is, in countless details, a realistic picture of the totalitarianism of the present. For instance, there is nothing novel in damning up the sexual instincts and canalizing them into political directions—into leader-worship, hatred, and war hysteria" (*The Paradox of George Orwell* (West Lafayette, Indiana: Purdue Research Foundation, [c]1961), 87). *1984* can also be viewed as having one foot in the present and the other in the future.

INDEX